Roger Vailland
The Man and his Masks

ROGER VAILLAND
The Man and his Masks

by J. E. Flower

HODDER AND STOUGHTON
LONDON SYDNEY AUCKLAND TORONTO

Some books by the same author:

Intention and Achievement: An Essay on the Novels of François Mauriac (1969)
A Critical Commentary on Mauriac's Le Nœud de Vipères (1969)
Georges Bernanos: 'Journal d'un Curé de Campagne' (1970)
France Today: Introductory Studies (1971 and 1973)
A critical edition of *Mauriac: Un Adolescent d'Autrefois* (1972)

ISBN 0 340 18447 7

Printed in Great Britain for Hodder and
Stoughton Educational, a division of
Hodder and Stoughton Ltd,
St Paul's House, Warwick Lane,
London EC4P 4AH by Butler & Tanner
Ltd, Frome and London

Contents

Acknowledgements

My debts in preparing this book have been many. In particular I should like to thank Jean Recanati for his generosity in allowing me to consult freely and in my own time the Vailland manuscripts in his possession; René Ballet for his assistance concerning Vailland's career as a journalist; and Elisabeth Vailland for her hospitality and for the interest with which she has followed this book's progress. My thanks are also due to the Editor of *Modern Languages* who kindly allowed me to reproduce in Chapter Four material which had already appeared in slightly different form in his journal; to the Directors of the Ernest Cassell Educational Trust for a grant which helped finance some of the early stages of the work in Paris; to Professor Philip Thody and to Gunther Kress for passing a critical eye over the manuscript and for suggesting various improvements; to Andrew Best for his support; to the University of London Press for their encouragement and efficiency, and to Joy Hardiment for the labour of typing. Needless to say, in the time honoured phrase, all unacknowledged peculiarities and errors are entirely of my own making.

John Flower,
Norwich, 1974.

For permission to reproduce copyright material the publisher wishes to thank the following:

Editions Gallimard (*Ecrits Intimes, Lettres à sa famille, Beau Masque, La Fête, La Loi, Monsieur Jean, La Truite*); Editions Grasset et Fasquelle (*L'Eloge du Cardinal de Bernis, Le Regard Froid*); Editions Bûchet/Chastel (*Un Jeune Homme Seul, Expérience du Drame, 325.000 francs, Les Pages Immortelles de Suétone: Les Douze Césars, Drôle de jeu, Bon Pied Bon Œil*).

For I.

j'en exige [...] de la pénétration et nulle
sensibilité, l'art de tout imiter, ou ce qui
revient au même, une égale aptitude à
toutes sortes de caractères et de rôles.

D. Diderot, *Le Paradoxe sur le comédien.*

je changeais souvent de rôle; mais il
s'agissait toujours de la même pièce.

A. Camus, *La Chute.*

Il m'est absolument nécessaire d'écrire et
que ce que j'écrive soit lu: c'est ma seule
manière de me mettre en circulation (mes
peaux successives d'œuvre en œuvre) sinon
je resterais enfermé dans moi comme un
propriétaire dans sa propriété.

R. Vailland, *Ecrits Intimes.*

Introduction

When in the spring of 1956 Vailland returned to France from Moscow where he had heard President Krushchev denounce the corruption and atrocities of the Stalin regime, he at once replaced the portrait of the former Soviet leader which hung above his desk by a photograph of 'la joueuse de flûte qui orne le trône de Vénus du Musée de Thermes, à Rome'.[1] Such an action might appear typical, symbolic even, of a man who was seen by many to oscillate irregularly between two high points of interest—politics and the erotic. Certainly such a view is not without foundation. Vailland's increasing involvement with the Communist Party during the forties and fifties caused him to emerge as one of the most interesting of the left-wing intellectuals of these years; at the same time his fascination with the erotic and with the figure of the eighteenth-century libertine has prompted many to see in him a lonely, aristocratically aloof figure in many respects not unlike his contemporary Henri de Montherlant. Yet, however attractive it may appear, any attempt to define Vailland quite so readily in these terms would, as a study of his life and work will show, result in oversimplification.

When he died from cancer on 12 May 1965 reactions were often guarded and uncertain; furthermore, with such a short perspective yet available it is difficult to estimate just how influential Vailland was. Yet there can be no doubting his popularity and importance. As a man of letters the award of the Prix Goncourt for *La Loi* in 1957 (his first novel *Drôle de jeu* had won the Prix Interallié in 1945) guaranteed a certain prestige and ensured that all of his work would be eagerly scrutinized. A wide reading public in France was also acknowledged by the publication during his life of all but three of his novels in the *livre de poche* collection, and abroad by the translation of several—in particular, *Drôle de jeu*, *325.000 francs*, *La Loi* and *La Fête*—into a wide variety of languages including English. The filming either commercially or for television of five of his novels[2] together with his own work in the cinema, notably his adaptation with Roger Vadim of Laclos' *Les Liaisons dangereuses* in which Gérard Philippe played the part of Valmont and Jeanne Moreau that of Mme de Merteuil, his essays, critical writing (especially on Laclos) and his immense journalistic output, ensured that his name was brought frequently before the public eye.

Yet Vailland's career as a literary figure is only one aspect of his life, albeit perhaps the most significant. Born in 1907, he was, like his close contemporaries Nizan and Sartre, too young to experience military service during the first World War. After the war he grew up first in Reims and later in Paris where he came into contact with the Surrealists and with a world of bohemianism and journalism, and where he turned, particularly after his first marriage in 1937, to drugs. From these years Vailland emerged to take his part in the Resistance and after the Liberation moved with increasing steadiness towards the orthodox left-wing position shared by many French intellectuals.[3] This period of political commitment, highlighted by some of his best writing, was followed after 1956 and the Moscow trials by a period of disillusion, and by a renewed taste for a private, insulated existence in which he became intensely concerned with the qualities of individual objects and of works of art in particular. During the last months of his life in 1964 and 1965 he gave signs of turning once more to politics and to the revolutionary situation in South America.

Even from such a minimal outline of his life it should emerge that Vailland was neither a man who could endure stasis for long, nor one who was prepared to allow himself to be absorbed by any single interest or passion indefinitely. Instead he moved from one experience to another, led on by an ever-renewed conviction that it was the one which would finally provide him with the intense personal satisfaction he was constantly seeking. In this respect he was rather like an actor who had a total conception of how he could display his talent, but could never find the particular role which best suited him. The result is not so much a paradox as a duality, a tension developed between the desire to become involved (what he termed *aller à*) in anticipation of self-fulfilment, and the realization that all collective activity ultimately destroyed individual aspirations. Hence we find Vailland on occasions siding with people like Politzer, Nizan and Sartre in rejecting bourgeois society for the very values which it attempts to perpetuate—elitism, conservatism, complacency, religious and political bigotry, for example—and on others looking to it for material comfort and security. Similarly, he accepts unquestioningly Communism and the Stalin mystique especially as it was cultivated during the post-Liberation years, yet is quick to reject it once it was shown to fall short of his *personal* conception of it. And in his novels and plays it is precisely this highly developed sense of individualism which is constantly at odds with society in its various forms—the family unit, marriage, political groups, for example—and which creates in them a tension and gives them their interest. Even in his most deeply committed political period, for example, Vailland could never have produced such disciplined (but ultimately dull and tendentious) works as his friend Pierre Courtade's *La Place rouge* (1962) for all that he admired it, or Aragon's *Les Communistes* (1949–51).

Where precisely then is Vailland to be situated in the history of ideas and literature in twentieth-century France? Was he because of his intense individualism and egocentricity ever more than a peripheral figure—albeit an important one—of the literary, intellectual and political circles of his day? Certainly he never enjoyed during his life the kind of international prestige and influence of, say, a Sartre or a Camus or a Malraux; nor did his work provide the regular reading matter for any particular social class in the way that Mauriac's did for the Catholic bourgeoisie for instance. Perhaps for the present he most usefully belongs to that body of writers and thinkers which already includes people like Céline, Nizan and Drieu la Rochelle whose works are increasingly being seen as an invaluable commentary on the social and political circumstances of their time.

Within four years of Vailland's death the first two of what proved subsequently to be an ever-increasing body of critical works appeared: *Les Saisons de Roger Vailland* by François Bott (1969) and *Roger Vailland. Tentative de description critique* by Jean-Jacques Brochier (1969). Neither book claims to offer more than a brief introduction to Vailland and his work. As the title of Bott's study suggests it is a survey—based on a theory of regular 'seasonal' development in which Vailland himself believed—of the principal stages of Vailland's life; Brochier's book is more general and attempts some interpretation of what Vailland understood by sovereignty and heroism, for example.

The real pioneering work, however, has been done by Jean Recanati to whom Vailland's manuscripts were entrusted by his widow, Elisabeth, after his death. It was by Recanati's efforts that the publication was made possible both of the *Ecrits Intimes* (1968)—a fascinating collection of selections from Vailland's private diaries, letters, articles and drafts of work which never materialized—and of the *Œuvres complètes*.[4] Yet in addition to filling the role of the perfect secretary, Recanati has also made an important contribution to Vailland studies in the form of a substantial psychocritical analysis, *Esquisse pour la psychanalyse d'un libertin: Roger Vailland* (1971). Recanati's thoroughness and intimate knowledge of Vailland's work cannot be questioned; his critical method, however, is, by its very nature, limited. Heavily influenced by the work of Charles Mauron, Recanati directs his attention at Vailland's formative years and at the impressions made upon his subconscious by his relationship with his parents and with his grandmother. The result is a persuasive thesis, carefully illustrated and charted through a body of published and unpublished material alike. But, as Recanati freely admits in his Introduction, his approach is selective, and much that concerns Vailland's *conscious* development as a writer in particular has been ignored.

In 1972 Michel Picard's *Libertinage et Tragique dans l'œuvre de Roger Vailland* appeared to which all future students of Vailland's work will owe a great deal. Originally a *doctorat d'état* thesis, Picard's study is a mine of detailed, carefully sifted and documented information. His scholarship is daunting (even the published version of his thesis contains nearly 100 pages of foot-notes!) so much so that any attempt to summarize his work does it scant justice. However, his approach is a mixture of psychocriticism not dissimilar to Recanati's—though he places greater emphasis on

Vailland's relationship with his mother than the earlier critic—and a sociological study whereby he relates Vailland's work to the particular social and political pressures and circumstances to which he was subjected at various stages in his life. In a somewhat brief and disappointing conclusion he traces Vailland's own attitude to his work and carefully underlines the various psychological and ideological blocks and contradictions from which he suffered.

It is only fair to say that ultimately both Recanati and Picard are as much, if not more concerned in a very special way with Vailland the man as with his work, an approach which has prompted his widow in various interviews and more particularly in the book *Roger Vailland* (1973) which she prepared in conjunction with the novelist René Ballet, to attempt to redress the balance. Yet she too is guilty of a certain, if more understandable partiality. For her Vailland was not a man of letters, and her concern is to establish him as a committed left-wing political figure who, despite various difficulties arising from his background and family influence and despite the events of 1956, consciously and purposefully pursued his beliefs throughout his life. *Roger Vailland* is a curious little book; an imagined monologue by Elisabeth Vailland addressed to her dead husband, the text of a dialogue—which centres on the 1956 crisis—between her and Henri Bourbon, and a more conventional chronological outline of Vailland's political activities amply illustrated by quotations lifted mostly from the *Ecrits Intimes* by René Ballet. The volume closes with a useful selection of Vailland's journalism.

These five books together with an important volume in the *Entretiens* series edited by Max Chaleil in 1970, and a handful of articles, constitute the body of Vailland criticism to date: almost without exception all of it has been written in French.

To attempt to present to an Anglo-Saxon audience a man who for so long seemed enigmatic and difficult to categorize in his own country is perhaps not so much ambitious as rash. In view of the absence of any serious work in English to date,[5] I decided to adopt a strictly chronological approach. Within this general framework my emphasis is on his imaginative writing and in particular on his novels. In this way in addition to providing a critical biography I try to place more emphasis than previous critics upon the novels as individual works in an attempt to show that Vailland was also much more of a conscious artist than has hitherto been suggested. The shortcomings and pitfalls of such an approach are many and various; I can only hope that I have managed to avoid some of them. On occasions I have felt obliged to provide brief summaries of those works which may not be known to the majority of readers. Inevitably too I am selective. A number of questions which I treat inconclusively or merely allude to are thoroughly dealt with by Recanati and Picard whose works should be consulted. There are others, however, like that of the influence on Vailland of certain writers and thinkers—especially Laclos, but also Stendhal, Hemingway and Flaubert—or of the development of his style in all its aspects, which remain unexplored. As an introduction to the man and his work I can only hope that this book will serve (as all introductions should) to send more people to Vailland with curiosity and enthusiasm.

Chapter One

The Formative Years

Toute sa vie était dans l'avenir
Drôle de jeu.

Middle-class, Catholic, patriotic (and, one suspects, anti-dreyfusard), valuing education and believing firmly in the sanctity of marriage, Vailland's family could hardly have been more representative of the society of its time; it was, to use René Ballet's words, 'un microcosme de la société française de la "Belle Epoque" '.[1] Roger's father, Georges Vailland, though born in Paris, belonged to a family originating in the Haute-Savoie—a fact of which Vailland was later to make a great deal. He was educated first in Annecy and later in Paris at the Lycée Charlemagne where he failed the stiffly competitive examinations for admission to the Ecole Polytechnique by half a mark. Instead of retaking them he passed a surveyor's examination and went to work for the French government in Madagascar[2] where he also became a free-mason. On his return to France he met Anna Morel who, deeply attached to her widowed mother, only agreed to marry him on condition that he would remain in France. Dutifully Georges Vailland bought a 'cabinet de géomètre expert' at Acy-en-Multien to the north of Paris, and after a year's engagement the marriage took place on 27 September 1906; on 16 October of the following year Roger Vailland was born.

During the first few years of his life Vailland was, it seems, pampered to an unusual degree even for an only child. Surrounded by four women—his mother, his two grandmothers and a maid—he was, as his sister Geneviève has remarked 'l'enfant-roi, l'enfant adoré, un enfant que l'on choyait, que l'on dorlotait, toujours tiré à quatre épingles...'.[3] From this period one event in particular should be recalled. Suffering from general fatigue Vailland's mother was advised against feeding him. Weaned abruptly at four months the young child reacted violently it seems, pushing his bottle away to the floor in temper. While the psychological harm which this kind of rejection can inflict is today widely recognized, there was less concern at the time, and while we may not wish to make of it quite as much as Recanati has done, there can be no doubt that this pattern of sudden change from inclusion (affection) to exclusion was one which was to become a regular and determining feature of Vailland's adult life as well.

In 1910 the family moved to Paris where Georges Vailland, having sold his practice in Acy-en-Multien, took up a government post. Here the same comfortable, middle-class, protective life continued. In 1913, however, the young Vailland experienced the harsh realities of the outside world in the form of his first school, the Ecole des Feuillantines: 'Je suis terrifié pendant quinze premiers jours à l'Ecole Communale par les petits voyous et par le maître—les maîtres'.[4] Vailland's recollection is almost certainly correct. His mother's reaction was predictable, Vailland being withdrawn from the school and taught by her at home to read and write. The following year, however, he returned and quickly established himself as one of the best pupils.

With the outbreak of the war the Vailland family life was disrupted once more. Georges Vailland, rendered unfit for military activity by his short sight, was none the less inspired by his sense of patriotism to join up as an unpaid volunteer. In 1915 he was drafted to Dunkerque where he renounced his free-masonry, and, in a way that was not untypical of many of his generation, turned instead to Catholicism.[5] During the war years Anna Vailland, her mother-in-law and the two children (Geneviève had been born in 1912) remained fairly mobile. At first they spent short periods in Versailles and Switzerland; later in 1916 when Anna Vailland found herself obliged to work, the two children were evacuated for a year to a country house (the 'pavillon' to which Vailland was often to refer later in his letters and diaries) in Monthléry near Villejust. This, for the first time, was a period of complete escape ('Nous menions une vie sauvage, heureuse')[6] and was followed shortly after by a similar but shorter spell in Teilhède in the Auvergne. In 1918 the family resettled in Paris and Vailland, now eleven years old, attended the Lycée Henri IV. But the stay was brief; in the following year Georges Vailland was posted to Reims where he worked as an architect in the restoration work which had to be carried out after the war. It was here in the avenue de Laon that the Vailland family inhabited the 'maison particulière' which would become the focus of the first part of what is in many ways his most autobiographical novel, Un Jeune Homme seul (1951).

In spite of the importance attributed by Vailland to the formative influence of the years of childhood and adolescence it is important at this point to draw attention to the considerable distortion to be found in much of what he was to say during the later years of his life concerning this period in Reims and his subsequent move back to Paris.[7] Certainly parental disapproval of and opposition to many of his activities and ideas increased. At the same time, however, it would be dangerous to see in these few years very much more than a re-enactment of an adolescent revolt, albeit a fairly healthy and well developed one with the classic symptoms well to the fore—a minor crisis over religious faith, a sense of guilt concerning masturbation and a schoolboy obsession with sex, arguments with his parents about his clothes, the discovery of certain writers (Rimbaud in particular) seen as kindred spirits, some experimentation with drugs (carbon tetrachloride and opium paste) and a need, in part satisfied by some boxing lessons, to gain more physical confidence.[8]

For all this Vailland continued to be an outstanding pupil[9] with a particular gift for imaginative writing. Already in 1921 when only in the Quatrième (the equivalent of the English third form) he organized together with Roger Gilbert-Lecomte, a small poetry magazine *Apollo* which eventually brought them to the attention of a philosophy teacher René Maublanc, through whose efforts they both had a poem published in a local literary review, *Le Pampre*, in April 1923.[10] Vailland's literary activities continued; at the same time his personality began to develop and arguments with his father, who appeared to find his son's literary activities somewhat unmanly and unsuitable training for the future, increased. At the end of January 1924, for example, we find Vailland writing to Maublanc asking that he should contact him concerning his poetry 'par l'intermédiaire de mon ami Lecomte'.[11] Inevitably as parental opposition increased so too did his own determination to rebel:

> Notre désir d'échapper à la médiocrité de la petite bourgeoisie était si passionné, notre ignorance des conditions de vie de toute autre classe sociale, notre ignorance du luxe, de l'aventure, de tout ce qui est en dehors de la routine de la vie du petit bourgeois, que nous conçumes pas d'intermédiaire possible entre cette situation intolérable et notre ambition d'être des princes de l'esprit. La difficulté de gagner de l'argent pour des garçons qui n'héritaient ni avaient espoir d'hériter le moindre capital accroissait l'intransigeance de notre position de principe: 'rien d'autre n'est souhaitable que de devenir un prince de l'esprit' (poète).[12]

Between 1922 and 1925 these feelings of revolt against what Lecomte later defined as 'cet étouffement de la source vitale de la pensée enfantine'[13] found expression in the activities of a group which he, Vailland, Meyrat and René Daumal formed and called, with what they imagined to be a striking disregard for the conventions of spelling, the Phrères Simplistes. Known to one another as Anges and renamed according to their position within the group or to particular characteristics,[14] they proclaimed their absolute freedom, scorned convention of any form, practised extra-sensory communication under the sign of their god, Bubu,[15] and attempted to inject some life into Reims ('Reims-la-plate' as they called it) with a number of activities which ranged from adolescent horse-play to young thuggery. It seems likely, however, that while to many of his fellow pupils Vailland may indeed have appeared extraordinary enough, within the context of the Simplistes he was the most conventional. Indeed the most accurate picture he provides of himself at this time would seem to be the one he gives in *Pour et contre l'existentialisme* (1948):

> Je préparais mon baccalauréat de philosophie. J'habitais chez mes parents qui étaient de petits bourgeois catholiques. Je n'avais la permission de minuit qu'une fois par semaine et pas assez d'argent pour aller au bordel, même pas assez pour inviter une jeune fille au cinéma et payer ensuite la chambre d'hôtel.[16]

Yet for Vailland the very fact that he belonged to such a group provided him—if at times only vicariously—with another existence, a chance to escape from the protective, inhibiting atmosphere of the 'maison particulière' in the avenue de Laon.

The other image which Vailland in later life was retrospectively to cultivate about himself was of the young bourgeois intellectual hungry for contact with the masses of the working-class world. The picture we have in *Un Jeune Homme seul* of Eugène-Marie peering furtively through the window of his father's study at the local factory girls as they pass by, may have been real enough, but however much a problem it was to become later, it can only be seen as one more expression of the need he felt at this particular time to escape.[17]

The opportunity was not far off. In 1925 his work in Reims having finished, Georges Vailland moved his family temporarily to Montmorency near Paris. Having passed his *baccalauréat*, Vailland, in October, entered the Lycée Louis-le-Grand (Daumal went to Henri IV while Lecomte, having failed his examinations, stayed on in Reims) in order to prepare for the Ecole Normale. Yet after the lycée in Reims he found Louis-le-Grand oppressive, 'un milieu étranger et presque hostile',[18] from which he now willingly returned each day to the comfort and shelter of the family home. In July of the following year, however, his father bought a practice near Antibes, and in October Vailland returned to Louis-le-Grand this time as a boarder. The break for which he had longed in Reims had now materialized yet, ironically, brought little relief. Certainly Vailland appears to have done his best to cut a figure with his contemporaries. According to Robert Brasillach 'Il était le Lafcadio de Gide incarné pour nous et, bien qu'il soit rare d'admirer quelqu'un de son âge, il est exact que nous l'admirions';[19] for Paul Guth he was someone '(qui) passait sur des semelles silencieuses, rentrant à des heures impossibles d'on ne sait où. Je n'avais jamais osé lui parler'. [20] Yet just how much truth or reality such recollections contain, or whether they indirectly acknowledge a pose Vailland had already chosen at this time to adopt, is difficult to assess. At the beginning of the school year in 1926, for example, we also find him writing to his father: 'je suis bien ennuyé que tu ne puisses plus me suivre dans mes études; finies nos bonnes discussions';[21] while in a letter to his mother from about the same time we read: 'sois certaine, ma chère

Maman, que je pense toujours très, très souvent à toi, que le dortoir m'est particulièrement pénible parce que ma Mme Labou ne vient pas me border...'.[22] Vailland, we should recall, was nineteen years of age...

It was not to be long, however, before independence once more became an issue. Although Lecomte had remained in Reims, Vailland and Daumal continued to see a great deal of one another: 'nous passons ensemble presque tous nos jeudis et dimanches et il vient tous les jours pour la récréation de 4 heures' (*Lettres à sa famille*, p. 50). In addition, regular correspondence with Lecomte kept the spirit of the Simplistes very much alive; furthermore, much in keeping with the literary fashion of the time, they had already discussed the possibility of creating a review which eventually emerged as *Le Grand Jeu*, a title chosen by Vailland himself.[23]

While the whole project of *Le Grand Jeu* may have served to provide some kind of focal point for his activities, in a more general way Vailland was becoming increasingly restless. In an important letter to his father in February 1927, Vailland attempted to explain what he described as 'ces deux tendances très contradictoires' (*Lettres à sa famille*, p. 56) which he felt within himself. On the one hand a reluctant respect for hard won but socially acceptable intellectual achievement, and on the other a feeling of attraction for instant reputation in the artistic and literary world of Paris which, he felt would establish his independence. At the same time, however, he clearly felt guilty: 'Je ne sais pas pourquoi [...] j'ai toujours peur que tu croies que c'est de la pose, non vis-à-vis de toi, mais vis-à-vis de moi-même' (*Lettres à sa famille*, p. 56). Indeed here, perhaps unwittingly, Vailland had pinpointed a characteristic which others already recognized in him and which was to dog him for the rest of his life.

In the spring of 1927 Vailland suffered a bad attack of scarlet fever after which he moved from the school to his grandmother Vailland's house in the rue Pétrarque, the setting for the wedding celebrations in *Un Jeune Homme seul*;[24] after the Easter vacation he left Louis-le-Grand altogether and began to study for a *licence en philosophie* at the Sorbonne which he completed the following year. For all that, however, Vailland was far from settled. Through the influence of Kafka's friend Richard Weiner, he managed to obtain a grant from the Czechoslovakian Foreign Ministry to enable him to undertake a short cultural visit to that country during the summer of 1927. Vailland hoped that he could be able to place articles based on his impressions of Czechoslovakia with the left-wing review *L'Œuvre*. While the project itself never materialized the experience of the trip was good training for him, the letters to his parents—on which the articles were to have been based—showing a sharpness of observation and analysis that was to characterize the best of his journalism in later life. But most important of all was the fact that for the first time in his life Vailland was completely alone and obliged to solve his own problems. A brief illness forced him into hospital in October. Having recovered he could write to his mother: 'Cela me fait de nouvelles expériences, j'acquiers de la "maturité"' (*Lettres à sa famille*, p. 99). Indeed his maturity was what he had above all to convince his parents about, for he was also contemplating marriage.

Vailland had met Marianne Lams in May 1926.[25] Five years his senior she became a member of the Simplistes-Grand Jeu group and adopted the name Mimouchka. Vailland's letters during the summer and autumn of 1927 suggest that the marriage, envisaged for June of the following year, had already been discussed.[26] Parental opposition was strong however; Georges Vailland stopped his son's allowance and for a few weeks they refused to write or speak to one another. Yet there would also appear to be some truth in Georges Vailland's view that it was just one more example of his son's defiance, 'ce parti pris d'opposition à tout prix' (*Lettres à sa famille*, p. 135). Whatever the reason it is clear that Vailland had been infatuated, and while the affair continued spasmodically for the next two years, his *volte face* late in April 1928 concerning a possible marriage, though sudden, was not all that inexplicable:

> Quand je réfléchis à cette pénible rupture j'en comprends de moins en moins les causes. J'y vois beaucoup plus le heurt du caractère de Papa et du mien, que cette stupide histoire de mariage à laquelle j'attache infiniment moins d'importance que vous. Cela me paraît tellement ridicule pour moi ce fameux rôle du jeune homme qui veut absolument se marier! (*Lettres à sa famille*, p. 133)

Yet even if the affair and its effect on his relationship with his father were less serious than Vailland in later life would have us believe, they did draw from him an important statement of what he at this time considered his position and attitude to life to be. For him the real cause of the discussion had been 'Les conceptions de la vie très différentes' (*Lettres à sa famille*, p. 137). He still maintained his total rejection of all material values, of all 'morale et surtout conventions sociales, (des) "garde-fous", dont les hommes s'entourent pour être tranquilles et n'avoir pas à chercher leur voie' (*Lettres à sa famille*, p. 137). For him poetry and the exploration of the unknown were far more vital in that they offered him the chance to create his own world on his own terms, an alternative to what he had described four years earlier to Maublanc as 'la même vie monotone'.[27]

Deprived of his family's financial support Vailland nonetheless managed to continue his studies in Paris and, having successfully completed his *licence*, even considered continuing with a *diplôme d'études supérieures* on Rimbaud. At the same time, however, his attention and energies were being drawn elsewhere as the preparations for the publication of the first number of *Le Grand Jeu* were rapidly coming to a head.

This clearly is not the place to undertake a study of the importance which *Le Grand Jeu* had within the Surrealist movement; nor is it necessary for the present study to explore in any detail the roles which René Daumal and Roger Gilbert-Lecomte in particular played in its development.[28] Vailland's own part, though significant enough, was never more than marginal. Certainly he had been one of the founder members and a long letter to Lecomte (2 August 1927), in which he discusses the lay-out, content and aim of the proposed review, shows a serious and positive approach to their intentions.[29] It was still to be some time, however, before material for Le Grand Jeu was ready for the printer. Vailland and Daumal had worked at its preparation and publicity, but it was Lecomte who increasingly assumed the leading role, bombarding Daumal with last minute corrections and instructions and writing the avant-propos for the first number. When it eventually appeared Le Grand Jeu contained two articles by Vailland, 'La bestialité de Montherlant' and 'Colonisation'.[30] If his intention in the first of these was to shock accepted opinion on sexual relationships, then by the young Simone de Beauvoir's reaction he certainly would appear to have had some success: 'J'avais l'imagination intrépide, mais [...] la realité m'effarouchait aisément. Je ne tentai pas d'approcher Daumal ni Vailland, qui m'ignoraient'.[31] In the second he attacked all systems of oppressive colonization and in words which could have been lifted from many a Surrealist text and which also looked forward to those used by Eugène-Marie Favart in Un Jeune Homme seul, championed the idea of complete revolution:

> Nous fraternisons avec vous, chers nègres, et vous souhaitons une prochaine arrivée à Paris, et de pouvoir vous y livrer en grand, à ce jeu des supplices où vous êtes si forts. Pénétrés de la forte joie d'être traîtres, nous vous ouvrirons toutes les portes! Et tant pis si vous ne nous reconnaissez pas![32]

In the second issue of Le Grand Jeu (May 1929) the same ideas reappear, this time in the form of an article on Rimbaud—'Arthur Rimbaud ou Guerre à l'homme'[33]—and in an unsigned 'Chronique de la vie sexuelle' with which Vailland's contribution to the review came to an end. His break with the group, however, had already occurred.

In July 1928 Vailland, desperate to find employment, had been introduced to Paris-Midi (later in 1930 to be taken over by Paris-Soir) by Robert Desnos. On 15 September an article signed by Vailland had appeared, entitled 'Chez les Gardiens de la Paix—L'hymne Chiappe Martia'. For André Breton such apparent approval for the established powers of the Third Republic and in particular the description of the prefect of police as the 'épurateur de notre capitale' provided the perfect excuse he needed to bring matters between the Surrealists and the Grand Jeu group to a head. Already he was concerned by the impact the latter had made and annoyed that one of his own disciples, Monny de Boully, should have changed his allegiance. A circular was sent to all avant-garde intellectuals to attend a meeting eventually held on 11 March 1929, ostensibly to consider the case of Trotsky who had recently been excommunicated from the Communist Party and exiled. In considering the moral position of all the invited groups concerning this issue Breton soon focused attention on the Grand Jeu. Vailland's articles were read, and their author accused. At first defended by Lecomte and by Georges Ribemont-Dessaigne, Vailland quickly found himself fighting a lone and losing battle. Eventually he accepted Breton's offer that an open letter in which he would disavow his articles should be published in the next issue of *Le Grand Jeu*. It was an undertaking which he failed to meet, however; instead on 14 March he wrote Breton a letter in which he once more protested his innocence: 'Ne savaient-ils [mes accusateurs] pas pertinemment que, profondément et réellement, je vomis toutes les polices? que quand je le déclare c'est tout mon être qui le déclare.'[34] But having got so far Breton was not going to lose now, and the letter which he summarily dismissed as 'un pareil tissu de palinodies'[34] was presented as the final evidence of Vailland's and, by implication, of the whole of the Grand Jeu group's lack of moral and political integrity.

There was, however, a further defence which Vailland claimed for himself in his letter to Breton which the latter chose to ignore, but which from Vailland's other correspondence of this period seems to have been valid enough. This, simply, was the need to earn a living: 'Ne savaient-ils pas aussi que [...] je n'attache aucune importance aux articles que j'ai écrits, écris et écrirai dans *Paris-Midi* ou autres journaux bourgeois pour gagner ma vie?'[35] Already in July of the previous year had he not maintained to his father that he felt 'une immense différence entre ces gens essentiellement superficiels et mes autres amis'? (*Lettres à sa famille*, p. 144.) Furthermore, no doubt warned by his friends of the danger involved in writing articles of the Chiappe-Martia kind,[36] he had begun by October to sign his articles with a pseudonym, Georges Omer. Roger Vailland—Georges Omer, an extension in name of the 'deux tendances contradictoires' of which he had written to his father in February 1927 and another pointer to the kind of role playing which he was to adopt in later years. In the same month too we find him writing to his sister in similar if somewhat dramatic terms: 'Ne me faut-il pas deux noms à moi qui mène une étonnante vie en partie double, tantôt avec les surréalistes et des métaphysiciens du Grand Jeu—tantôt avec les plus tristes imbéciles fripouilles du monde' (*Lettres à sa famille*, p. 148). Yet neither for Breton nor for his own Grand Jeu colleagues were these reasons sufficiently convincing and Vailland soon found himself once more alone. The whole affair had been a deeply humiliating one from which he was never perhaps to recover. Much, of course, hinged on his personal relationship with Lecomte of whom he wrote in 1956: 'Il faut dire que j'ai aimé Roger Gilbert-Lecomte, je crois d'amour'.[37] As we have already noted, Lecomte had naturally assumed the leadership of the Grand Jeu group, and for Vailland, whatever latent homosexual attraction there may have been,[38] he was, quite clearly, a hero, the incarnation of all Vailland's own unrealized aspirations. Indeed so influential was he that like Vailland's family he became part of a past which he (Vailland) tried on numerous occasions to exorcize, either subconsciously through dreams[39] or more overtly through some of his imaginative writing like *Les Mauvais Coups* for example, in which as Octave he is forced to commit suicide (*Œuvres Complètes*, II, pp. 82–8).

To a young man of twenty-two, however, the Grand Jeu affair saw the chance to realize an ambition which he had been nourishing for the past five years crumble in a matter of weeks. At first he turned, not for the first time, to his family for sympathy and protection: 'Quand je pense à vous, c'est comme à quelque chose de très calme et de très sûr, auprès duquel je pourrais aussi me réfugier si je "n'en pouvais plus" ' (*Lettres à sa famille*, p. 175). Yet Vailland's despair does not seem to have lasted for very long. He made arrangements to study at the Sorbonne for his *diplôme*, finished (according to his correspondence) a novel and 'trois petits textes philosophiques' (*Lettres à sa famille*, p. 175), and managed on the pretext of poor health to avoid military service. At the same time, however, he was forced, in order to exist, into the detested (so he continued to claim) world of journalism with its 'papiers superficiels' and 'fantaisie douteuse' (*Lettres à sa famille*, p. 180). For a while he withstood the pressure— 'C'est une [...] attitude possible que de rester hautainement en dehors' (*Lettres à sa famille*, p. 180)—but not for long. Gradually during the period 1930–5 the demands of a hectic but fragmented existence compounded by an acute feeling of loneliness drained his resistance. The double life about which he had written so enthusiastically to his sister continued, but it was now little more than a pose. In an attempt to find instant relief Vailland turned, with increasing frequency, to drugs and to women.

In April 1930 Vailland was obliged to spend twelve days in hospital for treatment to his right arm which had become infected after a morphine injection. On leaving hospital he abandoned his plans to continue his *diplôme* at the Sorbonne, moved back to his grandmother's flat in the rue Pétrarque and devoted himself to journalism. The amalgamation of *Paris-Midi* and *Paris-Soir* brought him more responsibility and work, and towards the end of the year he was sent first to Albania and later to Ethiopia where he was to cover the coronation of the new emperor Haile Sellassie. The second of these trips was, of course, more than just one more routine assignment. Here was an opportunity for him to follow in the wake of Rimbaud, and while in Ethiopia there was talk of a mysterious business affair ('une grosse entreprise d'élevage ou agricole')[40] which, however, seems to have come to nothing.

During his spell in Ethiopia Vailland's grandmother died and on his return to Paris his nomadic existence started once again. Apparently oblivious of his parents' growing financial straits[41] and in spite of considerable improvement in the material conditions of his own life, his letters for the next few years are regularly punctated by demands for money and often written in a tone of bitter rebuke:

> Je crois que c'est ni du 'genre', ni de la 'pose', ni de l' 'ingratitude' que de me plaindre. Mais c'est bien un fait que je ne puis en aucune manière me sentir soutenu par ma famille, alors qu'en des circonstances pareilles (emménagement, installation) il est, je crois, de coutume, qu'un fils le soit. Un fait aussi que je dois plus compter matériellement sur un étranger quelconque qui sait que je travaille et que je pourrai le rembourser un jour, ou sur une femme rencontrée par hasard, que sur vous. (*Lettres à sa famille*, p. 209)

But this reaction may also be seen as part of a defence mechanism; without support, Vailland argued, he was obliged to work at his journalism, if only for the sake of appearances—'je suis forcé de me débattre et de ne pas paraître pauvre' (*Lettres à sa famille*, p. 210)—and little progress in his literary and philosophical activities was possible. Yet if his letters are to be believed he was, especially by late 1932 and 1933, writing a good deal: 'j'écris presque un poème par jour'; 'j'achève une assez longue nouvelle sur un quartier de Paris'; 'j'ai commencé un long roman' (*Lettres à sa famille*, pp. 229, 248, 256). Of these little has remained, however, and it is hard to see Vailland's role at this time as being any other than that of a relatively successful journalist with a preference for travelling abroad and a certain skill in the accounts of his visits to foreign countries. Indeed his father's advice in December 1932 sounds eminently sensible: 'Mon cher Roger, tu as toutes les qualités voulues pour réussir dans ce genre. [...] Ne cherche pas à modifier artificiellement ton genre' (*Lettres à sa famille*, p. 244). Moreover the rewriting Vailland was required to do, the condensing of a wide range of other journalists' material into a single readable page of newsprint, was invaluable training.[42] For the moment, however, Vailland persisted in his belief that his real future lay elsewhere, with the result that he was neither journalist nor man of letters, a fringe figure who continued to turn either to drugs and to women for escape or found himself becoming increasingly isolated. But more important still was an awareness of his increasing age—'le vieux garçon que je deviens'[43]—and of waste: 'déjà sept ans que je suis seul à Paris; et qu'en reste-t-il?' (*Lettres à sa famille*, p. 273). In 1934 or early in 1935 Vailland met Andrée Blavette (known as Boule),[44] a night club singer, whom he was to marry the following year. Far from providing a steadying influence, however, the affair would appear to have prompted even more recklessness in matters of money and drugs, and in a letter to his father (17 May) he asks for a loan of 3,000 francs, his debts having risen to 5,000. A year later (25 April 1936) he would nonetheless write that his life was now 'beaucoup plus équilibrée que par le passé' (*Lettres à sa famille*, pp. 279–82); indeed with marriage to Andrée Blavette now certain—a civil ceremony was held unbeknown to Vailland's parents on 19 May—and with the completion of a book, there may well have been some truth in his words. For two reasons in particular this letter is significant. As Max Chaleil has suggested (*Lettres à sa famille*, pp. 260–61), the confessed difficulty Vailland had in writing it and of the dreams he had concerning his parents—'je rêve de maman ou de toi presque chaque nuit et de façon très pénible'—are indicative of a sense of guilt. Noticeable too is the fact that it is with his book, *L'Histoire d'un homme du peuple sous la Révolution*[45] that the first part of this letter deals, as though it were a proof of his new-found stability and serious intentions. Given that the book was written in collaboration with one of his journalist colleagues Raymond Manevy, it is difficult and perhaps unwise to look for too much in it that relates to Vailland's personal situation at that time. An historical novel set principally in the 1790s, it relates the life of Jean-Baptiste Drouet who by arresting the escaping Louis XVI and Marie-Antoinette is caught up in the maelstrom of revolutionary and counter-revolutionary politics and activities. Constantly trapped, he nonetheless always manages to outwit his opponents and eventually dies incognito but happy in the arms of his mistress, Christine Moenck. For Picard, Drouet's responsibility for the execution of Louis XVI and his queen can be related directly to Vailland's own subconscious attitude towards his mother;[46] he also sees in Drouet an early sketch of the 'vrai bolchevik' figure who dominates a number of the later novels,[47] while it is arguable, too, that when he leaves France for India to start a new life 'dans un pays où le nom de Drouet n'est peut-être pas encore parvenu' (*O. C.*, X, p. 168), Vailland could have been alluding to the hopes he had entertained when he set out for Ethiopia. Be that as it may, *L'Histoire d'un homme du peuple sous la Révolution* is probably more important for two quite different reasons: the first, that it was 'la première fois que j'achevais un livre commencé' (*Lettres à sa famille*, p. 280); the second, that it indicated a degree of political awareness, hitherto not particularly evident in spite of his regular claims of sympathy for the working-class world. Of these the former in particular is clearly important for, as his father recognized, Vailland had at last overcome an important psychological block in actually finishing the book. The second, however, must be qualified. Certainly, had Blum's Front Populaire been able to sustain its initial impetus, it is possible that Vailland's political affiliations would have crystallized much earlier and the next few years of his life been given a different direction. But this was not to be, and despite his retrospective claim in 1946 that *L'Histoire d'un homme du peuple sous la Révolution* had expressed a real political conviction, contemporary evidence is far more scarce. Neither the Front Populaire nor in fact the Spanish Civil War seems to have aroused in Vailland the kind of heartfelt response which we find in the work of writers of such politically different inclinations as Nizan (in his articles for *La Correspondance internationale*) and Bernanos (*Les Grands Cimetières sous la lune*) for example. Rather *L'Histoire d'un homme du peuple sous la Révolution* may be seen as an early sketch of a position which Vailland was not fully to reach for another fifteen years.

Clearly, therefore, the book failed to bring the stability he had hoped for. So too did his marriage. If Vailland's relationship with Marianne Lams had been an example of immature infatuation, that with Andrée Blavette was one of the Surrealists' *amour-fou*, an all-consuming passion which he recalls through Marat in *Drôle de jeu*, his first novel published in 1945 and based on his experience as a member of the Resistance movement: 'inégalable et intolérable, comme le feu, elle ne me laisse pas un instant de repos, elle me consume… Elle exige toute ma vie' (*O. C.* I, p. 204). In spite of the absence of contemporary evidence—Vailland's parents moved to Joinville-le-pont in 1937 and the correspondence stopped—it is clear from such fictionalized accounts as this, as well as from that in his second novel *Les Mauvais Coups* (1948)[48] and from Geneviève Vailland's recollections,[49] that the marriage was a turbulent one. Certainly Vailland is known to have had an affair with a working-class girl in 1937—perhaps the inspiration for the Paméla briefly recalled by Marat in *Drôle de jeu*—but it appears as well that he was beginning to tire of the bohemian style of life to which Andrée wished to bind him, and in 1938 he underwent his first *désintoxication*. In 1939 he became legal correspondent for *Paris-Soir* and, on the outbreak of war, was still deemed unfit for military service. In March of the following year, however, his classification was changed and only by being sent by *Paris-Soir* to Bucharest did he avoid being drafted into the French army. But the reprieve was short. He returned to France only days before Italy's declaration of war (10 June 1940), crossing the frontier at Menton just three hours before it was officially closed (*Lettres à sa famille*, p. 295). At once he was registered in the French reserves as a 'soldat deuxième classe' and posted at Narbonne where Andrée joined him with 'ses sœurs, les 3 voitures de la famille, les 6 chiens, des tas de bagages et un accordéon géant' (*Lettres à sa famille*, p. 295). On Vailland's advice she and her sisters left first for Spain continuing later to North Africa where Andrée contracted typhoid fever and was forced to stay for six months. From here she went to Mexico—where they had somewhat optimistically planned to join one another—and eventually returned permanently to France at the end of 1941. Demobilized soon after the declaration of the armistice, Vailland joined up once more with the *Paris-Soir* group of journalists first in Marseille, where quite independent of the Parisian organization a central office had been established, and later, in September, in Lyon. He continued to work for the paper until November 1943.

Although ostensibly a precautionary measure, Andrée's departure had a wider significance for Vailland. While, as we have already seen, no first-hand evidence of the tension between them is available, it is reasonable to assume that Marat's diary in *Drôle de jeu* is once again a faithful reproduction of Vailland's own at this time. With her departure her immediate influence upon him was lessened and Vailland seems to have begun to view their relationship with some degree of objectivity. In the entry for 30 September 1940, for example, we read: 'Pour la première fois depuis des années, l'esprit étonnement libre à l'égard de B. Serait-ce pour de bon la délivrance?'[50] Yet Andrée had had too deep an influence for the process of separation to be quite so simple. 3 November 1940: 'Très triste. En manque de B...'; 12 December 1940: 'Ai rêvé cette nuit de B...'; and above all, 25 May 1941:

> Journée mélancolique et d'asthénie brusquement et follement animée par une lettre de Mexico dans laquelle B. me raconte ses aventures d'après l'armistice, et proclame son désir de revenir près de moi... Qu'au travers de tous les aspects possibles de B., ceux que j'aime, ceux que je hais, ceux que je ne connais pas encore, existe une sorte d'entité B., à laquelle je suis irrémédiablement lié... B. est ma femme au sens le plus profond du terme: c'est seulement maintenant que je le comprends, que je l'admets... (*Drôle de jeu*, p. 209)

Just as he had been trapped by his own bourgeois upbringing Vailland was now trapped by his marriage, yet while recognizing his dilemma he could once again do little about it. Andrée returned to France at the end of 1941, and after a short stay in Lyon they had moved by the spring of 1942 to 'un petit hameau perdu en pleine Bresse' (*Lettres à sa famille*, p. 298) Chavannes-sur-Reyssouze. Here, despite some appearances to the contrary, the tension of Vailland's relationship with Andrée increased, relieved only occasionally and temporarily through drugs. During the early months of 1942 he became increasingly preoccupied by a projected *Méditations métaphysiques*: 'Trente méditations sur la vie, la mort, la liberté, l'amour et autres notions essentielles, chacune correspondant à une journée, comme les sept *Méditations métaphysiques*'.[51] Yet before this could be properly undertaken Vailland felt that for his thoughts to be entirely original he had to be certain of the authenticity of his own being and existence. At once the question of dependence (on Andrée or indeed on any system of thought or body of people) became evident. He found himself obsessed by the need to define the essence, not only of his own being but (rather like Roquentin in Sartre's *La Nausée*) of natural objects around him. To modify or qualify, shape or influence something (or somebody) immediately removed or at least reduced its *essential* quality and thereby its freedom:

> percevoir c'est être éveillé en face d'un objet. Nommer le noyer, c'est

une des actions possibles auxquelles m'invite le noyer, comme
l'abattre, le gauler ou le peindre. C'est aussi façon de le créer: en
disant noyer et tel noyer, je le crée pour moi. Toute action modifie
l'objet: celle de l'ouvrier modifie la nature et crée des objets nouveaux, celle du peintre modifie la couleur et crée des peintures; celle
du contemplateur modifie disons sa vision du monde et crée des
noms. (*Ecrits Intimes*, p. 72)

It is arguable, of course, that Vailland was simply experiencing the
symptoms of the kind of existential malaise so common among intellectuals
of this period. Yet when compared with many of his contemporaries
Vailland emerges as a figure of little importance or influence. Perhaps it is
true that much of what he wrote during the 1930s he destroyed, but what
has remained gives scant indication that he made any very positive impact.
Indeed despite the brief notoriety brought by the Surrealist 'trial' in 1929
his essentially peripheral role in the Grand Jeu enterprise would seem to be
characteristic of all his activities at this time. But above all else everything
became personalized for Vailland. The question of freedom was not the
profound metaphysical problem he claimed it to be but a private dilemma.
His upbringing and background, the presence of his parents—in particular
of his mother—and later that of Andrée, and, in spite of his claims to have
long since escaped its influence, religion, were all barriers which he had
still to overcome. In 1964 in his last article 'Eloge de la politique' Vailland
was to write that the definition of true freedom was the ability to act
positively—'agir au lieu d'être agi'.[52] It was the ultimate expression—
albeit here in a political context—of a belief which, as we have seen, he had
held from an early age but which in the 1930s he had unsuccessfully
attempted to realize either through drugs or by assuming a number of
different roles. Yet as his novels in particular reveal, Vailland's search for
freedom was not at an end; it continued through a variety of situations and
experiences of which the first and perhaps most significant was the
Resistance.

Chapter Two

The Search for Identity I

Je me sens beaucoup plus près de l'équilibre et de l'épanouissement que je ne me
suis jamais senti : j'y arrive en dépassant, en
résolvant des contradictions intérieures et
extérieures affrontées franchment.

Ecrits Intimes (26 January 1944)

Vailland's continued indifference to political events, including the Nazi-Soviet Pact in 1939 which caused such bitter disruption within the ranks of the French Communist Party, went on well into the early forties. He had nothing like the sense of political responsibility—nor indeed even the positive moral attitude—of the kind that drove Nizan to resign from the Party, for example, or that forced others like Thorez and Aragon to indulge in all manner of doctrinal casuistry in their attempts to reconcile approval for official party policy with their own sense of patriotism. In this he was not alone of course; like many of his generation Vailland remained basically unmoved, indifferent even. According to an entry in his private diary in June 1942, he felt completely *disponible*, too preoccupied with his own thoughts to be more than neutral towards events:

Je ne me sens pas suffisamment français pour prendre à cœur les intérêts des Français, pas suffisamment bourgeois pour défendre la classe bourgeoise, pas suffisamment prolétaire pour m'engager dans une action révolutionnaire; je n'ai jamais milité dans aucun parti politique: c'est que je n'ai jamais eu que des *goûts*, pas de 'convictions' en matière politique, je n'ai jamais senti de cause suffisamment mienne pour risquer un danger pour elle: les communistes l'appréciaient justement en se méfiant des 'intellectuels petits-bourgeois'. Tout mon bonheur, tout mon malheur, dépendent de moi et, me semble-t-il, ne dépendent que de moi; je n'ai rien à défendre que moi-même.[1]

Much of his time he spent studying local birds and wild flowers and reading the novels of Stendhal and Hemingway. Like Duc in *La Fête* (1960) he was indifferent: 'Les voisins parlaient des premiers maquis, il [Duc] écoutait chez eux les émissions en français de la B.B.C. Cela ne le concernait pas' (*O.C.*, XII, p. 187). Yet this attitude did not last for long. As he was to recall four years later in an essay 'L'Homme mystifié', he and many others with him suddenly became aware that they had been the victims of a massive confidence trick:

> Nous ne nous étions pas trompés en refusant le respect à Pétain-le-patriote. Mais on nous avait trompés en nous faisant croire que Pétain était un patriote.[...] Nous devenions nous-mêmes patriotes. La patrie de nos vingt ans avait-elle cessé d'être dérisoire? Pas du tout, mais *ce n'était plus la même*, les patriotes de profession nous avaient mystifiés, ils nous avaient fait prendre la France de *l'Echo de Paris* pour la vraie, afin que nous ne nous préoccupions pas de les empêcher de trahir.[2]

By the end of 1942, after the German occupation of the southern zone, Vailland found himself drawn towards the fast-growing Resistance movement. He voluntarily and successfully underwent a second *désintoxication* and then during the first months of 1943 convalesced at Chavannes: 'je n'en suis pas sorti une seule fois du 15 janvier à fin mars et la campagne et le printemps précoce m'ont fort aidé à rétablir complètement mon équilibre nerveux'.[3] There are no indications in any of Vailland's private writing at this time as to precisely when or how he joined the Resistance movement but, by the middle of the year, he was fully committed, working for the *Bureau Central de Renseignements et Action* (*BCRA*) and becoming a member first of the Vélites network and later of one known as Thermopyles in which he was responsible for the coordination and transmission of information—a responsible job indeed for one whose private life had given, and was to continue to give, evidence of considerable instability. Whether or not his new attitude can be attributed to any real change in his political convictions, however, is another matter, and as *Drôle de jeu* amply illustrates, his Resistance activities would seem to have been as much motivated by curiosity and personal challenge. Indeed, to quote Françoise Giroud, it seems very much in character that what Vailland principally sought in the Resistance was 'une aventure individuelle'.[4] Whatever the motives, what was significant about Vailland's decision was that it was a positive act—a major step away from his past and a genuine effort to create a new identity for himself. Before he had time to experience his Resistance activities very fully, however, another equally influential event was to occur. In April 1943 his father underwent an operation for cancer; a second followed in July and eventually Georges Vailland died on 17 August. For his son the death of a man to whom he referred in his diary as 'un dur adversaire'[6] acted as a further release. With his successful withdrawal from drugs, a growing awareness of the oppressive influence Andrée exercized over him and now the death of one who had largely epitomized the kind of bourgeois existence he had for so long claimed to abhor, Vailland was prompted once again to give voice to his revolt. Catholicism in particular became his target and he accused Catholics of being responsible for imposing or attempting to impose certain restrictive patterns on Western civilisation. In an important letter written to his sister on 29 January 1944 Vailland outlined—albeit in a relatively egocentric and limited fashion—a number of ideas which were to be essential to his work, fictional and non-fictional alike, during the following seven years. Religion, he argued, had been responsible for creating in people a sense of 'le besoin d'absolu' (Lettres à sa famille, p. 301); similarly it had established a set of general values by which individual cases were to be judged. And, above all, it had produced a breed of people—to which Vailland now accused his sister of belonging—who would always try 'directement ou indirectement, sur le plan individuel ou sur le plan social, à m'imposer[leur] méthode de culture humaine' (Lettres à sa famille, p. 301). Such an infringe-ment of liberty—'agir au lieu d'être agi'—was intolerable, and something which Vailland was to continue to fight against for the rest of his life.

By the time Vailland came to write Drôle de jeu, therefore, various key themes in his work were already beginning to crystallize. Moreover, his experience in the Resistance had brought him into direct contact with Communism, in which he was soon to believe he could discover the solution to his problem of acting and thinking in a personal, free manner within a collective situation. Yet, while his Resistance work may have done much to remove the stigma of having belonged to the ranks of the 'intel-lectuels petits-bourgeois', the Communists were wary of him. An applica-tion for membership to the Party made on his behalf by Jacques-Francis Rolland in late 1942 or early 1943 had remained unanswered, and Vailland was not to be accepted until June 1952.[6]

Having been cut off from his Resistance network in the spring of 1944, Vailland returned to Chavannes and wrote Drôle de jeu. Recent experience provided him with the kind of substantial material he could use with confidence: the action takes place in areas intimately known to him, Paris and the Bresse; the principal characters are based on people he knew and had recently worked with—Daniel Cordier (who replaced Jean Moulin in Paris), Jacques-Francis Rolland, and one of Rolland's student friends whose fanatical adherence to the Communist Party Vailland derided at the time in his private diary.[7] As a result Vailland's depiction of the problems facing the Resistance workers in occupied Paris, of the precautions they were obliged to take to avoid detection, of the methods employed for the transmission of information, of the derailment of the German train, of the black market restaurants and so on, all have an authenticity about them which can readily be checked against any of the standard historical accounts of the Resistance.

Yet Vailland was quick and eager to point out that Drôle de jeu was not simply another historical novel:

Si j'avais voulu faire un tableau de la Résistance, il serait inexact et incomplet puisque je ne mets en scène ni les maquisards ni les saboteurs des usines (entre autres exemples), qui furent parmi les plus purs et les plus désintéressés héros de la Résistance.[8]

Instead it is a much more personalized piece of writing, an attempt to formulate '[ma] conception du monde [...] c'est-à-dire cet ensemble d'idées sur l'homme, la vie, l'amour, le rôle de l'homme dans le monde, etc., que chacun porte en soi plus ou moins confusément'.[9] In other words we are back with Vailland's earlier project, the *Trente méditations*.... It is difficult therefore not to see such intentions as having a potentially limiting effect on the impact of the novel as a piece of imaginative writing. Indeed on examination it soon becomes evident that it is a very self-conscious book, artificially layered and constructed in such a way in order that our attention should constantly be focused on Marat/Lamballe, the principal character and Vailland's thinly disguised double.

As the closing reference to Xenephon's *Anabasis* and the accompanying exhortation to the Resistance fighters to be courageous and to continue their struggle suggests, *Drôle de jeu* deals with a period of time (about twenty days) selected almost at random from a continuing situation. In spite of this, however, very little changes, and as the novel develops only the derailment of the German train in Part III and the search for Caracalla in Part V provide any real impetus. Certainly many incidental episodes and descriptions like those of the Jewish couple Marat studies on his train journey to Lyon, the battle of wills between the curé and Jeanne or Elvire's dinner party, for example, are notable for the detail and acumen with which they are observed. But incidental they remain. Vailland deliberately establishes the context of the Resistance early on, thereby ensuring that the actions of his characters are neatly circumscribed and that the pressures to which they are submitted constant. Over and above this he uses a five-part 'classical' dramatic structure in order both to shape an action which becomes increasingly psychological and emotional, and to control the movements of Marat/Lamballe who in his dual role acts as both exponent and critic of Resistance activities.

With the exception of Marat, the characters in *Drôle de jeu* fall into two distinct categories: representatives of the French population in general, and a small group directly involved with the Resistance and who illustrate particular reactions to it. The function of those belonging to the former—Parisians and provincials alike—is self-evident; either they are targets for Vailland's scorn (for example, the cynical opportunists at Elvire's dinner party or the two journalists in Part I, Chapter Five) or they provide some extra depth to the general context and atmosphere (the anonymous dentist to whom Marat goes when he learns of Mathilde's treachery, the curé d'Etiamble, or Sidoine the engineer). For the most part they each appear once only, and occasionally, as is the case with Thucydide, the professional killer, at the risk of caricature. In general, however, they simply form part of the background against which the principal characters act out their parts. Here Vailland's taste for the discipline of the neo-classical theatre, which is to be a constant feature of his imaginative writing, can be seen to operate. With the exception of Annie whose actual appearance is strategically delayed until the middle of the book, we are presented with all the principal characters in Part I of *Drôle de jeu*. As the novel progresses it also becomes noticeable that apart from Marat, who is able to dissociate himself from them whenever he chooses, they remain faithful to the parts for which they have been cast. Four of them in particular show little development. Caracalla remains the 'machine à conspirer',[10] so devoted to his task that he pays little or no attention to people other than in the context of Resistance work, and whose only visible emotion when Marat takes him to a night-club is one of guilt (p. 130). Rodrigue, Marat's principal associate, remains young and un-formed to the end, uncertain how to take his friend's advice about women, unable to make known to Chloé his affection for her, and more importantly still, directly responsible for having disclosed the details of Caracalla's whereabouts to Mathilde. His emotional immaturity is counterbalanced, however, by a streak of idealism, expressed in his attempt (in Part IV, Chapter One) to persuade Marat to allow him to give money to the CACFM (Comité d'aide aux corps francs du maquis) and continued beyond *Drôle de jeu* into *Bon Pied Bon Œil* (1950). Chloé too, for all her undoubted maturity and experience both as a member of the Resistance and simply as a woman, is never allowed to enjoy more than a nominal role. She is the mother figure ('la bonne ménagère de la Résistance' (p. 126)) who appears as often in a domestic context as in an active political one. She also stands in complete contrast to Mathilde, Vailland rather naively indicating the differences in their moral qualities through his physical descriptions of them. On her first appearance, Chloé is described as 'une grande, forte fille qui, avant de se consacrer à la Résistance, était mannequin' (p. 110). Much later in the novel (Part IV, Chapter Three), after Marat has returned to Paris, we read: 'Vers onze heures survient Chloé. Elle porte, sous un léger manteau de demi-saison, une robe neuve faite d'un 'foulard' à pois qui joue sur la gorge. 'Comment tu es belle!' dit Marat (p. 303)'.[11] Within a few pages we are with Mathilde again:

> Mathilde vint lui [à Marat] ouvrir, dans une vieille robe de chambre tachée en maintes places. Elle releva une mèche de cheveux qui lui tombait sur les yeux. Elle avait les paupières bouffies, des traînées noirâtres sous les yeux, du rouge au coin des lèvres, elle s'était certainement endormie sans s'être démaquillée, le coup de sonnette venait de la réveiller (p. 306).

Here, as in Part I, her slovenliness contrasts sharply with Chloé's crisp elegance and is a clear, if somewhat unsubtle pointer to her role of traitor in the novel.

It is into this fairly clearly delineated group that Frédéric and Annie are introduced. Like its members they too are defined from the outset; unlike them, however, they are far less static. While it may be evident from early on just where their roles will lead them, they are nonetheless allowed to explore them as new experiences. From the first, Frédéric is shown to be an ascetic; he neither smokes nor drinks, is obsessed by physical cleanliness and is also, by repute at least, a virgin. Rodrigue remarks that 'il fait tout par principe avec principe' (p. 187) and Annie that 'il s'imagine Robespierre' (p. 257). He lacks subtlety; he pays court to Annie with as much vigour and enthusiasm as he practises his political convictions. But like Mathilde, whose consuming love for Dani eventually drives her into the waiting arms of the Gestapo, he allows himself to be totally overwhelmed by his passions, and is, in consequence, incapable of viewing situations objectively or of acting rationally. His eventual capture and presumed fate at the hands of the Nazis may have been very unfortunate, but, it is suggested, not all that surprising. Just as Frédéric's inexperience and refusal to accept advice or modify his fanatical views forces him again and again into an impasse of theorizing and high principles, so, in contrast, Annie is refreshingly cynical about the whole Resistance ethos.[12] Even so she too had allowed herself to be dominated by convention—social, educational and sexual. (While it is nowhere actually stated that she is a virgin, her sexual inexperience and inhibitions are evident.) Like Frédéric, there is an element of purity about her which Vailland again transmits through his first description of her:

> Ses traits sont d'une rare finesse. Le nez, la bouche, le menton, les sourcils, les tempes sont d'un dessin net, comme dans les estampes japonaises. La bouche petite, le nez menu avec le dos droit et l'extrémité arrondie, le menton qui prolonge et parachève l'ovale des joues, donnent une impression d'extrême délicatesse. Le cou, long et flexible, rend sa pleine signification au mot 'porter': il *porte*, avec une grâce infinie, le visage. La peau est blanche et presque transparente; sa finesse se manifeste tout particulièrement aux tempes, dont elle laisse voir le tendre réseau de veines bleutées. Le front est droit, haut, d'un dessin précis. Les cheveux blond cendré, très abondants, d'une extrême finesse, ondulés en larges vagues, encadrent le visage avec exactitude, puis, à la hauteur de la nuque, s'épandent fougueusement et tombent sur les épaules. Le visage d'Annie frappe par sa perfection: c'est un ouvrage fini, achevé, auquel on n'imagine rien pouvoir ajouter ni retrancher. (p. 244)

In her case, however, physical purity is not an indication of moral (or political) fanaticism. She has retained an independence of mind unknown to Frédéric, and while she may initially have been won over by him to Communism, it was a position which she soon rejected. Her real quality is that she is able to consider other people and events with precisely that degree of critical detachment which Frédéric lacks. (It is interesting to note that in Vailland's last novel *La Truite* (1964) the heroine who possesses the same qualities though in a much more developed form is named Frédérique.) Frédéric's blinkered attitude both to politics and to love results in disaster; Annie, eventually tutored by Marat, is more fortunate, and by the close of the novel she has, we may assume, reached that degree of maturity enjoyed by Chloé and is ready to take her place beside the others in their continuing struggle against the Nazis.

The situation of Marat, however, is deliberately more ambiguous. Certainly there can be no doubt as to his commitment to the Resistance movement: 'Depuis l'armistice, il n'était plus possible de "rester en marge", c'eût été quand même prendre parti et prendre parti contre les siens; maintenant donc, il combattait' (pp. 181–2). And when he describes to Caracalla what it is that has motivated the French people as a whole, he is also defining his own position:

> En 40, ils ne voulaient pas se battre parce que la bataille ne répondait
> à aucun besoin profond de leur être; maintenant ils n'aspirent qu'à
> se battre, en maints endroits ils se battent déjà, parce que l'Allemand
> et le milicien les ont opprimés et surtout humiliés; ils ont un affront
> à venger. (p. 121)

Significantly, however, Vailland presents his principal character both as *Marat* and as *Lamballe*, his historical namesakes being nicely indicative of the two quite different sides of his character: Marat the devoted, *pure* revolutionary (already glimpsed in *L'Histoire d'un Homme du peuple sous la Révolution* and central to a number of essays Vailland wrote during the 1940s) and Lamballe, a legitimized bastard son of Louis XIV and a perfect example of the eighteenth-century libertine. Furthermore we should note that Marat was Vailland's own *nom de guerre* during the Resistance, while Lamballe's Christian name, François, is, we may recall, that given to Vailland during the Simplistes-Grand Jeu years and later, in the form of Robert François, one of his pseudonyms as a journalist for *Paris-Soir*. It is hardly surprising therefore that while Marat may travel in first-class compartments, visit night-clubs or frequent prostitutes, it is more usually Lamballe who shares the illicit benefits of the Occupation enjoyed by those whose political apathy of the pre-war years has now changed into a passive acceptance of events and opportunism. It is probable in fact that Vailland's own attitude during the Resistance years continued on occasions to be a mixture of these two; nor, of course, should we forget Caracalla's dream of being able to opt out completely, to live in 'une petite villa dans la banlieue de Londres où quelqu'un raconterait des histoires sur la résistance en France, nous nous plaindrions d'être en exil, ce serait merveilleux...'[26] (p. 126).

But as Vailland himself was eager to underline, *Drôle de jeu* was not a 'Resistance novel', nor was his principal character—or indeed any other— to be considered as a vehicle simply for his own attitude to the Resistance. What we have in *Drôle de jeu* is the first extensive example in Vailland's writing of his attempt to exorcize his past and, masquerading under the intended philosophical reflections, his 'conception du monde', the portrayal of a new, ideal figure. It was his first real mask.

By the time he came to commit himself to the Resistance, Vailland was, as we have seen, a solitary figure still in the process of emerging from a period of complete intellectual and emotional disorientation. Now for the first time since the Grand Jeu affair he found himself presented with the opportunity of sharing in a collective venture which, at the same time, promised to satisfy his individual needs. But the memory of what happened in 1929 was still strong, and the letter to his sister and his portrayal of Frédéric show he was clearly all too aware of the dangers of total, blind commitment.[13] Yet this was the choice which faced him and which Vailland projected into his first novel.

Marat's recollections of his early years and the extracts from his diary in the first two parts of the novel prepare the way for his meeting with Annie to whom he readily and egotistically expounds his philosophy. In this way Vailland both writes out his past, provides information concerning his protagonist's (and his own) formative years and experiences, and brings Marat to the point where he can debate his new position. But Vailland's exorcism of his past also takes a more brutal form in the assassination of Mathilde—as it will too in *Les Mauvais Coups* (1948) with the death of Roberte—who, together with B., is clearly a projection of Andrée.[14] More significant still, however, is the age gap between Marat and his fellow Resistance workers. Rodrigue and Frédéric are twenty-one, Caracalla, Marat's superior, twenty-three, a fact to which our attention is sharply drawn at the end of the first chapter. Unlike Marat they have had little or no time for reflection; even as students they have plunged straight into action, committing themselves without hesitation to a cause which to them collectively is a just one. In consequence therefore there is an inevitable gap between them and Marat (picked up later in *Bon Pied Bon Œil*) which is more than just one of age: it is a problem of communication of which Marat shows himself to be aware on several occasions. He is, to use his own words 'un promeneur solitaire', 'un passant', and while not unnaturally, it is to *Marat*, the 'new' Vailland that our attention is increasingly drawn, and not to *Lamballe*, he remains to the very end an outsider. Indeed it is surely significant that at the close of the novel Marat should find himself alone in an unknown hotel bedroom equipped with a set of papers providing him with yet another temporary identity. The situation is further complicated by Vailland's various statements of faith in Communism and the Communists as the only coherent doctrine and body of people within the several which had come together in the common spirit of the Resistance. In one of the early extracts from Marat's diary for example, we read:

> Seuls les communistes disposent d'une doctrine qui leur permet une interprétation cohérente des événements. L'homme de génie sortira de leurs rangs; ce sera celui qui saura tirer du marxisme une explication du monde actuel frappante, évidente, universellement acceptable, et en déduire des règles d'action. (pp. 139-40)

Yet however convinced Vailland was, there was also, as he recognized, a considerable difference between political belief and the expression of that belief through action—a problem that was to become central to his work ten years later.[15] As Marat confesses to Annie: 'Je me bats aux côtés des communistes, j'adhère sans réserve à leur doctrine, je fais tout ce que je peux pour le Parti, plus peut-être que beaucoup de militants—mais je n'ai pas le *style* communiste...' (p. 284). However much he may have attempted to exorcize his past, Marat (Vailland) had retained—and not always too unwillingly—what he defined as the vices of his bourgeois class.[16] The only solution open to him then was to play his part, to pretend to belong in the hope that one day pretence would become a reality.[17] While therefore Vailland's presentation of his principal character is considerably more complex than that of any other, Marat does fit into the same dominant theatrical pattern of *Drôle de jeu*. Already the situating of Annie's first appearance in the central episode has been noticed, so too has the presentation of all the principal characters in Part I. Elsewhere we find other indications of this same concern: the stage-direction style of the openings to a number of chapters (One and Three, for example) followed at once by dialogue; the infrequency of descriptive passages; the manipulation of tense.[18] Not always, however, does such concern lead to happy results: in the final chapter, for example, coincidence (like the fact that Annie's aunt is absent from Paris) destroys the otherwise promising ironic interplay of scenes.

Drôle de jeu, therefore, is an interesting and important first novel. Interesting in that it shows Vailland already conscious of the need to provide an appropriate style and form for his ideas; important in that it is a clear pointer to his development both politically and personally during the next dozen years in particular. But while in *Drôle de jeu* Vailland could project himself into the idealized figure of Marat, Lamballe was to return. As much of his non-imaginative writing of the mid forties and his second novel, *Les Mauvais Coups* show, the problems were still far from solved.

After the war in late 1944 Vailland resumed his career as a journalist, this time working principally for *Libération*, edited by his former colleague and co-author Raymond Manevy and for the weekly *Action*. Yet while his ready association with such communist-dominated publications is significant, there is scant evidence to suggest that Vailland was in any way caught up in the political-ideological debate which centred on the question of communist power in post-war France. Nor does he appear to have had any meaningful contact with the left-wing *Comité national des écrivains*. Vailland shared his responsibilities for *Libération* and *Action* as foreign correspondent with Claude Roy and Jacques-Francis Rolland. Punctuating the normal accounts of war activities in, amongst other places, Alsace, Holland, Belgium and Bavaria, however, we occasionally find Vailland returning to his basic theme of freedom and restriction. One article in particular, which appeared in *Action* for 28 December 1945, challenges a review of *Drôle de jeu* written by his *Libération* colleague the Catholic, Louis Martin-Chauffier who claimed that Vailland was an 'inconoclaste par amour caché d'un Dieu dont il redoute à la fois la rencontre et désire l'approche'.[19] As we might expect, Vailland reacted strongly, accusing Martin-Chauffier (as he had accused his sister in the previous year) of adopting the kind of superior attitude born of religious conviction. His response, predictable enough, was yet another statement of the view he was to pursue during the next few years:

> Si j'ai quelque qualité, c'est bien, je pense, d'appartenir à cette lignée essentiellement française d'esprits libres qui mène depuis des siècles le combat singulier de la Raison humaine contre la notion du sacré sous toutes ses formes...[20]

By *sacré*, of course, Vailland—like Nizan and Politzer before him—designates not only anything that inhibits or restricts, but above all any elitist system of philosophy or belief created in order to provide security for those who subscribe to it. In particular the bourgeois class is guilty of this; two years later in an article entitled 'Questions de communisme', for example, we read:

> La bourgeoisie invente, selon les besoins de l'heure, les doctrines, les philosophies, les religions qui lui sont utiles. Les 'chiens de garde' s'accordent spontanément pour déprécier le rationalisme quand l'appel au sentiment de *sacré* devient nécessaire pour défendre les privilèges communs.[21]

Between 1945 and 1947 Vailland wrote a number of essays and reflections, all of which turned on this issue to some degree or other—*Quelques réflexions sur la singularité d'être français* (1945), *De quel monstrueux souci leur âme et dieu font-ils le poids?* (c. 1945), *Marat* (c. 1946), *Esquisses pour un portrait d'un vrai libertin* (1946), *Le Surréalisme contre la Révolution* (1947) and *Pour et contre l'existentialisme* (1947). While he recognized that he too had been guilty of evasion particularly through drugs ('une mystique sans Dieu')[22] Vailland now maintained that he had become fully aware of the need to think and act independently. Existentialism and more particularly surrealism (which had promised so much as 'une révolte contre la morale bourgeoise'),[23] had ultimately failed since they too in turn had both become systems of *évasion*, basically as guilty as Catholicism of having created and perpetuated their own mystiques. Yet the exposure of such systems, necessary if society were to make any kind of meaningful revolutionary progress, could only be achieved, Vailland maintained, in terms of a simultaneous realization of personal freedom. The two processes were inevitably linked: 'Chaque pas décisif dans la conquête du monde et la maîtrise de l'homme par lui-même a d'abord à dévoiler une mystification, à *désacraliser* un nouveau domaine.'[24] Already we find Vailland making references to Sade as the ideal figure—'une *âme forte*, il se *plaît à braver* Dieu et le Roi'[25]—the perfect *amateur*:

> L'amateur [...] c'est celui qui ne fait pas profession. Il n'est pas contraint par la nécessité. C'est volontairement qu'il s'abandonne à son goût, et il ne cesse jamais de le dominer. A ce dernier sens, nous retrouvons l'opposition cartésienne entre l'*action* et la *passion*. L'amateur n'est pas la victime, l'objet d'une passion, il n'est pas *agi*, il sait en toute occasion rester le sujet qui *agit*.[26]

For Vailland himself, however, the realization of this kind of freedom was in its earliest stages. As we have already seen, only during the early forties did he begin to make any real progress and, as *Drôle de jeu* in particular shows, there was a considerable division between the ideal figure and reality. It is hardly surprising, therefore, that much of Vailland's writing at this time is concerned with a discussion of his personal dilemma, the two unpublished essays in particular—*De quel monstrueux souci leur âme et dieu font-ils le poids?* and *Marat*—returning obsessively to the need to define himself. 'J'existe pour moi dans la mesure de ma souveraineté, c'est-à-dire de ma possession de moi-même et de mon autonomie dans le monde.'[27] Even so, once achieved, personal freedom (sovereignty) is in danger of becoming compromised through contact with society as a whole. Marat may indeed be Vailland's projected ideal, but he has after all accepted to play a role and in so doing has allowed himself to become an integral part of a more general scheme, and hence of something which threatens to limit and restrict him as before. Nor is it enough for Vailland to pretend that his character is free by allowing him to alternate between the part he chooses to play (Marat) and his real self (Lamballe). For freedom to be truly authentic it must be achieved without recourse to artificial props or aids of any kind. This precisely was Vailland's personal dilemma. Already he had begun to rid himself of those inhibiting forces which had so shaped his earlier life. But not entirely. While his Resistance activities and contact with a number of Communists may have already indicated a political solution, he had yet to achieve the kind of personal freedom necessary if he were to commit himself fully to it. In *De quel monstrueux souci leur âme et dieu font-ils le poids?* Vailland wrote: 'je n'ai d'autre loi que ma propre loi autant que je puis l'insérer dans le monde: ce que je veux c'est ce que je suis, et je suis ce que je suis dans la mesure où je puis l'être'. It was this degree of personal emancipation which he had not yet achieved which was to become a recurring theme in his work during the next few years.

On 27 November Vailland saw a performance of Camus' play *Caligula*. He found it humourless, arid—'ce n'est pas de l'humour mais l'idée de l'humour [...] chez un intellectuel petit-bourgeois après la deuxième Grande Guerre'[28]—yet it stirred him sufficiently for him to decide that he too would like to try his hand at the theatre. After some deliberation and exploration of various subjects both historical and contemporary Vailland settled on that of Heloisa and Abelard. Through it he hoped to project these obsessions which, as we have seen, formed the central core of his non-imaginative writings at this time. On 18 January in his 'Journal d'Héloïse et Abélard'[29] Vailland remarks: 'Assez pensé qu'il serait important pour moi qu'Abélard et Héloïse ait du succès: ce serait la liberté gagnée'. While with the recent (December 1945) award of the Prix Interallié for *Drôle de jeu* Vailland may have had no more than material independence in mind, it seems likely that he was also anticipating a sense of fulfilment. (It is worth recalling that the prize brought no instant financial reward, merely the prestige and promise of increased sales.) In fact, although *Héloïse et Abélard* did win the Prix Ibsen in 1950 it hardly contains much evidence for it to be called a theatrical success. Too much of a *pièce à thèse*, it mixes personal preoccupations—the questions of love, passion and possession—with wider issues —rebellion against the authority of the Church and State. Héloïse's cry—'Mon bonheur, à moi, c'est de faire ce que je veux, même contre le monde entier'[30], or the discussions concerning the *essential* identity of Abélard or the Prince, are, it should be clear, simple transpositions from any of Vailland's contemporary writings. So too is Héloïse's outburst in the final act against the fear which the Church has instilled in men's minds.[31] Whatever the play may lack in dramatic tension, however, there are a number of features which link it to *Drôle de jeu* and also anticipate Vailland's subsequent work. The enclosed nature of the basic intrigue ('à l'abri de cette monumentale serrure')[32] recalls the theatrical artificiality of the earlier novel; the Prince who for all his friendliness towards Abélard remains ultimately aloof and indifferent, playing people off against one another, is not unlike Marat; Abélard's castration is to become (as Jean Recanati has so amply demonstrated) a persistent theme in Vailland's writing; so too is the technical detail of the machinery controlling the entrance to Abélard's room. There is no indication in Vailland's diaries as to whether or not he was satisfied with *Héloïse et Abélard*. He was to return to the theatre within the next three years with *Le Colonel Foster plaidera coupable*, by which time his allegiance to (though not yet membership of) the Communist party had been much more clearly and publicly stated. Meanwhile it was in his novels that Vailland returned to the process of working out his obsession with *le sacré* in its various forms. The real exorcism of his past had begun.

In spite of their inherent promise as pieces of imaginative literature, both *Drôle de jeu* and *Héloïse et Abélard* may be seen to suffer from an imbalance caused by Vailland's overriding concern for a number of philosophical and technical considerations. *Les Mauvais Coups*, written between July 1947 and February 1948, is a much more successfully integrated piece of work. The exorcism of his past continues, and the tone of the book is one of conflict and crisis. Unlike *Drôle de jeu*, in which problems are presented through various situations and discussed by a number of characters, in *Les Mauvais Coups* the range is narrower and the focus, from the beginning, much sharper.

Milan who, like Vailland in 1947, is approaching 'l'équinoxe de [ses] quarante ans',[33] has retired to a small country village for a year. A man of intelligence and taste, he has made himself a successful career as an adviser on interior design. His marriage, however, has been less satisfactory. He has known his wife, Roberte, for fifteen years, and their relationship based at first on a mutual all exclusive passion has, as Roberte herself recognizes, now exhausted itself: 'Voilà quinze ans que ça dure. Maintenant, c'est la fin' (p. 58). The time has come for them to separate and put an end to their perpetual duel, yet they find themselves powerless to do so. In the village they become friendly with Hélène, the young institutrice, who, rather like Annie in *Drôle de jeu*, is a convenient but willing audience for Milan's views on love and freedom. Unwittingly she is the cause of Roberte's eventual death, for while Milan's relationship with her is no more than one of mild flirtation—indeed she is as much influenced by Roberte as by him—Roberte becomes increasingly jealous of her. Although there is no positive evidence for it, she appears to find a letter which Milan has written to Hélène and in which he expresses his dissatisfaction with his present life, leaves the house in a temper, becomes drunk and drives into one of the local swamps where she is drowned. Milan has not been required to make any effort; Roberte has ended their marriage for him.

The similarity between the fictive world of *Les Mauvais Coups* and the reality of Vailland's own situation is obvious. Following the award of the Prix Interallié for *Drôle de jeu*, Vailland returned to a life of alcoholism, drug addiction (morphine) and 'ballets nocturnes' in Saint-Germain-des-Prés and Montparnasse. In view too of the earlier insecurity of their married life it is not altogether surprising that Vailland and Andrée should separate once again early in 1947. Yet even though they were never to live together again on any permanent basis, the process of separation was long and painful.[34] Vailland was still held by the vestiges of their original *amour-passion*, and the tension of the love-hate relationship which developed during the last years of their marriage is suggested by the opening chapter of the novel where Milan and Roberte snipe at one another just as they snipe at the early morning birds. As the novel develops, their marriage is shown to be characterized by suspicion and spite, yet oddly tempered by occasional gestures or words of affection;[35] even after their brutal physical clash in Chapter Six, Vailland's description of them is deliberately ambiguous: 'Ils avaient tous deux les traits défaits et les yeux cernés comme après l'amour' (p. 133). The point of balance between love and hate is a delicate one indeed, though at the same time it is born of a much more deep-rooted emotion—fear. For Milan, Roberte (like B. and Mathilde before her in *Drôle de jeu*) is a reincarnation of the archetypal mother figure threatening his personal freedom and self-expression: 'J'ai peur de toi comme j'avais peur de ma mère. Je fais des rêves où le même personnage menaçant qui se dresse en face de moi a tantôt son visage, tantôt le tien' (p. 130).[36]

In consequence, Milan's assertions of his belief in complete autonomy have an empty ring about them; but it is also precisely because he is aware of this fear that we find an element of self-criticism in *Les Mauvais Coups* which was lacking in *Drôle de jeu*. Milan knows that he has to rid himself of his inhibition, that his theories must be given practical expression, and it is through his attempts to do this that a tension is created in the novel providing it with a unity which goes beyond one of structure and form.

On a first reading *Les Mauvais Coups* appears to divide itself into two more or less equal sections: the first containing those chapters which deal principally with the Milan-Roberte relationship, the second a series of seemingly incidental, even gratuitous episodes—the calving of Radiguet's cow (Chapter Three), the scene between Duval and Hélène (Chapter Four) or the evening in the casino (Chapter Five). Closer examination, however, suggests that these episodes in turn relate directly to the central theme of conflict and inhibition which in a more total way characterizes the Milan-Roberte marriage. They are all in their own right moments of crisis and tension, the outcome of which can only be success or failure; they portray extreme situations in which there is no room for half-measures, and from which there can be no turning back.[37] Once seen in this way they link in with the natural and primitive patterns which dominate so much of the rest of the book. As we have already noticed, the tone of *Les Mauvais Coups* is established in the hunting scenes of the opening chapter. More specific instances of it appear in Milan's nightmares about 'un grand oiseau qui tentait de me crever les yeux' (p. 16), his recollection of the young hare which he tried unsuccessfully to raise in captivity (p. 45) and above all in the crow which he pursues through the vines and brutally clubs to death, the 'sale bête [qui] ressemble aux oiseaux que je vois dans mes cauchemars' (p. 125). Clearly it is intended that the bird should symbolize Roberte, yet at the same time we should not forget that *un milan* is also a bird of prey, a deliberate ambiguity which reflects that of the title of the novel itself. Milan is therefore symbolically attempting to destroy not only his tormentor but that part of himself or even that version of himself which submits to such torment. It is also significant that in the same chapter (Chapter Six) Roberte should undertake the destruction of Milan's image of Hélène. Ostensibly giving her a lesson in the art of make-up, she carefully turns her from the fresh idealized young creature (again Annie in *Drôle de jeu* or Jenny Merveille) into 'le genre entraîneuse de boîte de nuit' (p. 126). But such vicarious expressions of hatred and spite can provide limited satisfaction only. Ultimately they must give way to reality and in the final pages of the chapter Vailland brings Milan and Roberte together in an open physical expression of their mutual hate. In spite of the ambiguous ending to the scene which we have already noted, events are now too advanced for there to be any real possibility of relief.

If, like *Drôle de jeu*, *Les Mauvais Coups* is considered in terms of the theatre it quickly becomes obvious that Roberte and Milan remain true to the roles cast for them from the beginning, and that their relationship is presented without recourse to the kind of artificiality which characterized so much of the earlier novel. What is more striking, however, is the manner in which Vailland has succeeded in providing *Les Mauvais Coups* with a synthesis that is absent from the earlier book. Dissatisfied with— or perhaps unable to provide—a neat solution to the human problem, he projects it into the wider context of an elemental and natural world of struggle and survival, of death and rebirth, of winter and summer. As I have already suggested, certain individual scenes only become fully meaningful when seen in this context, and indeed some—those describing the calving of Radiguet's cow or Milan's anger for example—are given too great an emphasis for them to be wholly acceptable. The first of these, as Picard has rightly emphasized, assumes the qualities of a fable and acts as a pointer to the meaning of the book as a whole.[38] Roberte, in successfully bringing the calf into the world, momentarily transcends the division between humans and animals and becomes an incarnation of the all absorbing universal mother figure of which Milan has such fear. Yet before the end of the night she has collapsed from the effects of the tension and of excessive alcohol, while the calf ultimately dies. Roberte has failed. There are at the same time a number of references in the novel to the superior strength and qualities of horses. In this particular scene Bourret, the vet, describes the speed with which a mare gives birth to a foal for example:

Une jument accouche debout, au retour du travail, sans préparation, sans avertissement. C'est à peine si tu t'es aperçu qu'elle est agitée, qu'elle est en sueur, que sa face est crispée. Elle se laisse tomber, elle se relève aussi vite, les sabots apparaissent, le poulain est expulsé d'un seul coup. La jument retombe apaisée, délivrée. C'est beau, une jument qui met bas. (p. 63)

Within two pages Hélène is described by Milan as 'une jument jeune, légère et grave' (p. 64). The contrasts and comparisons which we are being invited to make about the two women are, like those between Mathilde and Chloé in *Drôle de jeu*, obvious enough.

Similarly at the end of Chapter Six the symbolism of the poker for which Milan and Roberte struggle (and which Milan eventually wins) is given an extra dimension by the notion of phallic erection and ejaculation that is basic to Vailland's description of Milan's mounting anger as a whole:

Il connaissait bien sa colère. Elle naît dans les jambes, elle joue quelque temps dans les articulations des genoux, puis, d'un seul coup, elle fait l'ascension des cuisses et inonde le bas-ventre; là, le flot ne monte plus que lentement mais il est déjà puissant comme un fleuve en crue qui fait trembler les digues dans leur fondement; quand la colère atteint enfin le soleil de nerfs qui irradie au creux de la poitrine, il est trop tard pour l'enchaîner, elle jaillit comme un fer de lance et crève le cœur, le jet de sang inonde le visage et fait gonfler douloureusement jusqu'aux plus fines veinules des lobes cérébraux; toute conscience s'abolit dans une grande lueur rouge. (p. 129)

Clearly, such examples as these, however impressively written and significant they may be, threaten to obtrude and endanger the balance of the book as a whole. Fortunately they are few. Elsewhere the natural pattern of events is conveyed on a smaller scale altogether with references to the weather playing a particularly important part. Towards the end of the novel these increase and are frequently accompanied by suggestions of nervous tension: 'C'est le vent, dit Milan, le vent d'équinoxe. [...] Une rafale fit resonner les peupliers dans la prairie, au bas de la terrasse' (p. 110); 'Le grand vent énerve tout le monde...' (p. 115); 'Je suis nerveuse en ce moment. C'est l'approche de l'équinoxe' (p. 135) and so on. Moreover it comes as little surprise that the day of Roberte's death should be, precisely, 21 September: 'A l'aube le vent tourna à l'ouest. C'était le jour de l'équinoxe. Le ciel se couvrit peu à peu, mais il ne commença à pleuvoir qu'à la fin de l'après-midi' (p. 151).

There are, to be sure, some episodes which appear rather out of place, such as those recounting Milan's early formative years in Paris, for example, or the letter to Hélène in which he expounds his views on *l'amour-fou* and on the seasonal variations of life. It is also arguable that Vailland is still too firmly gripped by his personal problems for him to be able either to produce an entirely autonomous piece of imaginative writing or indeed to be able to project problems of the kind dealt with in *Les Mauvais Coups* in such a way that they become dissociated from him. Although in the guise of the fictional Roberte, Andrée has been physically removed, her influence, compounding that of the mother figure, has been too strong for it to be nullified quite so simply. It is surely significant therefore that in the closing words of the novel Milan should find himself actually incapable of admitting her death: 'Roberte, dit Milan, est restée au village' (p. 161). Although like *Drôle de jeu*, *Les Mauvais Coups* closes with its protagonist on the verge of a new situation, we have the impression that this too can only be a temporary refuge. In this respect *Les Mauvais Coups* is a more honest novel than *Drôle de jeu*; as Recanati suggests, while Marat had been the ideal, Milan is the real man.[39] The process of 'demystification' may still be far from complete, but Vailland has at least confronted it and continues to do so in his next two novels *Bon Pied Bon Œil* and *Un Jeune Homme seul*. At the same time, however, they go beyond *Les Mauvais Coups* in that they also show the extent to which Vailland's imaginative writing was beginning to be influenced by his growing involvement in political matters.

The last chapters of *Les Mauvais Coups* had been written in Czechoslovakia where Vailland had been attending a writers' conference. On his return he went in April to Italy with his Communist friend, the journalist and novelist Pierre Courtade, and with Claude Roy whose youthful support for the right-wing philosophy of Maurras' Action Française movement had during the occupation been replaced by a fast growing sympathy for the Communist Party, where he was to report on the Italian elections for *Action* and *Libération*. Since the 1946 referendum when the monarchy had been defeated, the Italian political situation had resolved itself into a basic struggle between the Popular Front on the Left and the Christian Democrats on the Right. Now in 1948 the Left, for the first time it seemed, had a real chance to assume control, due essentially to the rapidly increasing influence of Togliatti's Communist Party. For Vailland and his colleagues (as indeed for so many left-wing intellectuals in Europe at this time) the fate of the Italian Communist Party in particular would be a pointer to the potential of the Party in western Europe as a whole and it became fashionable to talk of the struggle in terms of a political crusade. Nonetheless, in as much as it affected him personally, Vailland was still only an observer—albeit a strongly sympathetic one. What he could see and approve as a general political situation was not one which he could as yet easily or even necessarily subscribe to unquestioningly himself. A sense of new-found freedom (though not in fact so fully realized as *Bon Pied Bon Œil* and *Un Jeune Homme seul* were to show), his ever-present readiness to dissociate himself from events in order, he felt, to be able to evaluate and criticize them to the full, and a typically egoistic pursuit of personal satisfaction were large and difficult obstacles to overcome. Yet in spite of them, Vailland was moving gradually to a position where he sensed that only by participating in a common cause, by committing himself to a collective programme, would he be able to find personal satisfaction. On 18 April 1948 the Popular Front was defeated—'Nous étions bien tristes, mais pas désespérés'[40]—and Vailland returned to France with Claude Roy to the latter's house in the Charente. Yet isolation in the depths of a French province in no way lessened Vailland's enthusiasm, and it was from here that one of the most complete definitions of his political stance at that time came.

Towards the end of May two articles by Jean Mijema and Jean Larnac appeared in *Action*, the first on a film version of Stendhal's *La Chartreuse de Parme*, the second on 'La Préciosité'. In them Vailland and Roy discovered a number of 'formules sur lesquelles nous nous sommes trouvés accordés dans le désaccord'.[41] Their response was to write a letter in which they outlined their views on revolutionary political activity and on the way in which, according to them, its essential motivating force was individual happiness.[42] The view that such happiness should be ignored in pursuit of a common political goal or in favour of trying to create a single social class was, they argued, a reactionary one. Instead people act as individuals:

> Celui qui se bat combat pour lui, tout de suite, pour lui présent à lui-même dans l'instant où il combat, parce que c'est la seule solution possible dans le présent pour lui s'il veut être heureux. (*Ecrits Intimes*, p. 142)

Only personal fulfilment therefore can provide a collective venture with its real energy and lead to true revolutionary action. Yet happiness is no divine gift: 'le bonheur ne vient pas à l'homme du ciel, il vient à l'homme de l'homme' (*Ecrits Intimes*, p. 143). The political implication is at once clear. Marxism, it is claimed, by making men aware of their present condition and hence of the need for change, provides the perfect incentive:

> Le marxisme n'appauvrit pas la notion du bonheur. Il l'enrichit. Il en rend le désir plus exigeant, parce qu'il fait prendre conscience aux hommes de nouvelles conditions et de nouvelles tâches. Etre communiste, c'est s'assigner un bonheur difficile, mais immédiat. (*Ecrits Intimes*, p. 143)

While the argument of their letter is clear enough, so too is its egocentricity. This is not to say, of course, that Vailland and Roy did not fully believe in the view they put forward; moreover they were active in the assistance they gave to a former Resistance colleague, Jean Pronteau: 'nous courions les routes de Charente, orateurs incertains (sauf Jean), communistes convaincus et compagnons heureux'.[43] But conviction can be as much an intuitive or even emotional response as an intellectual one, and, as Claude Roy has subsequently admitted, their letter to *Action* smacked of a certain 'romantisme doctoral'. Furthermore it is important to situate this view in the now fast developing attitudes of the French Communist Party's thinking during the late forties. The immediate post-war climate in which there was in general an unquestioning acceptance of the claims made on various fronts for democracy and free choice was changing. In particular American aid to Europe, the Marshall Plan, which the Party had allowed to go unchallenged, was now an issue. Prompted by the official Moscow line many of the Party's intellectuals saw America's commercial interests and Catholicism (with Cardinal Spellman prominent) as the first steps, to be resisted at all costs, towards an attempt to seize political control. It is hardly surprising, therefore, that such egocentric views as these that Vailland and Roy were proclaiming were unacceptable, lacking the necessary degree of hard-line conviction and, whatever they may have professed to the contrary, offering little evidence of a willing-ness to sacrifice personal indulgence in the interest of a common cause. Vailland was still the Marat figure of *Drôle de jeu*—or at least hoped to be, a 'fils de roi' or an 'homme de qualité'. But the pull of political action was increasing in strength and it was the tension thus created which, coupled with the strain of his private life, reduced him to a low point of despair. After his stay at Charente Vailland moved to Sceaux. His diaries during the last months of 1948 return obsessively to the theme of isolation, highlighted by his short essay 'Je suis ce soir triste à mourir' (*Ecrits Intimes*, pp. 146–50). In this the problem which he is to explore and partly resolve in *Bon Pied Bon Œil* soon becomes apparent. He realizes only too well that he belongs to an older generation and that political commitment for the contemporary communist demands an unswerving allegiance to a new life style:

> Nos amis qui parlent de la nécessité d'un style de vie bolchevik me font quelquefois peur. En temps de guerre bien sûr. Mais c'est toujours la guerre bien sûr. Mais j'ai quarante ans. Ah! Pierre [Courtade], je suis ce soir triste à mourir: c'est que j'ai si bien appris l'art d'être civilisé que quand la douceur de vie me manque (sauf dans le feu du combat mais le feu est une douceur) j'ai envie de mourir. Remarque bien que je parle de mourir et non de trahir. Il ne m'intéresse pas d'être civilisé dans ce qu'est devenue la civilisation bourgeoise. (*Ecrits Intimes*, p. 149)

The reference here to the 'style de vie bolchevik' is, presumably, to the new hard-line purist attitude encouraged by Moscow and frequently adopted with alarmingly little thought by many of the Party's intellectuals. Nearer to blind adoration than logical appraisal, it was an attitude which continued into the fifties when it became responsible for prompting vicious attacks on anyone who chose to voice their dissent—Sartre and

Malraux for example—over such issues as Soviet intervention in Yugo-slavia, labour camps and in particular the trials and executions in 1949 of Rajk and Kostov. Where for the present Vailland found himself in this debate is difficult to ascertain. Pierre Hervé, his *Action* colleague, and René Maublanc, his former teacher at Reims both readily adopted the Soviet line, yet if they had influence it has gone unrecorded. There is virtually no private writing by Vailland for the period 1948–9 and it would seem reasonable to suppose that his attitude, though more clearly defined than three or four years earlier, was still uncertain. It seems too that his feeling of despair was as much induced by his personal situation than by any external circumstances and was offset and relieved only rather patheti-cally by a number of brief sexual adventures. During these months Vailland's only main public statement, other than articles for *Action, Libération, Tribune des Nations* and *Horizons*, appears to have been the radio pro-gramme in the series 'Carte Blanche', *Appel à Jenny Merveille*, as we have seen a transparent projection of his private—even subconscious—pre-occupations. In the programme, the appeal made by the author-character for Jenny to appear ultimately remains unanswered; Jenny Merveille simply did not exist. But Elisabeth Naldi did.

In December 1949 *Héloïse et Abélard* was produced at the Théâtre des Mathurins in Paris. A lunch, organized by Gala Barbisan who hoped to transfer the play to Italy, brought together a number of interested Italians including Elisabeth Naldi, a friend of both Barbisan and the producer, Marcello Pagliero. At once she and Vailland were attracted to each other:

> A ce déjeuner, Roger m'a beaucoup impressionnée.
> J'ai trouvé qu'il ne correspondait pas du tout à ce qu'on avait dit.
> Dans ce maigre visage qu'il avait déjà, il m'a semblé tout de suite qu'il y avait beaucoup de tendresse, cachée peut-être, mais qui devait exister. [...] on s'est revus plusieurs fois.[44]

Already once divorced and on the point of leaving her second husband, Elisabeth Naldi appeared to match Vailland in his search for personal freedom. Boasting a record in the Italian Resistance and an allegiance to the Left which was altogether more convincing than his, she was to bring sta-bility and perhaps an element of greater maturity to Vailland: in many ways she acted as a catalyst, quickening the process of change which he was already experiencing. In a letter written to her on 24 March 1950, for example, we read: 'Je crois que j'arrive à maturité pour des décisions d'organisation, et de changement d'orientation de ma vie' (*Ecrits Intimes*, p. 192). Yet, inevitably, this was not to be achieved overnight and what-ever her influence, Vailland's diaries for the early months of 1950 contain repeated references to his sense of boredom and a failure (already ack-nowledged in 'Je suis ce soir triste à mourir') to have positively attacked the complacency and conservatism of bourgeois society in the way that others, like Politzer or Lefebvre for example, more totally committed to a revolutionary position had already done. Yet a concern for 'demystification', which as we have seen so preoccupied Vailland in 1946, continued and now assumed an extra dimension. The element of self-criticism or self-awareness in personal matters which distinguished *Les Mauvais Coups* from *Drôle de jeu* is now focused on his work as a whole: 'Mon œuvre, jusqu'à *Bon Pied Bon Œil*, a contribué à la mystification' (*Ecrits Intimes*, p. 194). Following an orthodox Marxist line on the purpose of literature, he maintains that his task from now on will be to devote himself to a literature which, by dealing with the concerns and problems of the people, would awaken his reader's awareness to them and hence contribute to the Revolutionary cause. *Bon Pied Bon Œil* was his preliminary attempt, and, to use his own expression, his 'adieux à la culture bourgeoise'.[45]

Despite Vailland's acute feeling of depression, *Bon Pied Bon Œil* was written, apparently with little difficulty, between December 1949 and March 1950. As we learn from the opening sentence of the novel, it is, albeit in a very loose sense, a sequel to *Drôle de jeu:*

> Les lecteurs de *Drôle de jeu* retrouveront dans le récit qui suit plusieurs des personnages de ce roman, qui obtint quelque audience du public, et dans lequel, aujourd'hui encore, certains critiques veulent bien voir l'une des peintures les plus fidèles de la France du temps de l'occupation et d'un milieu bien particulier de la Résistance.[46]

Of the characters of the earlier book, however, only Rodrigue, Marat and, to a lesser extent, Annie remain, the rest being summarily dismissed in the Prologue.[47] The point of focus has also shifted, with Rodrigue the younger man now assuming the principal role. Marat, who, we learn, was wounded during the winter campaign of 1944–5 and rendered impotent in the process, has retired to 'un beau domaine, sur le plateau de l'Aubrac' (p. 168) where he raises prize bulls. Although he still retains his contacts with the political scene and in particular with the Communists, he has for the most part opted out. His excuse is that certain foreign monetary transactions in which he has been involved would, if discovered, compromise the Communist Party, yet as the novel progresses it becomes clear that his real reasons are, as he confesses to Antoinette, much more personal:

> Si je ne descends pas plus souvent de ma montagne, c'est que je dispose présentement d'assez d'argent pour me tenir provisoirement *en marge* du conflit. Et je n'aime pas assez les hommes, ni ne me soucie assez de la gloire, pour renoncer volontairement à mon loisir, à mes jeux, à ma liberté, à mes plaisirs. C'est sans doute aussi que je suis *fatigué*. (p. 328)

Rodrigue, on the other hand, has become fully committed. The uncertainty and impetuosity which had characterized much of his behaviour in *Drôle de jeu* has been replaced by an unswerving allegiance to the Communist Party. Even so, there is a noticeable gap between the diffusion of Party policy and practical action. This, essentially, is the problem which Vailland has to bring himself to face (though does not solve) in *Bon Pied Bon Œil*, and continues to face throughout this period of committed writing. Yet Vailland is by now enough of an imaginative writer to realize the dangers implicit in a tendentious *roman-à-thèse*; he is aware of the amount of strong human interest his novel must contain if it is to retain the reader's attention. Rodrigue, acting with a generosity worthy of the Corneille character to whom he owes his name, marries Antoinette Larivière whose child he has fathered and who has been imprisoned for having abandoned it 'sur la voie publique'.[48] In so doing, he forfeits Annie who has become his mistress and enters into what Marat defines (and here one easily senses Vailland's own bitterness) as 'une institution sacrée [...] protégée par tous les talons de la tribu' (pp. 213–14). While not based on any deep passionate attachment, their marriage nonetheless proves during a year to be a stable and happy one with the respective feelings of duty and gratitude gradually developing into one of genuine affection. Moreover, in marrying Antoinette, Rodrigue acts against Marat's advice, the first real sign that he has escaped his tutelage, and by implication an indication too of Vailland's awareness that the time had come for him to adopt a more positive and independent role than before. In the second part of the novel, one of Rodrigue's friends, Albéran, is accused of having betrayed military secrets to Spain and is imprisoned. As a fellow Communist, Rodrigue also falls under suspicion and a search reveals that he has in his possession certain documents which, while being quite insignificant, are nonetheless ostentatiously marked 'Extrêmement secret', and he too is arrested as a political suspect. While in prison Rodrigue studies the history of the Convention and of Saint-Just; for him it is a period of political education during which he realizes how ineffective in political terms he has hitherto been. This realization is also made more acute by the appearance of Jeanne Gris, the young lawyer who acts in his defence and with whom he falls in love. Ultimately, Antoinette's intrigues and pressure to have Rodrigue released become embarrassing and Marat, who has information with which he blackmails a government minister, is obliged to intervene. But Rodrigue emerges from prison a changed man. His marriage to Antoinette and to the bourgeois world that she represents is at an end, though it is she who, realizing this, accepts Marat's invitation to go with her son to live with him in Aubrac. Having resigned from his government post, Rodrigue, we may assume, goes to live with Jeanne and according to a letter which he writes to Marat and Antoinette from Toulon finally finds satisfaction in direct political demonstration.

Even from such a brief and inevitably incomplete outline of *Bon Pied Bon Œil*, Vailland's intentions begin to emerge. As François Bott has observed, the novel is basically a dialogue which Vailland is having with himself.[49] In addition to the two-part structure which he is to use again in *Un Jeune Homme seul*, there is throughout a series of parallels and contrasts, two sides of a debate which, in spite of Vailland's apparent intentions to the contrary, is never completely satisfactorily concluded. Of these contrasts the most obvious is that already apparent in *Drôle de jeu* between the two generations represented by Marat and Rodrigue. 'Tu es resté l'homme d'entre les deux guerres' remarks Rodrigue at one point in the book (p. 191), a sentiment which both he and Antoinette continue to express in one form or another at regular intervals throughout.[50] Marat's points of reference against which he contrasts (sometimes patronizingly) present events are all, significantly, taken from the interwar or Second World War years. Discussing Antoinette's prison experiences with her, for example, he remarks: 'j'ai eu souvent l'occasion d'entendre parler du régime des prisons françaises. La Roquette, par rapport à Fresnes du temps de l'occupation, est un petit paradis...' (p. 218). For those familiar with Vailland's first novel, the fact too that Marat is now referred to almost constantly by his real name, Lamballe, is also an indication of the role the author has assigned to him. While, when asked by the police who Marat is, Antoinette not insignificantly remarks: 'Il a été assassiné par Charlotte Corday' (p. 251).

Despite the similarity of their ages, Antoinette too, as the novel progresses, appears to belong more naturally to Marat's generation than to Rodrigue's, and her final acceptance of his invitation to live with him comes as little surprise. Even from the opening description of her there is something physically mature about her (pp. 189–90) and her seduction of Rodrigue (whatever *his* account of the incident may be) makes him appear very much her junior and relatively unsure of himself (pp. 196–8).[51] In the second part of the novel Antoinette is interrogated and beaten up by the police, incurring an injury to her eye which eventually causes her to lose it. Like Marat she too is physically disabled, prematurely aged; as she admits in her farewell letter to Rodrigue: 'J'ai mille ans de plus que toi (et le visage mutilé, comme un vétéran). Je ne peux pas continuer de vivre avec mon arrière-petit-neveu' (p. 371).[52] Antoinette is also, and more obviously, set against Jeanne whose simplicity is underlined from the beginning:

> Il trouva devant lui, de l'autre côté de la petite table du parloir, une jeune fille, bras nus, tête nue, robe de toile imprimée, une serviette sous le bras, comme une écolière. [...] Elle avait les joues rouges comme une petite paysanne. (p. 297)

And later in the book, outside the context of the prison and Jeanne's work, Vailland's description of her contains nothing of the suggestion of vulgarity which characterizes that of Antoinette at the dinner party where Rodrigue met her for the first time:

> Jeanne avait enfin trouvé le temps d'aller chez le coiffeur; les cheveux rejetés en arrière, en *coup de vent*, dégageaient le front, qui est haut et large. Elle tournait à tout propos vers lui son visage, les joues sans fard; elle riait. [...] Il se sentait comblé qu'elle fût près de lui si fraîche, si nette. (p. 355)

Clearly we are intended to see in Jeanne an idealized union of physical beauty and intellectual integrity; unlike Antoinette she knows—and indeed has always known—the direction her life is to take. For Rodrigue she is to appear as a saviour figure who will lead him from the claustrophobic atmosphere of the bourgeois world in which he has been accustomed to living, into the simple but principled world of the working class. Yet there is also something romantic, even sentimental, about her and their relationship particularly in their taste for the same films and in their discovery that they have both been born in the 'treizième': 'Je suis né dans le treizième, tu es née dans le treizième, nous sommes nés dans le treizième' (p. 356). For all his political convictions and association with the Left, Vailland's picture of the working class world is here a naive and unrealistic one.

It has always been easier, however, to destroy and to reject than to rebuild; and what is more, a realization of what should be done has never been a substitute for actual practice. Rodrigue may well indeed be correct when he accuses Marat of belonging still to the 'phase romantique du mouvement ouvrier' (p. 185), but as he comes to realize, there is in his own case a considerable gap between what he knows to be the policy and aims of the Communist Party and what he personally has achieved:

> Evidemment, la lecture des quotidiens et des périodiques du Parti, la préparation des *exposés* à ses camarades de cellule, lui ont permis de se faire une idée claire des problèmes de l'actualité en France et dans le monde. Mais il ne faudra pas qu'on le pousse trop loin sur la doctrine (pp. 282-3).

Rodrigue stands midway between the romantic revolutionaries of novels by Malraux and Hemingway who like Marat, he contends, are more interested in personal adventure than collective political action, and a new political figure represented in *Bon Pied Bon Œil* by his fellow political prisoner Albéran—'le combattant communiste, le bolchevik, un type d'homme absolument nouveau' (pp. 211–12).[53] But Albéran, already partly prefigured by Drouet in *L'Histoire d'un Homme du peuple sous la Révolution*, never makes an appearance in the book: we hear of his political activities, of his record during the war, of his ability to convey his convictions to others and win them over to the Communist faith, but that is all. Indeed in his failure to portray Albéran, Vailland is guilty of one of the errors which Sartre in *Qu'est-ce que la littérature?* accuses communist novelists of making in their attempts to project their political allegiance in as positive and favourable a way as possible. Moreover the derivation of his name from the Latin word for white and the French *aube* (dawn) suggests that we should see him as an exemplary and prophetic figure rather than as a man of action. In Nizan's novel about a group of self-styled young revolutionaries, *La Conspiration* (1938), Carré the Communist makes a fleeting appearance only and is little more than a symbol for a doctrine which we do not see put into practice. At the other end of the political spectrum Carentan in Drieu la Rochelle's *Gilles* (1939) a panoramic survey of life in inter-war France, leads a hermit-like existence propounding fascist-type views which, if taken into the public arena of political activity, would necessarily undergo modification. Vailland's problem in *Bon Pied Bon Œil* is similar. In the second half of the novel Rodrigue undergoes a political education. What was before, on occasions, little more than an intuitive response to a general political and social situation, becomes hardened into a critical awareness. By the end of *Bon Pied Bon Œil* Rodrigue has perhaps reached a point from which he may the more easily emulate Albéran, though the only account we have of his new political activities is that given in a tone of euphoric enthusiasm in his letter to Marat and Antoinette from Toulon.

The agents of this education are Saint-Just, (together with Robespierre of course one of the Communist Party's principal Revolutionary heroes) whose life and works he decides to study during his prison sentence, and Jeanne Gris. As we have seen, Rodrigue, in rejecting Marat's advice concerning his marriage in Part I, shows that he does have the will-power to escape his influence. At the same time, a comparison between the author's third person singular account of his seduction by Antoinette and his own, reveals an adolescent male pride which suggests that he is still some way from being the fully mature person who will make a successful political figure. This immaturity is also underlined by the mildly erotic dream Rodrigue has about Chloé during his second night in prison:

> Il rêva qu'il était auprès de Chloé. '*On les met en prison*, disait-elle, *avant de les envoyer à l'école.*' Elle ouvrait son corsage, l'attirait contre elle, et il posait la tête entre deux gros seins ronds et blancs. '*Pauvre gosse*, disait-elle, *mon pauvre gosse.*' Elle le berçait. (p. 293)

For Jean Recanati, Chloé, already seen in *Drôle de jeu* as the 'bonne ménagère de la Résistance', is one particular incarnation of what he terms the 'femmes-mères'.[54] What is equally important if not more so, however, for an appreciation of the novel is the point at which this dream occurs. A sense of utter insignificance is experienced during his period of recreation and is compounded by the ultimate indignity of being searched:

> Rodrigue était nu.
> —Courbez-vous, dit Patachon.
> —Non, dit Rodrigue.
> —C'est le règlement, dit le gardien-chef.
> Rodrigue avait lu quelque chose sur l'astuce du *plan*, étui d'os ou de métal que les bagnards dissimulent dans l'anus. Il se courba, se releva, regarda droit dans les yeux le gardien, qui détourna la tête. (pp. 291-2)

This is the lowest pitch to which he is reduced, and a dream in which Chloé appears as the comforting mother figure is psychologically justifiable. Metaphorically, Rodrigue has to grow up again and it is from this point on that his political re-education begins. Fittingly, the following day ('il se sentait léger, dispos, presque allègre' (p. 293)) he makes his decision to study the work of Saint-Just and also meets Jeanne Gris for the first time.

In Saint-Just Rodrigue discovers the same principle which, of course, Vailland and Claude Roy had expounded in their letter to *Action*. Revolutionary activity could only successfully be achieved if it were based on happiness, and it was this discovery ('Le bonheur est une idée neuve en Europe') Saint-Just argued, which transcended and gave full significance to those other essential revolutionary prerequisites of discipline and virtue. As we might expect, Jeanne Gris is also acquainted with Saint-Just's revolutionary speeches: 'Mon grand-père me les faisait apprendre quand j'avais onze ans' (p. 303). In fact, her whole upbringing and spiritual and political inheritance have made of her a 'bolchevik de nature', more easily accessible to Rodrigue by virtue of the physical attraction they have for one another than Albéran. Yet there remains something unreal about Rodrigue's experience. The time he spends in prison is an idyllic interlude:

> pas de travaux ennuyeux à faire, pas de mains sales à serrer, pas de soucis d'argent, aucune sorte de responsabilités, il était hors de combat, hors de jeu, il *comptait pour du beurre*, ses camarades assumaient son destin à sa place. Il allait enfin faire ce qu'il voulait. (pp. 301-2)

But like Stendhal's Fabrice del Dongo whom he so admires (p. 205) and on whom he is partly modelled, Rodrigue is in danger of preferring the inactivity of prison life where commitment need be no more than an intellectual exercize and where he is assured of regular visits from Jeanne, to the harsh reality of the political world outside. Indeed, there is more than an echo of Stendhal's irony in Antoinette's attempts to have Rodrigue released (pp. 318-19; p. 353). But whereas Stendhal's heroes in *La Chartreuse de Parme* are allowed to remain aloof, Rodrigue must eventually emerge and take his place once more in society. Vailland's problem is to show how this is achieved, how Rodrigue translates his new political awareness into effective political action.

His first task is to rid himself of the vestiges of his previous bourgeois existence—the security of his government post and of his home. On both counts he is forestalled: before he has time to resign his employers give him an unusually rapid promotion in order to render him suspicious in the eyes of his fellow Communists, while Antoinette leaves to stay with Marat before he is able to inform her of his decision to leave her. But Rodrigue sees neither of these events to be in any way a reflection on his failure to act first. Instead he justifies himself in terms which would not sound amiss were they to be expressed by Marat: 'Il pensa que, comme il a beaucoup de chance dans la vie, les problèmes pour lui se résolvent en même temps qu'ils se posent' (p. 371).

This element of self-satisfaction is also to be found in the account of his conversation with the Yugoslav worker in the last chapter of the novel. As it develops their meeting becomes a kind of parable and can also be taken, of course, as signifying Vailland's increasing readiness to accept the 'new' Communist line over Yugoslavia. Originally from a prosperous middle-class family, the Yugoslav has, since the German occupation of his country, been reduced to a state of lonely despair, earning his living as an unskilled refugee worker in France. For him salvation can come only through war, but his reasons are entirely selfish: 'quand on est soldat, on mange à sa faim. J'aime mieux être tué à la guerre que de continuer à mener cette vie de chien...' (p. 366). Rodrigue's reaction is, as we might expect, one of scorn mixed with relief that he is not in the same situation. With a gesture in which the symbolism jars heavily he offers the Yugoslav his coat, but cannot refrain, once the other has left him, from congratulating himself that he at least recognizes the value of the brotherhood to which he belongs, and from indulging in a grandiloquent reflection on Man. Indeed at the end of the final chapter, Rodrigue, for all his rather naive optimism, is as self-centred as the Yugoslav worker was self-pitying.

The short Epilogue with which the *Bon Pied Bon Œil* closes would seem at first to underline Vailland's professed intention to reject bourgeois values. When he was about to write it he remarked in a letter to Elisabeth: 'Je veux que ça soit *grandiose* [...] c'est ce qui donnera toute sa signification au roman' (*Ecrits Intimes*, p. 194). Certainly, from the opening description of Marat's isolated farm, perched like a castle in a Gothic novel on the 'plateau de l'Aubrac', an instant change in tone is noticeable. But Vailland's ambition is more wide-ranging and is concerned with the novel's meaning as a whole. Here in the heart of France, Marat, who, as we already know, is impotent, confesses himself to Antoinette, symbolically rejecting his past. But, as in the case of Antoinette, through whom Vailland has projected certain aspects of himself, he continues to enjoy the author's sympathy.

Antoinette's eye is artificially but beautifully restored, and Marat, like Jake Barnes in Hemingway's *The Sun also rises*, is left in peace to contemplate on his own values, and to 'pêcher cette vieille truite que personne n'a jamais pu attraper' (p. 380). What is more his cynical reaction to Rodrigue's letter—'Notre Rodrigue [...] a pris Toulon' (p. 380)—is not, as we have seen, altogether unwarranted.

Bon Pied Bon Œil is not therefore quite such a straightforward rejection of 'la culture bourgeoise' as Vailland had once hoped it would be; nor does it successfully convey in fictional terms his growing private conviction that his art should serve to further a particular political programme. Certainly Rodrigue emerges as the new political man and in so doing provides a neat and valuable commentary on Vailland himself. As we have seen, he happily accepts the required self-discipline, but we have no positive evidence of his having achieved very much. Marat, on the other, hand refuses or is unable to do this; he prefers an aristocratic withdrawal, keeping his personal values—however unrealistic they may have become—intact. It is arguable therefore that the debate which underpins this novel remains inconclusive, with Vailland nostalgically clinging to certain values almost in spite of himself. On 23 May 1950 Vailland noted in his diary: 'Je suis (ou je tends à être) un bolchevik et non un carbonaro' (*Ecrits Intimes*, p. 221). The parenthesis is important. His political activities during the next few years were not only to increase but were to be firmer-based and were eventually acknowledged in 1952 by his being accepted as a member of the Communist Party.[55] For the present, however, there was still some way to go; as we shall see his next novel, *Un Jeune Homme seul*, portrays very much the same problem even though the hero, Eugène-Marie Favart, is shown to achieve more than Rodrigue and finally to commit himself through action. But, as François Bott has observed,[56] what is more significant still is that *Un Jeune Homme seul* marks the end of a period in Vailland's writing during which he has himself been the principal subject. In this novel the process of exorcizing the past takes its final step back into the years of Vailland's childhood and adolescence.

Chapter Three

The Search for Identity II

Les romans les plus justement illustres
peignent une éducation, c'est-à-dire la
métamorphose d'un adolescent en homme.
Expérience du drame.

With *Bon Pied Bon Œil* completed, Vailland left Sceaux for Italy towards the end of April 1950. Here he remained—initially in Rome and later, and more importantly, in Capri—until the end of September 1950. During these months he wrote, in addition to articles for *Action* and *La Tribune des Nations*, a small study of the Vatican[1] (*L'Impérialisme Vatican contre la paix*), two essays (*Les quatre figures du libertinage* and *La Cruauté de l'amour*) and the first drafts of his second play, *Le Colonel Foster plaidera coupable*. At the same time his relationship with Elisabeth Naldi was growing deeper, though not without problems. The fear both of public scandal and of family disapproval was not easily ignored, and only for fleeting moments when they often literally barricaded themselves in rooms or apartments did they feel safe. For Vailland too, of course, with the experience of one unhappy and, in the end, unsuccessful marriage behind him, the prospect of committing himself again was a daunting one. Yet despite a number of moments of doubt, his diaries for these months reveal how increasingly necessary Elisabeth was becoming to the whole pattern of his life. In an entry for 6 June shortly before his departure for Capri, for example, we read: 'à la passion elle ajoute la tendresse [...] c'est une femme de tête, qui m'aiderait à mettre dans ma vie l'ordre nécessaire à l'exécution de mon plan triennal'.[2]

As we have already seen, Vailland had by now convinced himself of the political direction his work was to take—'[Je suis] plus décidé que jamais à ne plus travailler qu'avec le peuple organisé dans le P.C.'[3]—and even in his two essays we find him projecting discussions of love and libertine behaviour into a context of dialectical materialism. This is particularly noticeable in the second, *La Cruauté dans l'amour*, where Vailland takes up a theme which is to become a permanent and crucial one in his work, that of the possessor and the possessed. In terms of the human couple possession acknowledges the right to use or abuse, and may lead therefore to tyranny. But if all men (and women) are free, they have the right both to object to being tyrannized and also to exercize tyranny themselves.[4] Translated

c

into economic terms the same paradoxical situation develops, Vailland
argues—albeit with a somewhat idiosyncratic interpretation of the original:

> la Déclaration des droits de l'homme, [...] proclame simultanément
> que tous les hommes ont des droits égaux, c'est-à-dire sont également
> souverains, et que la propriété est sacrée, laquelle pour la classe
> bourgeoise, dont la déclaration marque l'accession au pouvoir, autorise
> et implique l'exploitation de l'homme par l'homme, c'est-à-dire la
> tyrannie.
>
> Le libertin souverain, qui mutile et tue l'objet également
> souverain de son plaisir, place dans une lumière éclatante la con-
> tradiction qui permet au patron-citoyen d'acheter et de vendre
> comme une marchandise le travail de l'ouvrier-citoyen.[5]

In so far as the essay concerns a sexual or an erotic relationship between
two people, a solution to the problem is realizable through ritualization.
Only when each member of a couple fully acknowledges the right of freedom of his or her partner can the problem of tyranny and exploitation be
overcome: 'il implique des acteurs égaux en souveraineté, respectueux l'un
de l'autre. L'œuvre de cruauté sera le jeu sain et triomphant d'une
humanité heureuse et rajeunie.'[6] While Vailland may have found in Elisabeth Naldi a partner with whom he could and indeed eventually did resolve
his own situation,[7] his concern for the present was for political issues and
La Cruauté dans l'amour was somewhat abruptly dismissed as an 'aide-
mémoire pour les loisirs futurs'.[8]

By June 1950 money from the performances and translation rights
of *Héloïse et Abélard* gave Vailland the independence to write at his own
pace and under his own conditions. Curzio Malaparte, the Italian writer
and producer whom he had known in Paris and who was currently
making a film in Tuscany, generously allowed him to use his house in
Capri. Here Vailland spent the summer months, an idyllic interlude
during which intense intellectual effort was matched by a complete
physical enjoyment of his new surroundings and was punctuated only by
rare meetings with Elisabeth. His diaries for these weeks vibrate with an
enthusiasm and happiness unknown to him since those he had experienced
during his period in the Resistance, and with an almost unprecedented and
increasing sense of achievement. In fact, the summer of 1950 marked the
beginning of what was to be the most intensely productive and, in many
ways, successful period of Vailland's life. In a way therefore, it is ironic
that his first project, the book on the Vatican, was never published.

The principal aim of *L'Impérialisme Vatican contre la paix* was to
discredit the Roman Catholic Church on as many different counts as
possible, not only religious but economic, political, social and moral.
Vailland traces in very general terms the history of the Church, arguing that
whenever it has sought to establish a pact with bourgeois democracy or

with socialism, it has done so simply in order to facilitate the preservation of its own values and beliefs, and to work towards the restoration of its position of power and authority in the world. Such pacts therefore, however promising they may at first appear to, say, the socialist, are simply a means to an end and are to be rejected as soon as possible. On the other hand, he asserts, since the Catholic Church by its very hierarchical structure is a tyranny, pacts which can be made with a single political leader are to be encouraged and preserved.

> Le catholicisme romain est fondamentalement théocratique, et donc, par essence antilibéral, antiparlementaire, antirépublicain, antipopulaire, antidémocrate. Par opportunité tactique, le Vatican encourage les catholiques à lutter *aussi* sur le plan de la démocratie bourgeoise, quand les circonstances historiques l'exigent. Mais dès qu'à présent l'ombre du centre catholique a grandi un parti autoritaire, dès que sous l'aile d'une 'troisième force' toujours chancelante, parce que l'alliance des catholiques et des socialistes ne peut être que provisoire, un tyran a pris assez de forces pour voler seul, le Saint-Siège exige que le parti catholique se suicide au profit de la tyrannie. (Chapter VII)

The narrowness of Vailland's general interpretation is only matched in the book by his attacks on more specific aspects of the Church's policies and practice—the scheme for the training of religious missionaries to be sent to Russia, the complicity during the Second World War between Pius XII and Nazi Germany, the medievalism of the Thomist revival in the twentieth century, for example. But the real centre of focus of *L'Impérialisme Vatican contre la paix*—like that of Garaudy's *L'Eglise, le Communisme et les Chrétiens* which had appeared in 1949—is what Vailland sees to be the Roman Church's attempt to establish a Catholic European Federation which, with the financial support of the United States, would be sufficiently strong to resist the (for him inevitable) progress of Communism. Such an arrangement would also meet the Vatican's objection to the United Nations, namely that it was an organization which brought together a number of individual national sovereignties and was therefore illegitimate. Nor would America suffer, for a Federation of this nature based on such an agreement would provide her with a ready market for her exports, and would relieve her at the same time of the need to retain—and hence finance—her European industrial plants.

By the end of the book it is clear that Vailland's real target is not so much the Catholic Church as an organization guilty, in his eyes, of *mystification*—an approach which he might have adopted only a few years earlier—but a much wider political issue. And, while as an indication of where in the ranks of the Left in France Vailland now saw himself standing it is a valuable piece of work, it is also where the real weakness of the book lies. Certainly there are occasions, especially in the first two chapters, when he completely captures, for example, the mixture of awe and devotion which moves Catholics to Rome in pilgrimage. His descriptions as well of the *braccianti* (the papal missionaires whom he defines as the 'cosaques du Pape'), of the bourgeois Catholics who, for fear of disease, kiss the statue of St Peter only through their hand and of the Pope himself (Chapter II)[9] are brilliant cameos in his best journalist style. As soon as he moves out into the history of the Catholic Church or into a consideration of its role and power in the contemporary world, however, so the impact of the book diminishes. Persuasive as his arguments may at first appear, they are seen, on closer examination and by comparison with those in Garaudy's work, to lack both structure and rigour. There is never any single point of focus for his attack—indeed by the close he is as much if not more concerned with American influence and power as he is with the Catholic Church—while the Communist alternative is never presented other than as something which will emerge naturally and inevitably as an historical phenomenon. At no point can Vailland's enthusiasm for his undertaking be questioned, but the book betrays the fact that it was written in a hurry and with inadequate preparation. It is also evident from his diaries and letters to Elisabeth, that his new project, a play, was demanding an ever-increasing amount of his time and energy. And what is more important still, perhaps, is that even a non-imaginative work like *L'Impérialisme Vatican contre la paix* once more illustrates the problem of writing within a political perspective. Personal conviction is not sufficient; it must emerge to the reader in the form of persuasive argument and demonstration.

That he was aware of these problems, aggravated as they were by his personal situation, is clear from an important letter which Vailland wrote on 9 August to Pierre Courtade. In it he turns to the question of responsibility, the question which had haunted left-wing intellectuals certainly since 1934, when *Commune*, the review of the *Association des Ecrivains et des Artistes révolutionnaires* (*A.E.A.R.*) had issued a questionnaire on the subject and which Sartre had reopened more recently in *Qu'est-ce que la littérature?*: 'écrire pour qui, pour quoi?'.[10] Much of the letter recalls what Vailland had noted in his diary at the time when he was finishing *Bon Pied Bon Œil:*

> Il faut avoir l'audace de dire qu'il n'y a pas de culture en dehors du peuple. Que quiconque parle d'Art et de Culture en soi est un mystificateur et un contre-révolutionnaire, qui masque ainsi la défense de ses privilèges.
>
> Il faut, pour éclaircir le débat, définir le peuple: c'est la masse des non-privilégiés. [...] Le peuple c'est la masse des individus qui ne sont pas des personnes. (*Ecrits Intimes*, p. 194)

But to recognize and even to define one's public is no solution to the problem of how or what one should write. This, he admits, is the weakness of *Bon Pied Bon Œil* (whose only virtues he now maintains are ones of style): 'C'est trop dans la perspective communiste pour toucher les non-communistes sauf par malentendu, et trop en dehors des préoccupations des masses communistes pour avoir de l'effet sur elles' (*Ecrits Intimes*, p. 270). As we have seen, *L'Impérialisme Vatican contre la paix* was hardly any more successful, in spite of Vailland's claims in this letter that in writing it 'je ne me suis attaché qu'à des objectifs actuels, dans notre perspective' (p. 271). But his passionate conviction that the problem could be solved was to urge him on, and though not perhaps entirely in the manner he anticipated, *Le Colonel Foster plaidera coupable* was both to make an impact and finally put a seal on his relationship with the Communist Party.

In view of the way in which he was now moving steadily towards an orthodox left-wing position it is hardly surprising to find Vailland adopting without any sign of hesitation or question the official Party line on the Korean situation: 'Il est normal, logique, juste, nécessaire, honnête, fondamentalement juste que l'URSS où le peuple est au pouvoir soutienne le peuple coréen dans la lutte contre la bourgeoisie [...] la *camaraderie* l'exige' (*Ecrits Intimes*, p. 274). For him, as for the majority of the Party's intellectuals, it was unthinkable that the North could have attacked first; instead the responsibility for the war lay with President Rhee and the Southern forces who with American aid were threatening not just another people but the whole notion of democratic government and freedom. Instantly, therefore, the war became seen as the expression of a straight ideological conflict with the inevitable, and by now familiar, pattern of attendant justification and propaganda. Accounts of capitalist opportunism and ruthless purges in the South were sharply contrasted with those of the increase in the number of schools or of the redistribution of land in the North. American forces were viciously attacked in the communist press for their use of napalm and bacteriological warfare. All of this Vailland appears to have accepted, and even if in his letters to Elisabeth he could admit the possibility of defeat for the North Koreans, his confidence in the ultimate triumph of communism was no less strong: 'La Corée peut être vaincue, provisoirement, mais l'ensemble des pays communistes ne peut plus être "mis à genoux", même provisoirement, il est assez fort pour ne plus connaître que des échecs locaux' (*Ecrits Intimes*, p. 304).

Given this attitude, it comes as no surprise that he should write in August 1950 to Malaparte that his play was to be 'une violente et efficace critique de l'impérialisme américain [qui] va certainement faire un beau scandale' (*Ecrits Intimes*, p. 274). Originally the work was to have been called *Le major Brown est porté disparu*. Brown himself ('plutôt brave type et même un peu progressiste, ex-universitaire, à lunettes' (*Ecrits Intimes*, (p. 264) was to be shown as someone who was genuinely convinced that he was fighting in the cause of freedom and who only when it was too late realized his mistake. The conflict, both ideological and psychological, was promising. After a few weeks Vailland changed the play's title to *Le Colonel Foster plaidera coupable* (possibly in order to associate the name of the protagonist with that of John Foster Dulles, the American Foreign Secretary) and with the works of Mao Tse Tung and Lenin at his elbow to guarantee the accuracy of the political views expressed, and those of Shakespeare—Racine and Corneille having for once failed him—to provide a theatrical model, it was written on a wave of sustained enthusiasm between 14 August and 28 September. Basically the theme which he had originally set out to illustrate remained the same and on 14 November, after he had returned to Paris Vailland read his completed manuscript to the 'section idéologique' of the French Communist Party: 'Samedi soir lecture de ma pièce chez Leduc, devant la 'section idéologique' du Parti, presque au complet, accueil chaleureux, et après accord de Duclos, qui semble sûr, j'aurai *l'accord matériel et moral* total du Parti...' (*Ecrits Intimes*, p. 319).

In its final form the play shows only a number of relatively minor alterations and modifications, most of them made in order either to prune its physical shape or to reinforce its ideological message. Foster remains the liberal at heart whose 'idéaux humanitaires' and 'convictions progressistes'[11] are eventually only overcome by his military training and conditioning;[12] Paganel, whose Catholic formation causes him to regard the war as a crusade, nonetheless also admits to similar feelings but is at once suspected of betraying the section's instructions to the partisan forces; Jimmy McAllen represents the archetypal young American soldier full of racial and political prejudice. Of the local population Cho is the collaborator—as long as the American forces seem likely to provide the best protection for his business concerns; his daughter Lya, who has been a Communist for some years plays the dangerous and difficult game of betrayal inside the American Command Post, and Masan, the Communist, who is captured and finally executed, is clearly intended to go unflinching to his death (not unlike Katow in Malraux's *La Condition humaine*) with the message for all mankind to hear on his lips. In spite of the undoubted promise of Vailland's original design and intention the result is disappointing. However oversimplified such observations as these may be, there can be no disregarding the fact that *Le Colonel Foster plaidera coupable* has few redeeming features and is essentially a loaded and simplistic dialogue between American (Western) imperialism and Communism. The most obvious manner in which Vailland uses his stage directions in the last act reinforces this impression. Victory for the partisan forces is accompanied by the dawning of a new day; the American prisoners now stand in the places formerly occupied by Masan and the two thieves. Perhaps most artificial of all, however, is the conversation which Lya and Masan have immediately before the latter's execution and which is punctuated by such pregnant statements as 'Dans l'instant même où ils nous tuent, ils ont honte de n'être pas communistes' (IV, 2, p. 298) or 'C'est parce que nous sommes les plus humaines que nous sommes communistes' (IV, 2, pp. 299–30). They also share a vision of the promised city in which Communists from all over the world will unite in peace.[13] It is arguable, and not without justification, that to select examples of this kind from a play must necessarily give an incomplete account of it only and reduce it almost to the level of caricature, but no matter how carefully *Le Colonel Foster plaidera coupable* is scrutinized, there is little to redeem it.

The fact that Cho is allowed (presumably at least) to escape remains an enigma: either it indicates a token attempt by Vailland to introduce an element of balance into the play, or it suggests a more sinister degree of sympathy between author and character, or it has simply been overlooked. The last, I suspect, is more likely, though there is an interesting analogy with *La Condition humaine* where the opportunist Clappique is allowed to find his way to safety. The question of the extent to which Lya allows her ideals to become compromized through her complicity with the American forces, and Foster's inner struggle between his humanitarian ideals and his belief that American forces are fighting in the cause of freedom, do give them each a little psychological depth. Similarly the final scene is interestingly ambiguous. Does Foster plead guilty to having been responsible for certain atrocities against the local native population or on a much grander scale to having perpetrated imperialist aggression against his better and more humane judgements? The second interpretation is temptingly and no doubt intentionally present. A more important consideration, however, is that in addition to reading like the work of someone with firm, even rigid views (the critic Pierre Berger privately warned Vailland that he should 'atténuer largement cette partisanerie'), *Le Colonel Foster plaidera coupable* is also a *destructive* rather than a *constructive* play, and in this respect fails to provide a solution to the problem which has already emerged in *Bon Pied Bon Œil*. Lya and Masan may well be totally convinced of eventual Communist victory, of a time when 'les jeunes filles seront bien plus belles [...] parce qu'elles seront heureuses' (IV, 2, p. 301), but once again personal conviction falls well short of explanation and demonstration.

However dated and typical of its time *Le Colonel Foster plaidera coupable* might seem to us now, it was enough, as we have seen, to make a favourable impression on the French Communist Party intellectuals at the time. In addition, the stability of his relationship with Elisabeth Naldi was beginning to change Vailland's reputation as an individualist and a libertine, a fact which Courtade had already noted would be a necessary concomitant to eventual membership:

Dans un seul domaine je ne crois pas le compromis nécessaire (ni juste): c'est celui de l'adhésion au Parti. Cela oui, il faut le faire, maintenant surtout. C'est presque une question de style. Mais naturellement il vaut mieux savoir d'avance (mais tu le sais) que ta chasse au bonheur en sera rendue singulièrement plus difficile! (*Ecrits Intimes*, pp. 288-9)

Vailland left Capri at the end of September and spent October with Elisabeth in Florence and Paris. On her departure he found himself now much more fully immersed in and accepted by the Left. His articles in *Action* and *La Tribune des Nations*—in particular an open letter in the former which was outspokenly critical of the American Senator Brewster who advocated the use of the atomic bomb against the Chinese—earned him wide acclaim. *Bon Pied Bon Œil*, favourably reviewed by left-wing newspapers, was considered for the Prix Goncourt, though only for a short time, his hardening political position gradually alienating those with power and causing—according to Vailland at least—the influential *Le Monde* and *Le Figaro* to ignore it altogether.[14] Success and recognition made him more determined than ever to prove himself, and only Elisabeth's absence lessened in any way the pleasure and satisfaction he experienced during these few weeks. Commissioned by *La Tribune des Nations* to go to Indonesia, Vailland left Paris at the end of the year. On 1 December he had written to Elisabeth: 'Nous ne nous quitterons plus à partir de mon retour' (*Ecrits Intimes*, p. 342): when he returned in February 1951 the period of separation was at an end.

Indonesia under the leadership of President Sukarno had proclaimed her independence in December 1949. Whatever the post-war intrigues involving the Dutch, the Americans, the Japanese, the British and a number of conflicting internal factions had been, this example of a nation which had succeeded in throwing off the yoke of more than three centuries of Dutch imperialist rule was a perfect subject for Vailland's left-wing interpretation published in 1951 under the title of *Boroboudour*. 'Je suis certain que le monde va bouger beaucoup plus vite que nous le croyons en Europe,' he wrote to Elisabeth from Bangkok, (*Ecrits Intimes*, p. 360) but it is to his credit that only rarely is his account to any noticeable extent distorted by his own revolutionary enthusiasm. Certainly it appears from time to time, especially in the letters which he wrote regularly to Elisabeth where there are a number of references to the 'historical perspective' so necessary for a proper Marxist interpretation of events. His method too is completely orthodox: 'Je fais une étude systématique et très en détail du pays [...] je commence par le commencement, c'est-à-dire par les fondements économiques et politiques' (*Ecrits Intimes*, p. 368). And to help ensure that he remained within the clearly defined limits imposed by his method, Vailland took with him the collection of Stalin's articles and speeches given between 1913 and 1934 on nationalism and colonialism, *Le Marxisme et la question nationale et coloniale*, which had been published in French in 1950: 'c'est

simple, clair, lucide, solide et définitif, ça me fait gagner un temps considé-
rable dans la compréhension des choses ici' (*Ecrits Intimes*, p. 365).

Although Vailland had already 'proved' himself through his press
articles, *Le Colonel Foster plaidera coupable* was known only to a small
number of people and these for the most part, at least, convinced Communists already. *Boroboudour* was therefore an important book; a public
verification on a relatively large scale of his political convictions. It was this
no doubt which prompted the otherwise unnecessary confession-like
rejection of his past[15] and statement of his new belief in mankind:

> Aujourd'hui, j'ai retrouvé la communauté des hommes. Ma prédi-
> lection ne s'attache plus aux fauves. Le voilier sur la mer, c'est
> l'homme qui se sert de la tempête pour aller contre la tempête, et
> l'oasis c'est le canal d'irrigation ajouté au désert, voilà comment j'aime
> désormais la nature. Pour moi aussi, '*les rages, les débauches, la folie—
> tout mon fardeau est déposé...*' (p. 49)

This apart, *Boroboudour* is a balanced book, with history, geography,
anthropology, and folklore intermixed in the best travelogue fashion.
Vailland's eye for detail, whether it be in the technically precise descriptions of Javanese orchids or in the politically coloured reflections on the
rickshaw ('moyen de transport populaire par excellence') and his interest
in the erotic decor of the Buddhist temples or the highly ritualized Bali
dances, provide the book with a personal dimension as well. For all this,
however, the basic political intention is never far away. The attack on
imperialism and capitalism inevitably directed for the most part against the
Dutch, is, wherever possible, turned as well against the Americans and
the French. Against the background of the Korean and Vietnam wars,
Vailland never loses an opportunity in *Boroboudour* of underlining the
immense gap which exists between the white man in Asia and the native
population:

> un Blanc qui veut créer un contact humain avec un homme du pays
> doit:
> 1⁰ S'excuser d'être un Blanc;
> 2⁰ S'il appartient à une nation du bloc occidental, prendre nettement
> position contre l'intervention occidentale en Corée;
> 3⁰ S'il est Français, se désolidariser de la politique de nos gouvernants
> au Vietnam.
> Il est alors récompensé par un regard presque tendre, qui lui fait
> oublier bien des avanies. (p. 111)[16]

But such moments are rare (p. 175),[17] and not until the whole edifice of
imperialist exploitation has been destroyed will it be possible for them to
increase. Fortunately the younger generations of Indonesians possess
that blend of revolutionary fervour and virtue which Rodrigue admired

in Saint-Just and which is enabling them gradually to transform their country politically and economically. The implication is clear, and in the last few pages of his book Vailland is as much concerned with France as he is with Indonesia.

The arguments in *Boroboudour* are persuasive, and more so than in *L'Impérialisme Vatican contre la paix*, for example, on account of specific instances of progress to which Vailland can point; there is in fact a positive, constructive side to his argument. At the same time, it is difficult not to wonder whether his own revolutionary fervour was not still conditioning his interpretation too forcefully. His vision early in the book of 'de grandes fêtes, frivoles et délicates, sur les terraces de Boroboudor, des bergeries où les vraies bergères seraient toutes les reines' (p. 51) is, for all its lyricism, intended as a serious political comment. It is a transposition into a socio-political context of that state of perfect harmony achieved through a mutual acceptance of certain rules which Vailland had outlined in *La Cruauté de l'amour*. But it does not follow that what may be ritualized and thereby preserved at a personal level will also necessarily be so when expanded in this way. *Boroboudour* is an enthusiastic book; it may also be somewhat naïve, but it contains in essence the duality that was to characterize Vailland's work to such an extent during his Communist period— the search for personal happiness and a total commitment to a political cause.

On his return from Indonesia in February, Vailland and Elisabeth (who had now separated from her husband) lived in Paris, but only for a month. Almost at once he realized that the pressures and distractions of Parisian life could only harm his ambition to become 'un grand écrivain',[18] and they moved away from the capital to Les Allymes, a small village near Ambérieu-en-Bugey. During the next five years Vailland was to immerse himself fully in the political activities of the region:

> tantôt je gagnais les cités ouvrières de la vallée de l'Albarine, où se traite la soie artificielle, tantôt je descendais jusqu'au dépôt du chemin de fer d'Ambérieu-en-Bugey. Je participais aux réunions où se préparaient les *actions* politiques, je parlais dans les meetings, je défilais avec les militants, je dansais dans les *goguettes* du Parti communiste.[19]

The political mask which had so attracted him during the previous ten years or so but which he had not been able to accept he now assumed with increasing confidence and authority as his own. More important still was the impetus which such participation gave to his writing. As Jean Recanati has noted: 'Il écrit et il milite, il est heureux. C'est pour lui la saison de la fraternité. Elle sera jalonnée autant par les livres qu'il écrit que par les *actions* auxquelles il est mêlé.'[20]

At the same time one important further step still had to be made, for the process of exorcizing the past, though well advanced in *Les Mauvais Coups* and *Bon Pied Bon Œil*, was not yet complete. In his next novel, *Un Jeune Homme seul*, Vailland returns to and rejects the remaining influential period of his life, the formative years of his childhood and adolescence. In this respect *Un Jeune Homme seul* is, as a number of critics have noticed, the last novel in which Vailland takes himself as his principal subject. But it is also more. In it, the kind of problem facing him as a committed political writer which he had failed to resolve in *Bon Pied Bon Œil* is present once again. Now, however, more sure of his own position and with the shadows of the past fully wiped away, a solution begins to appear.

Like *Bon Pied Bon Œil*, *Un Jeune Homme seul* is divided into two parts. The first, largely autobiographical, describes the conditioning influence of the home, background and upbringing of Eugène-Marie Favart: the second, in which the action takes place twenty years later, is a projection in political and moral terms of these early influences. For the most part, therefore, *Un Jeune Homme seul* is, necessarily, a carefully constructed book, with a network of recurring motifs and images, reflections and resonances, linking the two parts together.

The tone of Part I is set from the opening scene. Eugène-Marie, who is returning home from school by bicycle, is involved in an accident with a Polish worker. As soon as he realizes that the man is injured he begins to wonder how he (the Pole) will exploit the situation: 'Les ouvriers trouvent tous les prétextes bons pour réclamer des indemnités à rien plus finir, on appelle ça incapacité de travail. Ils sont terribles sur ce chapitre-là, *tout le monde le dit*'.[21] But whatever initial fears he may have, Eugène-Marie also knows instinctively that simply because he lives in 'une maison particulière' and his father is an engineer he is safe; he is the child of a privileged class, conditioned in his thinking and protected by its institutions. Yet, as the Pole limps away, his feelings are mixed, and relief rapidly gives way to humiliation. But his sense of guilt is shortlived and from this incident Eugène-Marie quickly passes into the insulated world of his bourgeois family where the incident is never again mentioned. The six remaining chapters of Part I are concerned with the invitation to and the wedding itself of Eugène-Marie's uncle, Lucien.

The 'maison Favart' is occupied by three generations of the family: Godichaux, Eugène-Marie's maternal grandfather, his parents Michel and Victoria, himself and his sister Béatrice. Isolated externally ('entre deux maisons en ruine' (p. 9)), internally it lacks any sense of real communal living; rooms and objects belong to individual people (*le coin à maman, le casier d'Eugène-Marie, la chambre à Béatrice*, for example) cutting them off from one another and hence exacerbating any friction or tension which already exists. As a social unit the family lives, as Lucien comments later in the book, 'à l'écart de tout' (p. 126). The Favarts rarely receive visitors and consider themselves superior to the rest of the family, yet they are themselves an object of scornful amusement at the wedding, and Michel is ill at ease at the inaugural banquet of the 'Association des Savoyards à Reims', which he attends at the insistence of Victoria who has refused to go. Vailland emphasizes this sense of separateness both from society at large and from one another by dwelling on each of the characters in turn and in particular on Eugène-Marie and his parents.

In spite of his sister's claim to be the contrary, there is very little doubt that Vailland has, albeit with a certain degree of admissible literary distortion, drawn Michel and Victoria Favart from the models presented by his own parents. Michel is shown as a weak man, slapped and humiliated by his mother when he failed his Polytechnic examination, hoodwinked in business by a distant cousin, forced by family pressures to change his freemasonry for Catholicism, browbeaten by his wife and ever ready, it seems, to seek refuge in his study. In appearance timid ('tes airs de premier communicant' (p. 54)) his physical frailty and middle-class complacency are symbolized by his *pince-nez*. (He is mockingly referred to by the wedding guests as *le binoclard*.) Yet there is sympathy in the way he is presented, too. Michel is a sensitive, cultured man whose taste for the abstractions of mathematics is matched by a love of poetry. As a result the attitude he inspires in his son is ambivalent—a mixture of scorn and respect—but more indicative of Eugène-Marie's state of mind than of what Vailland considers to be his own shortcomings. While Michel may well be guilty of having allowed himself to become absorbed by bourgeois society, he is harmless enough. He is a private man used and even ridiculed by others, but he remains without malice and passes from the novel unnoticed.

By contrast, however, his wife Victoria Favart is shown to exert a much more pernicious influence. When she first appears we are at once struck by her awkwardness:[22]

> Elle a la démarche brusque et gauche des fillettes qui n'arrivent pas à dépasser l'âge ingrat, la poitrine plate et le visage sans âge des femmes qui vieillissent avant d'avoir vécu. [...] Sa présence crée un malaise analogue à celui qu'on éprouve à la vue d'un organisme inachevé, qui se flétrit avant d'avoir mûri. (pp. 15–16)

But her presence is nonetheless imposing and her influence at once noticeable. Already Eugène-Marie's first thoughts at the time of his accident have been about what his *mother's* reaction will be; it is she who is obstinately refusing to recognize Lucien's marriage. Vailland portrays her as a bigoted, hypocritical creature, conserative in the extreme and shocked (or claiming to be) at the slightest challenge to her system of values, social and moral alike. Almost with the intensity of a character from a Mauriac novel she is obsessed above all by her social rank and public image, and she holds her mother-in-law entirely responsible not simply for having pre-

vented Michel from entering the Ecole Polytechnique but, more importantly, for having thereby denied them the early assurance of a comfortable
middle-class existence. Appearance, however, is all important. A piano,
which, as Eugénie Favart points out, neither Victoria nor anyone else in
the family can play (p. 14), is kept simply as a status symbol and remains
with Victoria throughout the novel as a reminder of what she considers to
have been her better life. But the façade is thin. Concern for money ('Il ne
suffit pas de gagner de l'argent, il faut savoir le conserver' (p. 27)) results
in miserliness: Eugène-Marie is refused leather gloves during the winter,
there is no electricity or heating in the bedrooms and no bath.

Given this attitude, it is no surprise to discover that Victoria's objec-
tions to the wedding are equally blinkered. Ignorant of the real reasons
behind the marriage, she triumphantly and accusingly points to it as proof
of her middle-class ideas concerning those she considers to be socially
inferior. It follows that since workers are workers they must necessarily
be both dirty and immoral. For her they are a threat to her security and to
be avoided at all costs: 'On est toujours puni de fréquenter des gens qui ne
sont pas de son monde' she remarks later in the book, after Madru and
Domenica have been arrested (p. 207). It is from this world, associated as it
is in her mind with everything from foul language and the bistro to
revolutionary activities, that she struggles to preserve her son.

In one sense, of course, what we have in *Un Jeune Homme seul*
is no more than a classic example of a perfectly normal family situation, and
for all her narrow-mindedness there is nothing vicious in the way Victoria
treats Eugène-Marie. Vailland's concern, however, is to project the boy's
rebellion in such a way that it eventually becomes politically as well as
psychologically convincing. Already at the close of the first chapter,
Eugène-Marie's doubts about the privileged class to which he belongs are
clear. These doubts are prolonged in his relationship with his father; on
the one hand he accepts and enjoys the quiet, cultured and assured world
of the 'professions libérales', but on the other he senses its artificiality and
lack of real contact with the outside world:

> Le bureau de son père est réconfortant [...] C'est le bureau d'un
> homme dont le métier n'est ni de fabriquer, ni de vendre, ni d'acheter,
> qui n'est pas dans les affaires, mais qui n'a quand même pas de patron,
> qui est à son compte, comme on dit, qui ne touche ni salaire, ni
> appointements, ni commissions, ni gratifications, mais des honoraires;
> tel est le privilège des professions libérales. Pour Eugène-Marie, son
> père se trouve, par rapport aux pères de la plupart de ses camarades,
> dans une position analogue à celle des lycéens qui font du latin et du
> grec par rapport à ceux de la section moderne. Ce n'est pas qu'Eugène-
> Marie aime le latin, et il n'a fait du grec que pendant deux ans, mais il
> se sent flatté d'appartenir à l'élite. (pp. 62–3)[23]

With his mother his relationship is more emotional and more complex. Concerned at her distress following a brief dispute with Godichaux, he attempts to comfort her by adopting the games, words and poses of a small child.[24] The scene takes place, fittingly, in the *chambre à maman*, a room which, by its Louis XV furniture, soft pink and blue colouring and sentimental objects, bears far more evidence of her tastes than those of her husband. For a while he succeeds, readily agreeing with her as she gives vent to her feelings concerning the marriage. But the success is shortlived once Victoria turns from the marriage in particular to religion in general, and to Eugène-Marie's refusal to attend Easter mass. This, together with his reference to the students of the private Collège Saint-Joseph to which she had wanted to send him as 'des petits cons', prompts in her a horrified and increasingly neurotic outburst (pp. 40–3) from which he rushes to seek shelter in his father's study. As an example of adolescent rebellion or of a possessive mother's despairing attempts to retain control over her child, the scene is convincing, and however deeply felt, such moments of rebellion as this, whatever their significance for his subsequent development, are here little more than expressions of adolescent unrest. Furthermore, Eugène-Marie's vision of the working-class world is deliberately shown to be immature and sentimental. For him it is typified by the groups of girls who come from the local brick factory, their colourful, bright clothes contrasting strongly with the fussy, subdued interior of the Favart household:

> Les châles de laine, à larges bandes parallèles, de couleurs crues, rouge, bleu, vert, orange et noir, sont superbes dans la poussière blanche de l'avenue de Laon, faite de craie, comme toute la ville et la plaine qui l'entoure. (p. 68)

He watches them from his father's study, indulging in adolescent sexual fantasies; they tempt him like the prostitute in the *Apocalypse*, but he knows already that his position is hopeless: 'On reste un enfant tant qu'on ne gagne pas sa vie' (p. 71). But rebellion has no future; as he already knows from past experience, the pressures of his family and of his society are too strong, and at the end of Chapter Five he stands in the position where, symbolically, he is to remain for the next twenty years, 'derrière le carreau de la baie vitrée' (p. 74).

Whatever the autobiographical elements in the first five chapters of *Un Jeune Homme seul* may be, Vailland's analysis of a certain kind of middle-class existence in France in the early twenties, with its prejudices and distorted values, is impressive. So, too, is his description of the archetypal conflict between mother and child. The temptation, of course, is for Vailland to side with Eugène-Marie, to use him as a vehicle for his satire and criticism. Happily, however, he avoids this. Like Nizan, who in *La Conspiration* shows Rosenthal to be as much conditioned by and part of the very society he is attempting to undermine, Vailland portrays Eugène-Marie both as victim and beneficiary of the social system to which he belongs. He is, as Sartre has Hoederer say about Jessica in *Les Mains sales* (1948), 'à moitié victime, à moitié complice, comme tout le monde'. At the same time, in view of the political intention of the novel, Vailland clearly felt it necessary to give some indication of his young protagonist's ultimate role. Occasionally the results are unfortunate, especially in an awkward use of the future tense: 'Il ne se rendra compte que...' (p. 63). 'Il ne comprendra que beaucoup plus tard...' (p. 65), or the diatribes on religion or the 'professions libérales'. Less noticeably, however, it is through Godichaux that Vailland makes his intention clear. He, too, is a misfit in the Favart household and a sympathetic bond links him and Eugène-Marie together.[25] In this way the generation of Michel and Victoria is bridged, Eugène-Marie being compared by Godichaux to his paternal grandmother, Eugénie: 'Tu es fait du même bois qu'elle' (p. 21). There is also the similarity of their names. Although she does not appear in the first five chapters of the novel, Eugénie, by her imperious letters to Victoria, already dominates events. She stands as the founder of a race, a kind of Mauriac genitrix figure, and the descriptions of her which Godichaux provides ('Glorieuse, mais pas fière' (p. 24); 'orgueilleuse comme un roi' (p. 22)) and which therefore apply indirectly to Eugène-Marie as well, point to what Vailland ultimately considered to be the key to a proper understanding of the book.

The contrast between the insulated world of the Favart's 'maison particulière' and the teeming labyrinthine apartments of the rue Pétrarque where the wedding celebrations are held is immediately noticeable. Vailland's purpose in the last two chapters of Part I of *Un Jeune Homme seul* is twofold: on the one hand he is exposing Eugène-Marie to a new range of experiences and attitudes (most of which are projections of his own at various points in the past); on the other he continues to stress the confusion which exists in the boy's mind and which, whatever his initial reaction (p. 82), prevents him from accepting and being accepted by his new surroundings. In Paris Eugène-Marie finds himself immersed, if only for a short while, in the working-class world he had glimpsed and envied through his father's study window. He is invited to 'prendre l'apéritif sur le zinc avec nous' by Lucie (p. 81); he hears the words *socialiste* and *communiste* used freely and with respect for the first time in his life; he meets Marcelle the working-class girl he might have seen walking along the avenue de Laon, as well as Madru the Communist and Domenica, both of whom are to fill such important roles in the second half of the book and in his development. He also learns for the first time of his grandfather Favart's anti-clericalism, of his escape from the seminary and of his activities during the Commune. But these experiences—all of which occur, together with the account of the wedding feast and of the dance, in Chapter Six—have no pattern to them; it is as though Vailland wished to present them simply as a kaleido-scopic array to which Eugène-Marie should be exposed. Some of them make a deep impression on him, but in general terms he is too conditioned by his background to be able to absorb them properly. Inevitably, once removed from their insulated bourgeois world the Favarts become objects of scorn: Victoria's hat, Michel's gold teeth and his *binocle* and even, ironi-cally, Eugène-Marie's suit[26] are all emblems of different values and are strikingly out of place. But more significant still is Eugène-Marie's attitude. His anger at the traditional *Ronde des cocus*, for example, is not felt simply because his father has been singled out more than any other for special attention; it is much more deep-rooted, recalling, as we have seen, Vailland's own attitude to society in the late twenties:

> Les voilà les Gaulois, murmurait Eugène-Marie, entre ses dents crispées. La voilà donc la bonne vieille gaieté gauloise. Canailles, crapules, je vous crache à la gueule. J'ai honte d'être Français. Malheur à moi que les Allemands n'aient pas gagné la guerre. Vite une escouade de Prussiens, pour faire taire toute cette racaille à coups de crosse dans les reins...(p. 100)

A point has been reached where Eugène-Marie automatically and in-stinctively finds it impossible to participate any longer. Moreover his reaction, with its appeal to violence as a remedy, is unpleasantly authori-tarian and right-wing. The same kind of reaction also emerges in his behaviour with Marcelle. As we can see from the earlier chapters of the novel, Eugène-Marie's view of working-class girls is related directly to his sexual fantasies. He fondly imagines that Marcelle will be an easy conquest and when she refuses to submit to his adolescent attempt at seduction he at once resorts, pathetically, to insults and force. Fortunately he is saved from further humiliation when Madru, who has been watching the inci-dent, intervenes, but Vailland has made it quite clear that he sees Eugène-Marie (as indeed he now sees himself to have been) as no more than an immature schoolboy who is left at the end of the first part of the novel to return to his 'maison particulière'.

In view of the direction which the novel takes in Part II, it would have been relatively easy for Vailland—and not without some advantage—to have shown Eugène-Marie especially in Chapters Six and Seven giving far more positive hints of his future political development. That he did not choose to do so may be attributable to three reasons: firstly, that any sudden alteration in Eugène-Marie's make-up in such a brief period of time would not have been psychologically justifiable; secondly, that historical authenticity was necessary if the political impact of the book was to be properly felt, and thirdly, that Vailland was indulging in a good deal of confessional self-criticism. Of these the second is vital for a complete understanding of Part I, in the last chapter of which Eugène-Marie is subjected to his uncle Lucien's disillusioned analysis of the state of contemporary French society:

> La morale aussi fout le camp; on n'a jamais vu tant de monde dans les dancings et les boîtes de nuit, et les jeunes filles se coupent les cheveux et se maquillent comme les filles. Tout fout le camp. Quand tout fout le camp, les hommes prennent peur et essaient de se planquer. Après cinq ans de guerre, Lucien sait tout sur tous les genres possibles de planque. Etienne Fleuri s'est planqué dans la police; c'est sa manière à lui de se défendre. Victorien Fleuri est un imbécile; il a sa manière à lui de se planquer, qui est une manière d'imbécile; les imbéciles aussi ont droit à la vie. Le père d'Eugène-Marie se planque dans la religion, c'est une planque comme une autre. (p. 129)

Lucien in the past has been both a socialist and a pacifist and it could be (especially when we recall that the first part of *Un Jeune Homme seul* relates to 1923) that through him Vailland is attacking the socialism of people like Barbusse and Rolland; a socialism which, whatever it may have professed to the contrary, tended to concern itself more with general humanitarian principles and with the notion of the universal brotherhood of man, than with direct revolutionary political action. For all their apparent contented gregariousness and even their talk of revolution which make them so attractive to the young Eugène-Marie, these people lack any real sense of political ambition and motivation. They are, in fact, almost as guilty as the bourgeois world to which Eugène-Marie belongs, for having done nothing to arrest the economic, political and moral disintegration of the French nation. Certainly there are exceptions—Madru, Domenica and Eugénie Favart herself—but their presence is not felt politically until the second half of the novel, by which time both the political climate and Vailland's own position, in as much as autobiography continues to constitute part of *Un Jeune Homme seul*, have altered as well.

As in Part I, the action in Part II spans a matter of days only. Its main impetus derives from an investigation carried out by a Vichy police inspector, Marchand, into a series of sabotage incidents in the railway depot where Eugène-Marie is principal engineer. During the most recent attempt Madru has been killed. In the course of the investigation the whole question of the Resistance and in particular of Eugène-Marie's position is gradually brought into focus. Vailland's method is basically the same as in Part I: information concerning the past, here in the form of police reports, enable us to trace Eugène-Marie's development and career, all of which condition the present; the second part of the novel similarly closes with a ceremony, here Madru's funeral. In Part I the wedding provides Eugène-Marie with an introduction to the working-class world which he so admires; in Part II the funeral becomes a kind of initiation ceremony by which he

finally commits himself to the Resistance forces and after which he proves
his worth through action.

From the beginning of the second part of *Un Jeune Homme seul*
Eugène-Marie is shown to be the solitary figure of the title. Like his parents
before him, he, too, lives in a 'maison particulière' which, he feels, seals
him off from the working-class world around him; unlike the house in the
avenue de Laon, however—but the significance escapes him—it adjoins
the local *cité ouvrière*:

> Regardez ma maison, poursuivait Favart, on la voit d'ici, une jolie
> villa, presque une maison de riche, une maison particulière. Mais
> regardez où elle est placée: elle ouvre sur l'avenue de la Gare et mon
> jardinet est fermé par une grille en fer de lance; mais elle touche
> par-derrière à la cité ouvrière et le mur de mon potager est mitoyen
> avec le mur du potager des hommes d'équipe. Transportez la même
> maison sur la Côte d'Azur ou avenue Henri-Martin, je serais un riche.
> Mais parce que ma porte ouvre sur l'avenue de la Gare, je ne suis
> quand même pas un pauvre. Et les pauvres ne veulent pas de moi.
> (p. 176–7)

Eugène-Marie's bourgeois image is further maintained by his style of dress
which clearly distinguishes and again separates him from 'des hommes
d'équipe en bleus de travail' around him: 'il portait une veste de sport,
des pantalons de golf, des guêtres de cuir. Cravate de lainage écossais nouée
négligemment' (p. 140).

While such social appearances as these suggest that Eugène-Marie
might be ready to accept the Vichy régime,[27] his political attitude is, in fact,
ambiguous, closely resembling Vailland's own in 1942.[28] He is torn between the temptation to join Madru and the others in their Resistance
work, and a sense of wishing to remain unaffected. Superficially, at least,
his attitude has been one of utter impartiality, though, in spite of Ronce-
veaux's accusations to the contrary (p. 168), he has already morally
committed himself by failing to denounce recent events as possible acts of
sabotage, by his hostility towards Marchand and by his refusal to be more
than officially correct in his dealings with him. But for Eugène-Marie
moral commitment of this kind, even were he to recognize it as such, is
clearly not sufficient; it is instead the longing to be involved and accepted
as a person which creates the real tension in him, and in order to be accepted
he must first of all provide positive evidence of his political allegiance. His
attempt to overcome the barrier between himself and his men by offering
them drinks each evening in the bistros is of course misconceived and has
only served, ironically, to make them more wary, and his solitary position
even more acute. Even in his own house he is necessarily isolated, and
however much faith Domenica may have in his eventual political 're-

covery',[29] he is kept in complete ignorance of the part she plays in the Resistance.[30]

As Marchand's inquiry progresses and the net tightens around the Resistance workers, it becomes increasingly difficult for Eugène-Marie to maintain his role of impartiality. His moment of truth arrives at Madru's funeral when he places himself at the head of the procession next to Jeanne (the dead man's wife), Eugénie Favart, who has arrived from Paris, and Domenica. This, for Eugène-Marie, is a public demonstration of his ultimate allegiance, a fact which is conveyed both by the description of him at the head of the procession[31] and by the subsequent attitude of the railway workers: 'Les cheminots serraient la main de l'ingénieur, avec une intention particulière, qu'il traduisait: "Tu es donc des nôtres. Pourquoi ne l'as-tu pas montré plus tôt?"' (p. 219). In many ways the position reached by Eugène-Marie at this stage is not unlike that in which Rodrigue found himself in Bon Pied Bon Œil after his prison sentence: conviction must be translated into action, and it is here that Eugène-Marie goes further than his predecessor when in the final chapter he helps Jacques Madru escape from the police. Ironically he himself is caught and imprisoned, but the all-important act of commitment has been made: Eugène-Marie belongs. As Eugénie Favart remarks in the last words of the novel: 'Il a retrouvé les siens' (p. 236).

Politically, therefore, there would seem to be little about Un Jeune Homme seul that is particularly complicated. Eugène-Marie Favart moves, especially in the second part, from a position of bourgeois indifference to open political involvement which may well cost him his life. Moreover in doing so, he has found happiness and self-fulfilment. The message is apparently clear. But why then does Vailland devote so much attention to Eugène-Marie's childhood? Why are the motifs of the houses in which he lived, of the piano, of the 'gifle qui fait voir rouge' repeated so regularly? Why is Marchand described in such detail and not, surely, without some sympathy? And what, precisely, is the sense of 'les siens'? It is only when we consider Eugène-Marie's case as an individual, personal dilemma—not necessarily in auto-biographical terms—and subsequently apply it to society as a whole, that some of the full significance of Un Jeune Homme seul begins to become clear. As Vailland observed in a long and important letter which he wrote in November 1951 to the critic Pierre Berger, Eugène-Marie has been conditioned: 'strictement défini par sa profession, ses origines familiales et son milieu social. Strictement mais pas totalement défini...' (Ecrits Intimes, p. 451). His efforts to overcome the barriers of social prejudice and preconception in order to rediscover the 'true' (according to Vailland) values of his working-class inheritance may indeed have a political relevance, but it is limited. In spite of the reactions of a number of critics, Vailland insisted that Eugène-Marie's development should not be seen to have occurred within the narrow perspective of any one political party; the Resistance attitude is shared by a range of people all of whom are placed at different points on the political spectrum:

> Mon *Jeune Homme seul* ne s'engage pas dans la voie de l'héroïsme en adhérant au parti communiste, mais en faisant acte de résistance, aux côtés d'un cheminot communiste, d'un cheminot chrétien (Ronceveaux membre de la CFTC), et d'anonymes dont je ne précise pas l'appartenance. Et la conclusion: 'il a retrouvé les siens' est exprimée par la vieille Favart qui n'est pas communiste, qui appartient à un réseau de résistance gaulliste...(*Ecrits Intimes*, p. 449)

But more important still is the intended sense of Eugénie's final words. Throughout the novel the stubborn, rebellious nature of the Savoyards has been stressed—'On dit bien: Savoyard cabochard, Savoyard Favart double cabochard' (p. 38); so, too, have their working-class origins—'Les Savoyards sont faits pour courrir les chantiers, dit Traboulez. Ça leur réussit mieux que de gratter le papier' (p. 55). It can be argued, of course, that autobiographical factors have determined this particular emphasis, but to do so would be to pay insufficient attention to the balance and contrast Vailland has attempted to establish between Eugène-Marie, Marchand and Madru and which give the novel both its general and its political significance.

As I have suggested, Marchand is portrayed in a manner that is not wholly unsympathetic. He is a cultured man who reads Proust; he is also an accomplished pianist. Although Eugène-Marie rejects Marchand's suggestion, there are a number of points of similarity between them in the way in which they have each only imperfectly realized the ambitions of their early years. They are also, of course, both solitary men, but whereas Eugène-Marie's solitude is largely the result of outside factors, Marchand's is deliberately cultivated. As his name suggests, he sells himself and his skills, which he regards as indispensable, to the highest or most powerful bidder: 'Les nouvelles autorités m'utiliseront contre les anciennes, ma technique est la seule dont aucun régime ne peut se passer' (p. 200). And he takes an immense pride in the clinical efficiency with which he carries out his duties.[32] When, finally, he is deemed to have failed in his investigation and is handed over to the Gestapo, his claims are shown to be misguided and the principle underlying them false. Marchand has simply made the wrong decision and is now paying the penalty. At the other end of the scale is Madru, the ideal figure, the 'vrai bolchevik':

> En arrière-plan j'ai esquissé la silhouette du héros accompli, le cheminot Madru; ce n'est pas un communiste quelconque; dans son éloge funèbre [...] j'écris, très à dessein: 'les communistes disaient qu'il avait été un "vrai bolchevik"'; c'est une forme d'éloge qu'il est

possible que certains communistes me reprochent, quoique je l'aie
entendu dans la bouche de certains d'entre eux, et des meilleurs, à
propos des meilleurs; et je n'entends pas bien sûr par ce mot bolchevik
une référence nationale, mais une distinction précisément entre les
héros et ceux qui ne sont pas moins bons 'en soi', mais qui les
reconnaissent comme modèles, entraîneurs, et meilleurs dans le
moment. (*Ecrits Intimes*, pp. 448-9)

It becomes clear from this that the term 'bolchevik' is meant to carry much
more than a simple political implication. Indeed it is a term which, as we
shall see, becomes increasingly central to an understanding of Vailland's
writing and thinking during the next few years. Madru is the complete
man, who has achieved personal happiness and fulfilment during his life only
through commitment to what he believes is for the betterment of society as
a whole. He is, in fact, that rare creature already glimpsed in Drouet and
Albéran, described by Vailland and Claude Roy in their letter to *Action* in
1948 or, to use a definition which Vailland had much more recently given,
'le héros, [...] l'homme qui sait mieux qu'un autre s'asservir à sa propre
volonté, c'est-à-dire réaliser son unité, c'est-à-dire grouper toutes ses
énergies et les porter au maximum d'efficacité, *au service de* ce qui est à
son époque la cause de la liberté positive' (*Ecrits Intimes*, p. 448). This is
precisely where Madru differs from Marchand, who had preferred to
remain solitary, confident that society will always need and indeed accept
him on his own terms. Between them stands Eugène-Marie who, by his
final actions, shows that Madru's example has not been in vain.

While, therefore, a political lesson is obviously to be drawn from *Un
Jeune Homme seul*, the real merit of the novel lies in the manner in which
Vailland has ensured that it is only one element—albeit ultimately the
most important—among many. Certainly there are some weaknesses: the
self-indulgent outbursts against the *pétainistes* or the quasi-sociological
diatribes on the *binocle* or the *professions libérales*, for example. Some, too,
might object to the stylized language and tone of the *éloge du mort*, even
though it may be seen to form part of what is after all a ritualistic event, or
to Vailland's customary alignment of physical and moral characteristics:
Eugénie's physical stature, Madru's strength or Marchand's hidden weakness—'la mâchoire empâtée, les paupières boursouflées révélaient des
faiblesses, une maladie de cœur et des vices' (p. 135). But these are relatively
minor blemishes in what was without question Vailland's most successful
piece of imaginative writing to date. The linking of the two parts by the use
of recurrent motifs and themes, the emphasis on the conditioning power of
social and provincial background, and the refusal to associate Eugène-
Marie's development with any specific political group ensure that the
book retains a general appeal without losing any of its political impact.
Furthermore, Vailland has at long last finally completed the exorcism of

his past. From now on, though the same problems and inhibitions may still manifest themselves in his imaginative writing, they will be externalized and controlled, projected in such a way that they become part of the world which he creates.

Chapter Four

The Years of Commitment

> Toute œuvre pose directement ou in-
> directement les problèmes de l'époque où
> elle a été écrite.
> *Quelques réflexions à propos d'une*
> *critique de M. Emile Henriot.*

'In literature as in politics', Trotsky once remarked, a fellow traveller is 'someone who, stumbling and staggering, goes up to a certain point along the same road which we shall follow much further.'[1] With *Un Jeune Homme seul* (though without this degree of difficulty) Vailland had reached the certain point to which Trotsky here refers. The novel had been a declaration of faith, artistically infinitely superior to *Le Colonel Foster plaidera coupable*, but more impressive still by the manner in which Vailland had, in various ways, met his friend and critic Berger's advice in advance and succeeded in toning down the partisan nature of the earlier work.[2] Yet it was still questionable whether or not *Un Jeune Homme seul* which, to use Berger's words again, was situated 'dans les limites de ce qu'on peut appeler le militantisme littéraire, le militantisme en marche',[3] was sufficiently revolutionary to be wholly acceptable to the Communist Party. Berger not only found in it an unwarranted amount of what he termed naturalist writing but also, and more significantly, evidence that 'le libertin n'est pas encore tout à fait effacé'. Such criticism from one whom Vailland admired and whose opinion he much respected inspired the piece of explanatory self-defence to which reference was made in the last chapter. In addition, however, to those parts of it which deal specifically with *Un Jeune Homme seul*, Vailland's letter contains an outline of his attitude to literature and its place in a changing society. Naturalism and the vogue for populism which had developed in the late twenties and early thirties—the attempt to convey as accurately as possible the conditions and behaviour of working-class people—he rejects out of hand. Of paramount importance instead, he argues, is the shape of a work of art, its physical development. Life, Vailland maintains, is essentially dramatic in the way it evolves. Similarly therefore—and this is a theory which he picks up again and discusses more thoroughly in his essay *Expérience du drame*—literature which sets out to depict the reality of life can best do so if it has an internal dramatic development of its own: 'une situation donnée au premier acte contient un certain nombre de conflits qui se développent jusqu'à aboutir au dénouement, à une situation nouvelle, radicalement, ou en langage dialectique qualitativement différente de la situation initiale'.[4]

There is, in other words therefore, a progressive or revolutionary quality about such work. Yet it is perfectly natural, according to Vailland, that within such a system an individual will emerge as the leader or hero and he rejects as unreal the idea that heroism can be collective—a view which was subsequently to emerge with important implications in *325.000 francs* and *Beau Masque*. For him the modern hero may indeed be seen as the direct descendant of the supreme iconoclast, the eighteenth-century libertine; his duty is to fight and eventually overcome constraint in any form, thereby encouraging others to follow suit and enjoy a new freedom. No longer, however, is Vailland concerned with a self-indulgent 'chasse au bonheur'; Marat has given way to Rodrigue and Eugène-Marie, who in turn have as their model the 'vrai bolchevik' figures of Albéran and Madru. Yet Berger's criticisms remained valid. Near as he now was to the Communist Party, Vailland had not yet been accepted as a member. But not for much longer. On 9 May of the following year (1952) *Le Colonel Foster plaidera coupable* was due to receive its first public performance at the Théâtre de l'Ambigu. The Préfecture of Police, however, maintaining that the electrical system of the theatre was inadequate, had the performance cancelled 'in the interests of public safety'.[2] In the face of much criticism in the press the police subsequently allowed the play to be put on, but the performance was shortlived, this time disrupted by people Vailland later maintained had been planted in the audience by the police, and the play was subsequently banned. At once Vailland achieved a gloss of political notoriety that had previously been lacking. The incident was interpreted by many as being yet another of the Communist demonstrations so frequent in France in 1952 against the whole principle of N.A.T.O., against American influence in general and against the arrival as allied commander in Europe of General Ridgway who had been in charge of military operations in Korea. Towards the end of May various Communist leaders were arrested including Jacques Duclos, secretary of the French Communist Party. On 7 June Vailland sent his formal application for membership to Duclos in the Santé prison, on a copy of his banned play: 'En témoignage de respectueuse affection cette nouvelle édition de "Le Colonel Foster plaidera coupable" et en lui demandant d'accepter mon adhésion au Parti Communiste Français.'

It is arguable that Vailland had forced the Party's hand, and that in the circumstances his application could hardly be refused, but whatever the case, there is no doubt that the time had been fast approaching when membership would be a matter of course. On 3 July *L'Humanité* carried Vailland's carefully-worded public announcement of his new, regularized position:

Dans la résistance d'abord, puis aux combattants et aux partisans de la Paix, j'avais eu l'occasion de travailler avec les communistes, d'apprendre à les estimer, à les aimer. Preuve m'avait été faite d'année par année que le Parti Communiste constitue réellement l'avant-garde du combat pour la paix, pour la liberté et pour le bonheur des hommes. Dans l'instant où les arrestations illégales d'André Stil, Jacques Duclos et tant d'autres patriotes rendent la menace fasciste plus concrète qu'elle ne l'avait jamais été depuis le temps de Vichy, il m'est apparu comme la chose la plus naturelle au monde de prendre ma place au combat dans le parti de Marx, Engels, Lénine, Staline et Maurice Thorez.

Je suis très heureux de commencer à militer dans le parti dans la ville où j'habite, Ambérieu-en-Bugey, parmi les cheminots, les paysans, les cheminots-paysans et les paysans-cheminots qui sauront certainement s'unir contre le nouvel occupant, les nouveaux collabos, comme ils l'ont déjà fait pendant la résistance.

Already earlier in the year Vailland had begun work on his next novel, *Beau Masque*, but had, somewhat unusually, experienced difficulty in making much progress with it. In July, only a few weeks after his being accepted into the Communist Party, the military coup d'état in Egypt occurred and Vailland was sent by the recently founded left-wing review *Défense de la paix* to 'situer la nouvelle Egypte, celle qui était en train de se former sur le débris du trône, par rapport au problème dans le camp de la paix de celles qui la pousseraient dans le camp de la guerre'.[5] With the same kind of revolutionary fervour which had prompted him to write so enthusiastically about the Indonesians in *Boroboudour*, Vailland now finds in the Egyptian *fellahs* the ideal expression of those qualities possessed only by the people and so vital for revolution—quickness, intelligence, generosity and kindness. The pattern is predictable. He exalts the peasants and caricatures the rich and wealthy, all of whom, without exception, are presented as obese and corrupt;[6] wherever possible he finds points of comparison with the French Revolution. Within days of arriving, Vailland was arrested—together with his friend the Egyptian poet, Kamal, and others—on grounds of being 'un agitateur étranger', and found guilty of unspecified 'manœuvres visant à détruire les fondements de l'Etat'.[7] Vailland's account of the days spent as a political prisoner are the most moving and the most effective of the book, even though its original purpose thereby becomes somewhat lost and can hardly be said to be redeemed by a heavy-handed analysis of the contemporary political situation as a whole in the final chapter. Above all, they are marked by his sense of belonging. Whether handcuffed together with other prisoners on the back of a lorry or in the prison cell at Damietta, Vailland was deeply impressed by the strong feeling of comradeship which existed not only between prisoners (and which expressed itself in the way in which everything from messages to food was passed from one to another with little risk of detection), but also between prisoners and their guards. Here, he concluded, was further evidence of the gradual disintegration of the political hierarchy, and a clear pointer to its eventual overthrow. Vailland's experience also served—as had the uproar surrounding *Le Colonel Foster plaidera coupable* —to bring him further into prominence. Although seemingly a local affair only, news of Vailland's arrest was leaked both to the American Press Agency and to France, where *L'Aurore* and *Ce Matin* each published articles denouncing Vailland as a Communist agitator and encouraging the Egyptian government to deal with him severely. But Vailland's imprisonment ended almost as abruptly and as perfunctorily as it had begun, and by the beginning of September he was back in France.

Choses vues en Egypte was to be Vailland's last piece of lengthy reporting for more than ten years. After a number of visits during the winter months 1952–3 first with Elisabeth to Eastern Europe and later on his own to Russia where *Le Colonel Foster plaidera coupable* was being produced,[8] he returned to France and to a period of intense political, intellectual and creative acitivity characterized above all by a concern for the problem of literature as a vehicle for political and social ideas. In the space of the following three years he was to write *Laclos par lui-même*, *Expérience du drame*, *Batailles pour l'Humanité*, *La Bataille de Denain* (unfinished), a new version of *Beau Masque* and *325.000 francs*.

In view of his now much more clearly defined stance it is hardly surprising to find Vailland's first extensive efforts at literary criticism— *Expérience du drame* and *Laclos par lui-même*—written with reference to a system of Marxist values. In the first, a discursive, general study, Vailland expresses his views on the theatre both as an art form and as a medium through which certain ideas can be best expressed; in the second he devotes his attention almost entirely to an analysis of Laclos' *Les Liaisons dangereuses*, demonstrating how it had been inspired by the social and economic conditions prevailing in France during the second half of the eighteenth century, and from which Laclos (according to Vailland) suffered.

As has already become clear, the most successful and rewarding form of drama for Vailland was tragedy, the movement and development of which are directly comparable to those of life, a series of distinct periods (*saisons*) dynamically related to one another:

> Le vie d'un homme véritable est analogue à une bonne tragédie. Elle se dénoue dans une mort heureuse, après que l'homme ait [...] résolu, tels qu'ils se reflètent en lui-même en fonction de son temps, de son pays, de sa classe, de sa condition et de sa singularité, tous les problèmes de son temps, tous les conflits de son temps.[9]

Conversely, t follows that a study of classical tragedy will lead automatically to a proper understanding of the historical processes of life—
a fact which Vailland maintained he had been made aware of through
his study of Corneille at school. Events no longer appear 'un déroulement
continu et inorganisé', a dull accumulation of unrelated facts, but instead
a progression, albeit irregular, with one situation leading into another:
'le passage dramatique d'une situation à une nouvelle situation, radicalement, qualitativement nouvelle' (p. 134). Indeed, in his own case, Vailland
claims his reading of Marx, Lenin and Stalin has only added depth to what
had already been firmly established as a method for analyzing society during
his early years. But while the writer may be aware that his task in writing a
tragedy is precisely to convey this historical movement, literary creation
alone is not sufficient. Unlike the novel, drama is a public event, 'le rapport
de participation entre la salle et la scène'.[10] Consequently it is the duty
of the producer and his actors to establish this contact with their audience.
While each performance is potentially different, it nonetheless remains
organically whole, actors and audience meeting in 'un amical conflit'.
For this to be achieved demands of the actor the highest control of his
art. Like Diderot, on whose views in *Le Paradoxe sur le comédien* Vailland
draws heavily, he believes that the actor can only truly fulfil his role
and project it to the audience in the required manner, if he himself can
view it objectively. Only in this way can he fully contribute to the creation
of the unity of action, thereby causing the audience to become properly
aware of the issues at stake. More significantly still the actor's ability to
project himself ('l'acteur n'a pas à devenir son personnage. Il doit le
jouer'[11]) to separate wittingly his real self from the role required of him
by the play, in itself contains a lesson for society as a whole. We are back
with Vailland's overriding concern for the need for individuals to control
their emotional responses to a situation rationally, and by so doing to
become master of it. It follows that through the process of participation
within the theatre an audience will be brought to the point where it
believes that it too has a role to play outside: a new, revolutionary situation
has been created.

This same emphasis on change and revolution also underpins Vailland's
analysis of Laclos' novel. *Les Liaisons dangereuses* was written, he maintains, by a man who was both professionally at a disadvantage on account
of his middle-class birth, and disillusioned. It is well enough known that
as a young officer in the French army, Laclos had shown himself to be both
brilliant and ambitious, but in 1763 his promise was stifled by the treaty
of Paris which ended the Seven Years War. In 1779, instead of being sent
to serve in the American War of Independence along with a number of
officers drawn from the aristocracy, he was drafted to the Ile de Ré where
his task was to erect and maintain defences against a possible invasion by
the English which, in fact, never materialized. It was on the Ile de Ré off

the west coast of France that he began his novel. Vailland's interpretation of *Les Liaisons dangereuses* is essentially twofold. On the one hand he relates the novel to the prevailing social conditions of the late eighteenth century and attempts to demonstrate its relevance for the twentieth; and on the other he analyzes some of its internal patterns and structures, which constitute its value as a piece of imaginative literature in its own right.

Vailland's consideration of the novel as a social commentary rests in part, however, on the assumption that of the principal characters only La Présidente de Tourvel is a member of the bourgeoisie.[12] While there is no internal, nor indeed any direct historical evidence for this, it enables Vailland to see her as the only unambiguously sympathetic character of the novel, with Valmont, a member of the privileged aristocracy (again in historical terms a narrow and misinformed view),[13] as the principal target for attack. But the real key to *Les Liaisons dangereuses* as a commentary on certain social conditions is, according to Vailland, to be found in its portrayal of women. He refers to Laclos' essay, *De l'Education des Femmes*, in order to show how he (Laclos) believed in the equal rights of women. By nature physically weaker, woman has gradually become oppressed socially and economically as well, and Vailland quotes from Marx and Engels to show what the full consequences of Laclos' view are. In order to retaliate, however, she has developed her sense of cunning and her powers of persuasion and seduction, and *Les Liaisons dangereuses* is an illustration of the contest which must inevitably ensue. When the novel is seen in these terms it soon becomes clear, as Vailland admits, that Valmont is not simply a figure to be despised. He outlines and admires the way in which Laclos describes the military precision with which Valmont carries out his four-stage seduction of the Présidente (though he makes little of the former's confession of love at the close of Letter CXXV), and holds it up as a perfect example of true libertine behaviour. Like the tragic actor in the drama Vailland discusses in *Expérience du drame*, Valmont is always master of the situation in which he finds himself and of the emotional response it requires of him. Vailland largely ignores the possible moral interpretations which can be made of the end of Laclos' novel; for him it is essentially an illustration of a ritual involving both men and women and in which some (Valmont and Mme de Merteuil) are further initiated than others. Basically it is an expression of freedom: 'Le libertinage, jeu de société dramatique, pratiqué dans la seconde moitié du XVIIIe, mime théâtralement le défi que l'héroïque libertin des XVIe et XVIIe siècles portait à Dieu, à l'autel et au trône'.[14] Having defined libertine behaviour precisely in this way it is surprising that Vailland does not make more of what is one of the most striking aspects of Laclos' novel as a whole—its intense artificiality. The opera, the salon, the cab, the boudoir, even the garden provide stylized settings in which people act out their parts. Furthermore, the very nature of the epistolary novel is such that the author avoids direct confrontation of characters, and since, as Merteuil carefully instructs Cécile, any letter is necessarily written with the recipient in mind and is therefore almost invariably a distortion of the truth, even language itself becomes artificial. Indeed, in many ways *Les Liaisons dangereuses* is a theatrical novel, in that it selects and distills Laclos' views on society and develops them with the studied precision of a mathematical equation.

Already in *Expérience du drame* Vailland had spoken of the impact made by a novel on its reader in terms of a private experience; it could not, he claimed, command the kind of participation and response which a theatrical representation invited from its audience. Nonetheless it was to the novel and not the theatre that he was to return, aiming at 'un roman dont la lecture se précipite comme une action et qui provoque à l'action'.[15]

Beau Masque, to which Vailland reapplied himself on his return from Egypt, was greeted, particularly by the Communist press, as an unqualified success. André Wurmser, writing in *Les Lettres Françaises*, for example, saw it as a book which was 'ni "purement" psychologique, ni "purement" social [...] mais humaine dans sa "totalité". [...] Peu de livres aussi pleins sont aussi exempts de schématisme'.[16] In simple terms, the central theme of *Beau Masque* is exploitation—of the weak by the strong, of the workers by management, of peasant farmers by agricultural consortiums. Its principal action is the struggle between the silk manufacturers of le Clusot, the *Filatures et Tissages Anonymes* (*FETA*) and their employees, a number of whom are threatened by redundancy with the introduction of a new plan for streamlining the business in order to satisfy its American shareholders. The workers' leader is a young Communist divorcee, Pierrette Amable, whose marriage broke up when she discovered that her husband was spying for the *FETA* management. Mistress of her emotions as she is certain of her political views, she is utterly devoted to her fellow workers' struggle, and she finally succeeds in bringing together those less totally committed, or simply more cautious than herself, in the organization of a strike and massive demonstration against American interference. Yet her view of the management's attitude is necessarily limited by what she knows of *FETA*'s own internal problems. Here too, unknown to her, there is a struggle for power, with Emilie Privas-Lubas, the second wife of the present owner, Valerio Empoli, attempting together with Valerio's sister Esther, to obtain a majority of the shares and hence ultimate control. Emilie's two children, Philippe Letourneau (by her first marriage), and Nathalie, her step-daughter, also have their roles to play. Philippe, who, although due to inherit the *FETA* organization, has no business sense whatsoever, falls in love with Pierrette, and, in order to win her esteem, attempts, in vain, to betray his company's plans; Nathalie, dying of tuberculosis and almost an alcoholic, finally thwarts her step-mother with a Machiavellian maliciousness worthy of her father himself. Caught between these two groups is Beau Masque. An Italian immigrant and Communist sympathizer, Beau Masque has behind him a record of political action. He becomes Pierrette's lover, but always remains an outsider on the fringe of the local political activities, and becomes increasingly jealous of the time Pierrette devotes to them. Ultimately he is a victim of the situation, killed by the CRS as he and Vizille, a former local Resistance fighter, attempt to stage their own demonstration.

In addition to the struggle at a local level, however, Vailland also aims in *Beau Masque* at the French government's national policy and in particular at the unresisted influence of America in Europe. *FETA*'s normal supply of raw silk comes from China. A deal between the French and Chinese governments, whereby train engines will be offered in exchange is quashed when the American government threatens to withdraw financial support from French industry generally. At both a local and national level Vailland is once again pointing to what he (and the French Communist Party) considered to be the greatest threat to the nation's self-esteem.

While Wurmser's enthusiasm for *Beau Masque* may have been somewhat excessive, closer examination does show that Vailland was aware of—though not necessarily able to avoid—the dangers of schematization, and that while remaining for the most part faithful to the Marxist criteria of economic, social and historical determinism, he also attempted to introduce some degree of psychological depth to the struggle he set out to depict.

One result of this awareness to have as wide an optique as possible is a somewhat marginal consideration of the world of the small peasant farmer. Pierrette's uncle, Aimé Amable, and his wife are justified in terms of the story by their role as guardians of Pierrette's five-year-old son Roger. But they are also intended to be representative of a certain way of and attitude to life. Amable, who by deceit and exploitation has pieced his twenty hectares together over thirty years, now guards them jealously, unable to bear the thought that on his death his land might be split up again. Yet so conservative and short-sighted is he that he is unable to see that he too will be an inevitable victim of 'la grande culture', and part, in fact, of the process of exploiter and exploited to which he has already in his own small way contributed:

> Elle [Pierrette] pensa que, par le simple jeu de la concurrence les gros propriétaires de Beauce et de Brie étaient en train de dépouiller son oncle de sa terre, exactement de la même manière qu'il avait dépouillé de leurs terres les tout petits propriétaires du Quartier d'En-Bas. Eux, parce qu'ils avaient des tracteurs et de l'argent pour acheter des engrais, lui parce que, trente années durant, il avait prêté bœufs contre le travail des autres. [...] Elle avait pitié de

millions de petits propriétaires qui se trouvaient ou allaient se trouver acculés à la même ruine; la grande culture tuait aussi sûrement la petite exploitation que la machine à vapeur avait tué le tissage à domicile.[17]

While Pierrette's (and Vailland's) sympathy for the likes of Amable may be genuine enough, there can be no doubt that he is to blame. Like his neighbours Justin and Ernestine who, we learn in the Epilogue, have abandoned their small-holdings and moved to Grenoble in order to find more instantly rewarding factory work, he is guilty of betrayal. The implication, clearly, is that a corporate awareness of and reaction to the problem would at least be an initial step towards its solution, but it is an issue which Vailland chooses not to pursue, registering it nostalgically as a feature of modern life and devoting his attention instead to the pocket of industrial society in Le Clusot.

As we have already noted, the conflict between *FETA* and its employees eventually resolves itself into a confrontation of two massive blocks of power: on the one hand authority—represented variously by *FETA*, the French government, Johnston the American delegate, the *CRS*, for example—and on the other, by the united workers' front. But while, as the novel develops, the latter are shown to converge towards this position of solidarity, the former, whatever their façade of strength, are torn internally by dissension, rivalry, jealousy and irresponsibility.

With its origins in the eighteenth century, *FETA* owes its power and present position to a mixture of good fortune, the astute business sense of its various heads over the years and to ruthless exploitation. The last of the old style bosses Philippe's grandfather ('qui disait "mes ouvriers" et jugeait sa prospérité au nombre de travailleurs qu'il occupait' (p. 130))[20] has been replaced by representatives of modern-day capitalism for whom one such business concern is only a single element in a whole range, and who insure against loss in one quarter by investment in another. The present owner of *FETA*, Valerio Empoli, an influential Lyon banker, has only been so since 1932. Rarely visiting Le Clusot, the 'maître occulte de la *FETA*' (p. 147) as Noblet imagines him, nonetheless has everything under his control. Physically impressive, he is also a cultured man who reads and quotes Montaigne. But above all he owes his position of strength to his ability to interpret his employees' thoughts (he also reads Stalin's speeches) and, though he professes belief in the workers' ultimate success, to meet them on their own terms. Valerio's real concern, however, is not with the workers of Le Clusot, but with his own wife Emilie, whose plots with his sister Esther and her husband's family threaten his control. Quite remorselessly he resorts to underhand tactics. He pressurizes local investors and leaks to the press the details of the French government's agreement with the United States; moreover, he ensures that Philippe

D

will see the reports knowing that he in turn will pass them on to Pierrette for her to use in the workers' campaign against the company's reorganization. The outcome of this struggle for power, however, finally rests with Nathalie, whose six per cent of the company's shares is enough to provide an overall majority for one side or another. As an Empoli, her decision to support her father is as unhesitating as it is devoid of business reasoning: 'J'appartiens à l'une des grandes familles régnantes du monde...(p. 70) Le gouvernement doit comprendre ce qu'il en coûte d'entrer en conflit avec nous...'(p. 430).[18]

Like her father, Nathalie is a dynamic person who is clearly not without Vailland's sympathy. Aware that she is dying, she appears to challenge death by the very extravagance of her way of life, and deliberately flaunts her total lack of concern for accepted moral conduct by her relationship with her step-brother and with her cousin, Bertrande. She is an aggressive, spiky person who by her very independence and strength of character inevitably invites our admiration, and, as we shall see, is vital for our understanding of Vailland's own attitude.

In contrast to his step-sister's independence, Philippe seeks what he imagines to be the companionship and feeling of solidarity with the working class. For him the world is rotten—'Ce vieux monde s'est transformé en charogne' (p. 411)—but his flirtation with Pierrette and her colleagues is doomed from the start to be as empty and as unsuccessful as his earlier crazes for the theatre, publishing or Yoga. Certainly he has rejected much that is represented by the commercial world of *FETA*. His poetry, his love of painting and even the decor of his office define him as a sensitive creature, whose lack of concern for business is genuine. But by the same token it is impossible for him suddenly to throw his weight into the workers' struggle for a better deal. As Pierrette remarks when he takes the reports of the government's intervention in the silk industry to the workers' meeting: 'Il manque de caractère, [...] mais il est plein de bonne volonté' (p. 395).[19] Philippe is, of course, driven on in his new socio-political ambitions by his love for Pierrette. His letters to Nathalie (Part III) plot the development of this *amour-fou*, which, unreturned, eventually goads him into persuading Beau Masque that Pierrette has been unfaithful to him. Only after Beau Masque's death does he realize the real effect that his jealousy has had:

C'est un suicide, pensa aussitôt Philippe. Beau Masque s'est suicidé parce que je lui ai donné la preuve que Pierrette le trompait. Il n'a pas pu supporter la certitude de la trahison de celle qu'il avait cru la plus intègre des femmes. Il s'est suicidé héroïquement. Mais c'est moi qui l'ai assassiné.... (p. 454)

There is no alternative left other than to kill himself, and his suicide by hanging is a tragic if somewhat melodramatic ending to a life doomed to failure from the start. It is arguable and indeed significant that Philippe lacks his sister's ability to act with cold rationality whatever part she is required to play. He is in fact the actor condemned by Vailland in *Expéri-ence du drame*, who allows his emotions to take control. But he is also a victim of historical and social circumstances. Philippe oscillates between two worlds, attempting unsuccessfully to reject one yet never being accepted by the other; failure, however justified his intention to change his allegiance may seem, is inevitable.

If the society to which Nathalie and Philippe belong is shown to be founded on exploitation and corruption, so that of Pierrette and her colleagues is healthy and vigorous. Nonetheless, there is one important point of similarity. Valerio, and more obviously Nathalie, control and thereby, in a sense, rise above the sordid details of the commercial world to which they owe their power and fortune; Pierrette likewise has achieved a position of complete understanding and authority. Free from family and emotional ties she has devoted her energies entirely to the service of the working class: 'C'est que, peu à peu, dans cette période de sa vie, elle avait cessé d'avoir des problèmes personnels; elle ne connaissait plus que ceux de son action; elle était déjà presque une révolutionnaire pro-fessionnelle' (p. 95).

She has earned the respect of her employers by her assiduousness and political integrity—she even refuses, for example, to dance with Philippe 'parce que c'est mon patron' (p. 72). But more than this she is instantly recognized by Nathalie as 'une fille qui a de la classe' (p. 50), being clearly distinguishable from those around her, who for all their political good faith, tend to be dull in comparison and appear as little more than standard types: Mignot, the serious and unimaginative secretary of the local section of the Communist Party; Cuvrot, 'héros de la grande grève de 1924' (p. 44), now leader of the Communist minority on the town council and living rather in the past; Louise, delegate of the socialist *Force Ouvrière*, ever ready to compromise with the management (p. 346-7) yet sympathetic to and ready with her support for Pierrette; Marguerite, sentimental and politically naive 'qui ne pensait qu'à s'évader du Clusot' (p. 87). Yet at the same time Pierrette is almost too exemplary, a lone figure whose self-imposed solitude may have rendered her political activities easier, but which is also endangering her contact with other people: 'elle était devenue, en une certaine mesure, une étrangère' (p. 303). From this predicament she is rescued by Beau Masque, but only for a while. At first his admiration for her is absolute: 'Pierrette était son héroïne, c'était la première fois de sa vie qu'il rencontrait une héroïne' (p. 205). Their life together initially is idyllic, but domesticity and Pierrette's pregnancy gradually encourage Beau Masque to adopt an increasingly possessive attitude towards her and more importantly erode her political fibre. The extent to which this is so is seen in Pierrette's interview with Northemaire, during which she responds to what she considers to have been flattery:

> c'était la première fois qu'elle souriait à un représentant du patronat, au cours d'une discussion professionnelle. [...] elle savait bien que ce n'était pas le comique de la situation qui avait commandé son sourire. Pour être rigoureusement sincère avec elle-même, elle devait admettre que son sourire avait été un acquiescement à la confiance que Northemaire faisait à son intelligence. (p. 341)

This interview is followed within the next few days by a number of incidents all of which provide further tests for Pierrette's political integrity: she is presented with the compromise solutions reached by Louise and the *Force Ouvrière*, by *FETA*'s quite reasonable alternatives to its original plan, while a political reunion which has been especially called by Pierrette succeeds in attracting one person only. Despondent, she appeals to Mignot. His response, however painful to her, is nonetheless to the point:

> Ne crois-tu pas, [...] que les camarades t'accordent moins de confiance depuis que tu t'es mise avec Beau Masque? Vous n'êtes pas mariés. Je sais bien que vous vivez honnêtement, comme mari et femme...*Mais les camarades responsables se doivent d'avoir une vie privée irréprochable.* (p. 352)[20]

The 'class' which Nathalie had sensed she possessed is still present, however, and despite her own doubts, Mignot's insinuations and Beau Masque's jealousy, Pierrette reasserts her authority and successfully organizes the strike action and demonstration with which the American delegate's visit is greeted. But while such action may be proof of her political integrity and power of leadership, its effectiveness must remain in doubt. As we have seen, the reorganization of *FETA* in favour of Emilie and its American shareholders is successfully sabotaged internally by Valerio and Nathalie, and while the police arrest Pierrette, Mignot and Cuvrot as likely troublemakers, the real disruption of proceedings is carried out by Beau Masque and Vizille. In a sense, therefore, Pierrette and her colleagues have little to show for their efforts, at least in the short term. Their only real achievement is perhaps to have got the better of people such as Noblet the personnel manager, Tallagrand the engineer, and even Northemaire—mediocre men who merely carry out the orders issued by the family and who, when necessary, are themselves conveniently passed over. Aware of this perhaps, Vailland is careful in the Epilogue to underline the continuing solidarity of the workers and to suggest that what was happening in Le Clusot was only part of a revolution on a worldwide scale: 'L'histoire de l'homme était ainsi en train de prendre son "tournant décisif"...' (p. 461).

It is, at this point, worth recalling Vailland's remark in *Expérience du drame* concerning the novel 'dont la lecture se précipite comme une action et qui provoque à l'action'. Does *Beau Masque* have this kind of inner dynamism which Sartre, too, saw as an essential ingredient of the novel? Can it, by the very manner in which the intrigue is presented, sharpen our awareness of the problem? As we have seen, the influence of neo-classical drama on Vailland's writing had always been considerable, but, formulated in *Expérience du drame* and brought into line with his more clearly defined political stance, it is reasonable to expect that any tragic form which *Beau Masque* may have will be more successful than that in his earlier novels.

In a general way the five-part structure of the novel is not without its effect. Part I is largely expository, situating the characters in relation to the problem in general terms and to one another; Part II, in which Beau Masque becomes Pierrette's lover and Emilie begins to develop her campaign for gaining control of *FETA*, adds further psychological and emotional dimensions to the intrigue; Part III, which (no doubt influenced by the epistolary form of Laclos' novel) is a series of letters exchanged between Philippe and Nathalie, provides a commentary on the former's relationship with Pierrette and on the latter's cynical withdrawal from the scene of action, each of which serves to bring matters to a head more quickly; Part IV deals with the period of crisis in Pierrette's private life and shows its effect on her public role; Part V contains the final confrontation between the two sides, Beau Masque's death and the eventual end to the family feud. There is, too, an attempt to impose a unity of place—events rarely occur outside Le Clusot or Grange-aux-Vents where Amable lives—and of time. (The time span of the novel is approximately seven months—or a year if the Epilogue is included. Part IV covers the same period—June to October—as Part III.)

Our attention, therefore, is controlled throughout; moreover, the recapitulative and confessional episodes of the kind to be found in *Drôle de jeu* or *Les Mauvais Coups* are now absent, with the result that as the intrigue of *Beau Masque* develops and evolves, so, too, does our response to it. But a novel depends for its impact on the tension that develops between the contrasting personalities of its characters and the situations in which they find themselves. It is, by definition, a diffuse work of art quite different in kind from neo-classical tragedy with its close control and refinement. *Beau Masque* falls somewhere between the two. Certain characters—Pierrette, Nathalie and Philippe in particular—function rather like a Stendhalian elite, at once both representative of the principal issues at stake and yet by their very natures set apart from them. Elsewhere lesser beings, workers and management alike, are seen to be mere extensions of the context in which they have been placed. And apart from all others stands Beau Masque himself.

In a lecture Vailland had given two years earlier entitled *Le héros du roman*,[21] he had confessed to the difficulty he always experienced when asked to select the hero (or heroine) of *La Chartreuse de Parme*. His choice, he maintained, varied according to his emotional reaction to the novel on any particular reading, though he acknowledged that the 'hero' in principle at least, was Fabrice. The same kind of confusion surrounds *Beau Masque*. In the context of what we know to be Vailland's views on the hero and on the need for leadership within communal action, we are tempted to select Pierrette as the book's heroine. Indeed the title of the German translation of the novel was *Die junge Frau Amable* and of the Russian simply *Pierrette Amable*. But Nathalie has a claim, as does Philippe (if only by his *failure* to act heroically), and even Valerio. What then of Beau Masque? Clearly Vailland intends that he should be seen as the innocent (and thereby tragic) victim of a situation induced by the actions of an unjust capitalist system. At the same time, however, he is, in spite of his previous political actions, too much of an individualist to be considered a hero in the sense that Vailland applies the term. Indeed, when Pierrette prevents Vizille from ambushing the *CRS* and accuses him of acting in an individualistic way (p. 451) her words could well have applied to Beau Masque. For all that, he is undoubtedly intended to be a sympathetic character. There is, as his very name suggests, something false about him. His actions during the workers' demonstration, though spectacular and indeed effective, are also self-indulgent and anarchic.[22] Only, therefore, by underlining their essential futility and by stressing instead the need for corporate action on however small or local a scale initially, could Vailland convey the ideational intention of *Beau Masque*. Yet while Part V closes on a note of triumph—'Nous sommes vainqueurs. Nous sommes les plus forts' (p. 458)—it is in the Epilogue that Vailland chooses to express most forcibly his faith in the revolution. Indeed, it is arguable that he found himself dissatisfied with the bulk of the novel as a vehicle for the expression of his ideas, and that the Epilogue (whatever its function in terms of the plot) may be read as both a statement of faith and as a sop to possible left-wing critics. But what is perhaps more disturbing still is the pessimistic tone of *Beau Masque*. Certainly Vailland never maintained that social and political injustices could be instantly eradicated, nor that the necessary struggle would be easy, but *Beau Masque* curiously lacks the glow of *anticipated* success which characterizes the non-imaginative essays like *Boroboudour* and *Choses vues en Egypte*, and which Rodrigue imagines in *Bon Pied Bon Œil*. For it to be successful revolutionary activity seems to demand sacrifice, pain (Pierrette's private life is shattered for a second time within a few years) and solitude. Indeed it seems that Vailland was aware of this basic tension when in February 1956 he wrote: 'Je m'embarque dans une grande entreprise romanesque; au centre un révolutionnaire professionnel, ce que je n'ai pas réussi avec Pierrette Amable, la solitude du communiste quand il est vraiment à l'avant-garde, l'avant-garde est par définition seule'.[23] His new venture was not to materialize, however, and while in his next novel, *325.000 francs*, the nature of the central character and the situation in which he is placed have changed, the problem of contact, of exemplary behaviour on the one hand and that of integration on the other, remains unsolved.

Whatever problems Vailland may have been experiencing in his attempts to project his ideas through his novels, there was no evidence that they in any way affected his activities as a militant member of the Party. Marriage to Elisabeth (he and Andrée were officially divorced on 6 March 1954), and a move from Les Allymes to the house in Meillonnas where he was to live until his death, were the final stages in the process of the regularization of his private life which had been going on since the summer of 1950. In April 1954 Vailland's *Batailles pour l'Humanité*—a series of dramatic tableaux representing the various stages and periods of struggle during the history of the Party newspaper—was presented at the Vélodrome d'Hiver to an enthusiastic audience. Its success prompted Vailland, together with the critic Claude Martin and Henri Bourbon, Communist deputy for the department of Ain with whom Vailland became very friendly, to propose to the secretary of the French Communist Party, Jacques Duclos, that a whole series of such theatrical performances should be launched. For them the theatre had revealed itself as the ideal medium through which to make contact with the public on a large scale:

> Aujourd'hui, des spectacles comme *Le colonel Foster*, *Drame à Toulon* [by Claude Martin], *Batailles pour l'Humanité*, ont voulu servir d'arme d'agitation et de propagande pour notre Parti [...]. En donnant à un contenu politique, apparent ou non, une forme concrète, singulière, dramatique, tragique ou plaisante, le théâtre permet d'atteindre des couches de la population beaucoup plus vastes que celles que touchent les journaux, les tracts, les affiches. Pour les militants éduqués même, le théâtre crée une émotion, un sentiment d'urgence, qui les enthousiasme pour l'action. Il peut également avoir un rôle indirectement pédagogique et contribuer à 'l'élévation du niveau idéologique' de nos camarades.[24]

With the number of disused theatres (particularly on the outskirts of large towns) and the number of unemployed actors, the scheme was, they maintained, assured of success. Duclos was enthusiastic. Unfortunately, however, Bourbon could not be released from his political duties in Ain and it seems that the project must have been abandoned. Certainly Vailland never again refers to it in his private diaries or elsewhere, and during the next twelve months, he became instead deeply involved in local political activities, taking part in debates and attending meetings. In May 1955 he went to Eastern Europe to cover the 'Course de la Paix' cycle race, possibly the inspiration for the opening chapter of *325.000 francs*—'la presse internationale annonce que je prépare un roman sur le cyclisme...'[25] —which was to be his next and in many ways most significant project to date.

The origins of *325.000 francs* lay in a visit which Vailland made to Oyonnax, the centre of the French plastics industry:

> Je suis allé à Oyonnax et, dans un café, j'ai vu un manchot qui jouait aux cartes. On m'a dit qu'il jouait aux cartes toute la journée, qu'il ne faisait que cela. Il ne lui restait plus que ça à faire... Il tenait ses cartes dans un crochet fixé à son moignon. Le roman s'est organisé autour.[26]

Already Bourbon had suggested to him that he should write a series of articles exposing the exploitation of the workers in this industry and the conditions under which they were required to work. After a week of investigations, however, so strong was the impression which the visit made on him and so horrified was he by the high injury rate in the factories that Vailland abandoned the idea of the articles and wrote his novel instead: 'Ce ne sont pas des articles que j'écrirai mais un livre, car la portée sera plus grande. C'est trop important'.[27]

In terms of intrigue, *325.000 francs* is a much simpler novel than *Beau Masque*. It relates the attempt of a young worker, Bernard Busard, to realize his ambition of marrying a local girl, Marie-Jeanne Lemercier, and of leaving his native town of Bionnas. His opportunity appears in the shape of a snack-bar on the N.7 for which a deposit of 700,000 francs is required. His family's savings and Marie-Jeanne's dowry make up slightly more than half the amount, and he sets out to earn the rest by manning full-time a machine in one of the factories. This he does by sharing the work in eight-hourly shifts with Le Bressan. During his last shift at the machine his hand is smashed and while he has earned his money (and Marie-Jeanne) he is no longer acceptable as a manager for the snack-bar. Instead he becomes the owner of the local café and, after a rapid decline in trade, is obliged to consider returning to the factory where, because of his disability, he will earn less money than the average worker.

In its exposure of the corrupt world of industrial enterprise and capitalism, *325.000 francs* at first sight appears to follow the pattern of *Beau Masque*. Jules Morel, who like Valerio Empoli owes his industrial success to his native wit and astuteness, is no villain, however.[28] Certainly his control of the Bionnas people's working and private lives through Plastoform and the Cité Morel is total—only Busard's father remains passively independent to the end—but it is never shown to be vicious. As he is well aware, his is a position of strength; he knows as well as Chatelard, the local union leader, the arguments and cases that can be and are constantly put before him; he knows, too, that, as there is no alternative employment in Bionnas, strike action ultimately has a limited effectiveness. Because of the enclosed, isolated nature of Bionnas, Morel can act without fear of real opposition. Whatever the long-term implications, local political action will be briefly effective only, and indeed Vailland introduces an important new element into *325.000 francs* when he directs his criticism as much against the workers (represented by Busard), as against Morel and the management. As long as they are content to struggle at a local level, and hence on terms dictated to them by Morel, their lot will remain unimproved. This, precisely, is the problem. For them to rise above the conditioning factors of their economic and social background and environment demands heroic action and sacrifice. In the final analysis Busard fails because he is unable to see beyond the immediate confines of his personal predicament, or to requote Vailland's words to Pierre Berger, 'grouper toutes ses énergies et les porter au maximum d'efficacité *au service de* ce qui est à son époque la cause de la liberté positive'. When Busard abandons cycling for the machine bench and willingly accepts the conditions laid down to him by Marie-Jeanne, his stature is immediately reduced. As Vailland remarks half-way through the novel: 'Il me plaisait, tant qu'il voulait gagner le Tour de France. Maintenant qu'il fait des bassesses pour devenir boutiquier, il me dégoûte (p. 331).[29] Indeed, in *325.000 francs* Vailland may already be suspected of being as much, if not more, concerned with the relationship between Busard and Marie-Jeanne as he is with the need to expose the iniquities of capitalist society.

As we might expect, the structure of *325.000 francs* is, like that of *Beau Masque* though in a more controlled way, very much in the neoclassical mould. The time span is exactly one year, the place remains Bionnas and the action strictly limited. In all there are eight chapters: Chapter One recounts the cycle race; Two provides further essential information concerning Busard and Marie-Jeanne; Three establishes the action; Four deals with the social pressures to which the young couple are subjected; Five accelerates the action; Six contains the Juliette episode and allows Busard a glimpse of what he has missed; Seven recounts the climax and Eight the final ironic deflation of Busard's married life. In this respect Vailland's use of chapter division is conventional enough; the plot has a straightforward linear pattern with the author always in control of his material and able to manipulate it at will. Even the most cursory reading of the novel, however, is enough for it to become quickly evident that the chapter division only thinly disguises a more carefully prepared five-part dramatic structure. Chapter One functions as a Prologue; Two presents us with the principal protagonists and outlines their relationships to one another; Three to Six deal with the action and cover the longest period of time; Seven, separated from Six by two months, brings matters rapidly to a head; Eight, reflecting the opening chapter, acts as an Epilogue.

It is also interesting to note at this point that while it may have been simply coincidental or even convenient for the printer, each of these five sections is followed in the *livre de poche* edition of the novel by a blank page. There is no such division in any other edition.

Predictably the opening chapter of the novel offers an account—albeit in a different form—of what is subsequently to occur in the novel as a whole. The 'Circuit cycliste de Bionnas' (circular and repetitive like Busard's life) provides him with the opportunity to prove himself to Marie-Jeanne. He fails. Even though he fails through no fault of his own —indeed his technical knowledge and skill as a cyclist is not to be questioned —Vailland is careful to ensure that Busard never enjoys our unreserved sympathy. It is not that he shows himself to be insufficiently ruthless in his attitude during the race, that he failed to break Le Bressan when he had the chance; nor, whatever the appearances to the contrary may be, is it that fate is against him ('le peloton [...] se rapprochait, majestueux, inexorable' (p. 267)). Busard is here paying the first penalty for his intrinsically 'unheroic' nature. Although, should he win, victory is certain to guarantee him the chance to participate in more important races and hence to leave Bionnas, Busard regards the cycle race as a test of his devotion to Marie-Jeanne: 'Busard tourna la tête vers Marie-Jeanne— C'est pour vous, cria-t-il' (p. 269). He is unable to see it otherwise than in terms of his relationship with her and, though he is of course unaware of its significance, failure here anticipates what is to come. In the style of his classical models Vailland is making use of the omen. The pace of the cycle race—Busard's magnificent start and early success, his falls and injuries, and the flat anticlimax of the end—will be that of Busard's spell in the factory, his accident and failure to realize his ambitions. Indeed Vailland draws our attention to this by casually reintroducing the cycling theme of the opening chapter shortly before Busard's accident: 'Au coin de l'avenue Jean-Jaurès, un cycliste dérapa sur le pavé mouillé. Busard frissonna et rentra dans l'atelier' (p. 400). But more important is the fact that this technique creates an ironic distance between reader and characters. Busard's physical reaction here has no conscious meaning for him: only the reader appreciates its significance. As we shall see this technique is vital to the novel as a whole and for its success necessitates complete control by the author of his material. The result is that the action of *325.000 francs* is always tight, character development strictly limited, with the only really extraneous material appearing in the form of Vailland's own observations on events in his role of author-narrator or in his conversations with his wife, Cordélia.

By comparison with *Beau Masque* the characters of *325.000 francs* are fewer in number and, with the exception of the protagonists, fixed quickly and with an economy of detail. Paul Morel, for example, is 'un beau parleur' (p. 241) and yet 'encore assez peuple' (p. 323) for him not to be completely alienated from his workers. Chatelard, the local union leader, appears briefly, partly as a means of authenticating the political context of the plot, but more importantly as a point of contrast with the unheroic Busard (pp. 315–20). Others, notably Le Bressan and Juliette Doucet, have a more central role—in many respects not unlike that of a *confidant*—their attitude and way of life reflecting and contrasting with those of the principal characters. Le Bressan belongs to another world, 'un personnage presque mythique' as Vailland later called him.[30] Rather like a character out of a novel by Giono he represents the natural, primitive world of the Bresse peasant whose existence is as yet untouched by encroaching industry. A spontaneous person by nature he is full of an 'inébranlable confiance en soi' (p. 312–13), and his act of generosity at the end is as gratuitous and as selfless as Busard's suspicions are groundless. As yet he is free even though his future too is mapped out well in advance: 'En décembre, il sera appelé au service militaire. A sa libération, il se mariera avec la fille d'un voisin, qui lui apportera trois hectares en dot; cela était déjà réglé' (p. 292). Similarly Juliette Doucet enjoys the same kind of present carefree existence that is unknown to Busard and in particular to Marie-Jeanne with whom she is sharply contrasted.[31] Indeed in this novel, as in *Drôle de jeu* in particular, Vailland again relies heavily on the technique whereby physical appearance is directly indicative of moral and personal qualities. Compare for example the opening descriptions of the two women:

> Juliette Doucet est grande et a une belle gorge que les hommes essaient toujours de toucher. Elle se défend sans se fâcher. On dit d'elle: *quel beau châssis!*
>
> Elle renverse la tête en arrière. Elle porte longs ses cheveux noirs. Quand elle roule sur son scooter, que le vent plaque sa robe et soulève sa chevelure, elle est vraiment belle. (pp. 245–6)
>
> Marie-Jeanne Lemercier [...] s'avançait d'un pas tranquille au milieu des passants pressés. Sa veste de lainage blanc tombait bien droit. La coiffure en trois plis, sans un cheveu qui se rebiffe. Les bas, du calibre comme toujours le plus fin, parfaitement tendus. Légèrement maquillée: un trait de rouge sur les lèvres, un rien de bleu sur la paupière pour faire chanter le bleu de l'œil. (p. 240)

In comparison with Juliette, Marie-Jeanne appears isolated and aloof from the rest of Bionnas, her refusal to work in the Plastoform factory underlining her attempt at independence and playing an important part in her relationship with Busard. The allusion in this opening description of her to the disciplined existence of a nurse and a nun is given an additional dimension within a few pages by the introduction of the image of a medieval lady:

> Marie-Jeanne est lingère. Elle coud ou brode toute la journée, assise près de la fenêtre. Elle habite le seul baraquement de la Cité Morel qui se trouve en bordure de la route de Saint-Claude. Ainsi les

passants la voient tout au long de l'année, assise bien droite sur une chaise de paille à haut dossier, maniant des choses délicates, du linon, de la soie, de la batiste, rien que des blancheurs où ses ongles vernis posent des taches de rouge vif. (p. 242)

Indeed this 'medievalism' is to be found throughout; not only does the cycle race have clear echoes of a tournament—cycle/horse; handkerchief/ favour, for example, but the relationship between Marie-Jeanne and Busard is the highly ritualized one of courtly love demanding utter obedience from the male whose 'rewards' are always strictly controlled: 'Marie-Jeanne *autorisait* Busard à passer chez elle les soirées du mardi et du jeudi' (p. 275); 'On ne vit pas Busard à Bionnas pendant toute une semaine. Il revint chez Marie-Jeanne le mardi suivant, à neuf heures du soir, l'heure où il était *autorisé habituellement* à se présenter' (p. 289).[32]

When in late August, Marie-Jeanne eventually allows Busard to make love to her, it is as if she were granting him a favour even though, ironically, he hardly has time to enjoy it: 'Fin août, elle lui céda. Elle pensa qu'*il méritait bien cela*. Il dut partir presque aussitôt...' (p. 351). It is she who dictates the conditions for their marriage, and when towards the end of his spell in the factory, Marie-Jeanne visits him there and shows the first signs of disinterested genuine affection, it is too late. So conditioned has she become by her concern for appearance and reputation, that Marie-Jeanne is ultimately incapable of allowing their ritualized relationship to be replaced by a natural one based on genuine love. Unlike Juliette, she is playing a role which Busard's acceptance encourages her to continue. Through his interventions and Marie-Jeanne's conversations with Cordélia, however, Vailland ensures that another, less flattering view of Marie-Jeanne is maintained. His insistence on her polished (*poncé*) appearance,[33] her 'singulière unité de style' (p. 342), and the explicitly drawn similarity between her and the plastic dolls which lie near Busard during his final shift (pp. 405,407), underline her shallowness and superficiality; so, too, do the account of her earlier pregnancy, and the fact that she is still the object of Jules Morel's attentions as well as those of other 'hommes mariés [...] des vieux' (p. 332). Through her strict observance of a code of behaviour with Busard, Marie-Jeanne believes she is protecting herself: ironically (as Vailland takes pains to point out) she is also thereby making herself an object of unwanted attention:

Je commençais de comprendre pourquoi les poursuivants rôdent autour de sa demeure. Les hommes pleins d'âge mûr et les vieillards sont fascinés par les jeunes femmes pleines de retenue, les corps fragiles sous les vêtements stricts, les peaux très blanches dans les linges sans taches qu'exigent la chirurgie et l'amour, les épaules délicates, la saignée du coude et la saignée du genou quand la pondération du geste les dérobe perpétuellement à la vue. (p. 343)

Like Busard, she too has become conditioned by (and in consequence also a victim of) the part which she has convinced herself she ought to be playing.

Ultimately Busard's view of her changes and from the idealized creature of courtship she becomes the subdued partner in marriage, a victim of her husband's petty tyranny and suspicions. In a sense their roles have been reversed, but more importantly they have both been reduced in stature. In the true medieval tradition of courtly love, the knight's virtues are heightened and refined through his service to his lady. Busard's are not. His physical condition deteriorates, he invents the story of Marie-Jeanne's pregnancy and his dream of the snack-bar materializes as the local café. And most important of all of course he is finally disabled, symbolically castrated by the machine.

When, in Chapter Six, Busard remarks to Juliette: 'Tu es bien plus belle que Marie-Jeanne. Tu es meilleure qu'elle. Je me sens mieux avec toi. Pourquoi est-ce que j'aime Marie-Jeanne?' (p. 370) he is asking the question the answer to which provides the key to the whole book. Not only does Busard readily submit to Marie-Jeanne's domination; he *enjoys* doing so. Yet as Duc was of Roberte in *Les Mauvais Coups*, he is subconsciously afraid of her, and Vailland's descriptions of her repeatedly return to the theme of castration. The suggestion of the nurse in the opening description of Marie-Jeanne is picked up later in the 'linges sans taches qu'exigent la chirurgie et l'amour' (p. 343). There are also frequent allusions to cutting; for example, her needle (pp. 242, 320); her teeth ('elle a les incisives menues, bien alignées, coupantes comme une faucheuse le premier jour des fenaisons' (p. 281)); her eyes ('C'était comme si Marie-Jeanne avait posé de petites cuirasses sur ses prunelles' (p. 341)); her lips ('elle pinça les lèvres' (p. 249)). There is the suggestion of blood in the 'trait de rouge sur ses lèvres' (p. 240) and her 'ongles vernis' (p. 242). As Jean Recanati has argued, these are classic Freudian symbols of the castration complex, but whether or not we accept this analysis and trace their origin back to Vailland himself, and to his relationship with his parents and grandmother is of no immediate value for a study of *325.000 francs*. Suffice it to say that within the context of the novel they provide a key to Busard's character and to his relationship with Marie-Jeanne. They also prepare in a much more subtle way for the overt sexual symbolism of the machine (pp. 305–7) and for Busard's 'castration'.

What we are shown throughout the novel, therefore, is Busard ensnared by his own subconscious inhibitions, which in turn express themselves particularly in the artificiality of his relationship with Marie-Jeanne, and more generally in his inability ever to act in a truly independent, positive or 'heroic' manner. Moreover, as was suggested earlier, Busard's plight is reflected in the form and tone of the novel. Vailland's dramatic handling of the plot brings Busard, at the end of the book, to a new situation from which even the chance to escape is missing. The pattern of his life has become that of the cycle race or the machine—circular and repetitive. At the same time, however, the ironic distance which Vailland establishes between Busard's view of events and the reader's, ensures his control over the latter's sympathies. It is tempting, because like Beau Masque he appears powerless, to consider Busard to be the innocent and tragic victim of circumstance. But this would be to miss the point. Unlike the heroes of Corneille's tragedies who through becoming aware of their predicament were endowed with a certain grandeur, Busard has lost stature: '[il] ne faisait plus partie de la cohorte des héros...' (p. 324).

In January 1963 Vailland wrote that *325.000 francs* was 'le meilleur de mes romans, vrai rêve, rêve vrai, une vraie histoire qui peut être interprétée totalement par Freud, par Marx, et encore par bien d'autres, elle a toutes les faces possibles de la réalité'.[34] Whatever global significance Vailland wished ultimately to give the novel—and as we have seen there is evidence enough for his claim—it is in the context of his politically committed years that it must, initially at least, be judged. Like *Beau Masque*, *325.000 francs* has as its basic theme one of submission: Busard to Marie-Jeanne and her wishes; Marie-Jeanne to the image and reputation she has built up and around herself; the workers collectively to their machines and to Plastoform developed over the years like *FETA* by ruthless exploitation and opportunism; while even Le Bressan and Juliette lose their naturalness and freedom in time as they merge with society around them. Only Chatelard and Busard's father retain any degree of independence, yet they too are static, passively resistant but actively ineffective. Vailland also underlines this sense of confinement through the structural pattern of the novel, and it is noticeable that he refrains from the kind of somewhat ponderous intervention which characterizes the Epilogue in *Beau Masque*. There is also another, vital distinction between the two works. In the earlier novel Vailland focuses our attention on the workers' condition from a number of superior vantage points; in *325.000 francs* he explores it from the inside. This shift of position is critical.

At this point we might usefully recall Vailland's letter to Pierre Berger, in which he maintains that it is quite natural for a leader to emerge within any group engaged in collective revolutionary activity. Elsewhere, however, he implies that all members of such a group are potentially leaders and that only when this potential has been realized will there be a society in which 'toutes les bergères seront des reines'. Six years later he was to recognize that he had failed to suggest a solution to the problem expressed in *325.000 francs* of the worker who sought to 'sortir (s'affranchir) seul de sa condition ou s'affirmer ouvrier et homme de qualité en luttant révolutionnairement'.[35] From the beginning of *Beau Masque* it is clear that Pierrette Amable has already separated herself from her fellow workers; like Marat, Milan or even Rodrigue in *Bon Pied Bon*

Œil—though for different reasons—she is by nature different from those around her. She belongs to that line of 'vrai bolchevik' figures which, as we have seen, begins with Drouet, continues through Albéran and Madru and has as its supreme prototype Stalin himself. Does Nathalie not draw our attention to her 'class'? Busard, on the other hand, is different, and the implication of this distinction between him and Pierrette would appear to be therefore, not that Busard has failed because of his particular weakness and narrowness of vision, but rather that there is quite simply an *intrinsic* qualitative difference between him and someone like her. If this is so, then *325.000 francs* is not only utterly pessimistic in its affirmation of the workers' condition and of the real extent of the power and influence of bourgeois capitalism, but also and more significantly a revealing commentary on Vailland himself. Although in his public activities there could be no question of his commitment to the cause of the Communist Party, Vailland, nevertheless, experienced—almost in spite of himself—a need to retain an independence of mind and attitude to life that were not always compatible. The result was an increasing sense of futility and despair:

> Il arrive qu'un homme d'action mêlé à une action, accomplissant une action pour lui ou pour les autres, se trouve soudain séparé de celle-ci. Il croit qu'il continue de transformer le monde mais ses gestes ne déclenchent plus rien. Il ne le sait pas. Un voile le sépare de toutes les réalités du monde.[36]

With these words in mind, *325.000 francs* should be considered to be an unwittingly honest book. In its exposure of certain working-class conditions it is probably one of the best novels of its kind, but its failure to communicate any positive suggestion of how such conditions might be overcome reflect Vailland's own growing realization that the revolution was not to take place overnight.

Les Phrères Simplistes (left to right: Daumal, Gilbert-Lecomte, Meyrat, Vailland). Reims, 1925. *Collection: Elisabeth Vailland.*

Le Grand Jeu (Daumal, Vailland (at the top),
Gilbert-Lecomte, Meyrat). Paris. 1929.

Chapter Five

The Winds of Change

Tout se passe comme si, depuis les
événements qui suivent le xxᵉ congrès,
'changer la face du monde' ne me concernait plus.

Ecrits Intimes.

The following two years, 1956 and 1957, were to be crucial for Vailland. Whatever his private or even subconscious feelings and doubts may have been, he continued at first to work within the 'perspective communiste' which he had made his own at the time of *Bon Pied Bon Œil*. His task was made all the more easy by the immense popularity of *325.000 francs* —due in part to its having been serialized in *L'Humanité*—which now earned him the accolade he had sought for several years, that of being 'un écrivain au service du peuple'.[1] But the sense of pride and pleasure which he experienced at having finally been granted this mark of acceptance was short-lived. In February 1956, a secret session of the Twentieth Communist Party Congress was held, during which Krushchev exposed what he defined as the 'despotism' and the 'glaring violations of revolutionary legality' of the Stalin regime.[2] Rumours of the report had already filtered through to the West, when in April an opportunity to attend the Czechoslovak writers' conference took Vailland to Prague. From there he moved on to Moscow and to the truth about Stalin.

However prepared he may have been, the shock Vailland experienced when the earlier rumours of the report were confirmed, was genuinely traumatic. At once he returned to Meillonnas, removed the portrait of Stalin from the wall behind his desk (replacing it by a picture of the flute player on the Statue of Venus in the Thermal Museum in Rome) and for forty-eight hours was physically ill. On 21 May he wrote: 'On se croit à l'extrême pointe de son temps et l'on réalise soudain que l'histoire est entrée dans une nouvelle phase sans qu'on s'en soit aperçu. J'en reste un peu comme mort' (*Ecrits Intimes*, p. 483), sentiments which were later recorded in *La Fête*:

> Duc s'était trouvé comme mort. L'histoire de son temps et sa propre histoire qu'il croyait aller de concert, et il s'en glorifiait, lui avaient paru soudain aller à contretemps. Tout avait été remis en question de ce qu'il avait estimé le plus assuré.[3]

Yet it was not that Vailland now found himself in a position where he was obliged to reinterpret the patterns of history which was so difficult for him to accept. Far more distressing was the fact that he was compelled to reject Stalin, and not simply as a political figure but as one in whom he believed he had found the complete expression of the 'bolchevik idéal' and on whom a number of key figures in his fictional work had already been based. As Elisabeth Vailland recalled seventeen years later: 'Il aimait Staline, non comme un Dieu mais, au contraire, comme le symbole de l'Homme, celui qui peut tout, lucide et logique, libre et anti-métaphysique, le contraire en somme du petit-bourgeois'.[4] Now that Stalin had been exposed, however, and the image destroyed—and in consequence much of his own confidence and self-esteem as well—Vailland clearly felt that he should at least attempt to rationalize matters, and after a month of complete seclusion at Meillonnas, he began to take stock of the situation. As a result he found himself pushed back into a consideration of the dilemma which had already lurked beneath the surface of *Beau Masque* and *325.000 francs*. His private diary for the summer of 1956, the *Eloge du cardinal de Bernis*, *La Loi* and also his third and final play *Monsieur Jean* each in its own way illustrates and testifies to the extent to which Vailland's attitude to politics, to the Communist Party and indeed to life in general had been shaken.

The first few pages from Vailland's diary are of a recollective and confessional nature not seen in such intensity in his work since the time of *Les Mauvais Coups*. The break-up of his marriage to Andrée, the *désintoxication* in the Lyon clinic in 1942 and now the Stalin affair are neatly equated with one another as the inevitable points of crisis marking the end of any significant period of his development: 'dix ans voués à la passion d'amour, dix ans à l'opium, dix ans à la passion politique' (*Ecrits Intimes*, p. 492). But the equation is a false one. Certainly it is true that like a love affair or a drug, his relationship with Stalin had absorbed his whole being, but unlike them it had been brought to a close in a way that had been quite outside his control. And even though the dilemma surrounding the revolutionary hero had latterly begun to make itself felt with increasing poignancy, Vailland had allowed himself to be blinded both by his own ambitions to meet the requirements for becoming a Marxist revolutionary writer, and by the image of Stalin which he had cultivated for himself. His first reactions now were to attempt to explain the new political–personnal dilemma in which he found himself in the way he might have done at any point during the previous five years—in terms of the Marxist theory of historical perspective: 'déjà le bolchevik est un personnage historique […]. Un autre type d'homme est en train de se forger, qui ne devine pas lui-même ses traits, et qui ne ressemblera à rien de ce qui a encore existé' (*Ecrits Intimes*, pp. 486–7). But the attempt is unconvincing and we are left with the impression that Vailland is now not doing much more than going through the motions of a meaningless exercise. The rest of his diary continues much in the same vein; a bizarre jumble of reflexions and autobiographical and especially childhood recollections—some, like the account of his dream of Roger Gilbert-Lecomte, quite striking[5]—all of which are clear indications of the disturbed state he was in. The tone too is pessimistic. Happiness ('le bonheur est une idée neuve en Europe') as he and Claude Roy had conceived it in 1947, has lost its appeal; society has become dull, with local, private interests (Busard in *325.000 francs* and later Mariette in *La Loi*, for example) taking precedence over national ones. It is not surprising therefore that Vailland should decide, if only temporarily, to withdraw: 'Pour se retrouver et se situer dans le monde, il faut prendre ses distances' (*Ecrits Intimes*, p. 495). The time for a new mask was fast approaching.

Drained physically as well as mentally, Vailland left Meillonnas in July and went to Italy where he spent nearly four months on the Adriatic coast at Gargano, later to be used as the setting for *La Loi*. But like the patient convalescing after drug addiction, Vailland found that instant cure was not possible. He remained a member of the Communist Party for another three years when, on the advice of Henri Bourbon, he left it 'sur la pointe des pieds'. Meanwhile he became increasingly disillusioned by its failure in particular to respond to the diluting influence of socialism;[6] he was also sufficiently angered by the Russian invasion of Hungary to agree to a telephone request from Sartre to allow his name to appear alongside those of Roy, Sartre himself, Vercors, Simone de Beauvoir, Leiris, Cau and others on a letter of protest to the Communist Party sent on 5 November. Strongly reprimanded for his action he personally wrote to the secretariat of the French Communist Party on 14 November: already, three years in advance, it was in effect his letter of resignation:

> Je viens en effet de reprendre mes travaux littéraires, trop souvent interrompus, depuis un an, par des événements politiques qui m'ont profondément bouleversé. Et je souhaite n'avoir aucune sorte d'entretien à leur sujet, avant d'avoir achevé le roman en train. Bref, je sollicite de votre fraternité le loisir de me consacrer sans partage aux soins de mon métier. (*Ecrits Intimes*, p. 517)

La Loi to which he here refers was to be published six months later: meanwhile, the *Eloge du cardinal de Bernis* had already been completed.

This short account of the life of the eighteenth-century cardinal is an important text for an understanding of Vailland's feelings in 1956 immediately after the Moscow trials. Less concerned with his career as a diplomat and a man of the church than with his character, Vailland, in his portrayal of Bernis, clearly aims, as we might expect, both to focus attention on himself and in particular to explore more fully the dilemma which had been threatening to come to a head during the previous year or two in particular and which had now been finally thrown into sharp relief by recent events: that of the hero figure, the 'fils de roi'. A man of ambition, an 'athée conséquent, mais cardinal du meilleur ton. Pas du tout frondeur',[7] Bernis' moral qualities are best seen in the way he has educated his young mistress (whom Casanova significantly defined as 'religieuse, esprit fort, libertine et joueuse' (p. 162)) and in his never failing ability to face up (*faire face*) to adversity and change of fortune of any kind. He is shown as one who, in his maturity, has learned to remain aloof, to judge people and events only in the light of experience and not as mere allegiance or self-interest might dictate. The analogy which Vailland is asking us to make with himself is clear. But Bernis, 'homme de qualité' or 'fils de roi' as he is, belongs very firmly to the eighteenth century; he is both a product and an expression of an organized, centralized society, in which national prestige and happiness, Vailland maintains, took precedence over provincial interests. Vailland confesses that he had hoped for the time when twentieth-century society, too, would have developed in such a way as to provide the right kind of environment in which the modern 'fils de roi' could exist:

> Tous les hommes seront fils de roi, quand le milieu permettra à l'homme de développer librement toutes ses facultés, dans la 'société sans classes', quand 'l'exploitation de la nature aura succédé à l'exploitation de l'homme par l'homme', quand 'l'homme libéré ayant définitivement maîtrisé la nature [...] chaque homme pourra satisfaire à tous ses besoins matérials et culturels'. (pp. 204–5)

But, he continues, such hopes are, for the present at least, unrealizable: 'pour nous qui vivons dans la seconde moitié du xxᵉ siècle, en France, l'Age d'or dans l'avenir est pratiquement aussi éloigné que l'Age d'or dans le passé, et sans réalité pratique par rapport à notre vie' (p. 205).

The frenzied tone of the private diaries has here given way to a measured, realistic, if pessimistic, statement of acceptance. But while in terms of society as a whole Vailland sees little hope for any immediate change, he remains as ever obsessed by the enigma of the 'homme de qualité'. With modern society unable—at least in the forseeable future—to provide the right kind of political and social climate ('où toutes les bergères seront des reines'), Vailland returns with much greater conviction to the view which, as we have seen, lay behind the character of Pierrette Amable: 'un homme de qualité est *qualitativement* différent de la grande masse des hommes. [...] un homme de qualité est aussi différent du plus grand nombre des autres hommes qu'une licorne de tous les chevaux du monde' (p. 205).[8] Yet faced with the example of Stalin, he is obliged to carry his argument one stage further. This result is stalemate. History past and recent, Vailland contends, has illustrated only too well that 'l'homme de la plus grande qualité devient le plus abominable des tyrans' (pp. 208–9), a theme which he was to pick up again and explore more thoroughly in his commentary on Suetonius' *Lives of the Caesars* two years later. If he is to avoid such degradation therefore, the hero figure is doomed never to realize fully his potential; paradoxically, however, this very failure to do so is equally damning. There would appear in fact to be no solution; not only is the 'homme de qualité' as distinct from other men as the unicorn is from other horses, he is also as mythical, a figment of Vailland's imagination, a dream which in *political* terms at least, he now realizes he will never see become reality.

Yet the *Eloge du cardinal de Bernis* was only the first of the texts tracing Vailland's response to the events of 1956. In many ways it may be regarded as the most significant in that it does provide us with an immediate, spontaneous response; behind the thin eighteenth-century façade there is a portrait of a Vailland despairing and temporarily trapped by the dilemma which now faced him. Even so it is *La Loi* to which the majority of Vailland's critics have turned in order to justify the view that he had once and for all finally broken with the political *engagement* that had characterized his work during the previous five years in particular. The reasons for this are evident enough. The popularity of the novel form as opposed to that of the essay immediately guaranteed a wide audience; indeed while the *Eloge du Cardinal de Bernis* passed relatively unnoticed, *La Loi* was received with almost unanimous enthusiasm and approval[9] and the award, in December, of the Prix Goncourt, was in fact little more than a formality.

Certainly there is much in *La Loi* to encourage this particular interpretation. In some ways it is his most personal novel since *Drôle de jeu* or *Les Mauvais Coups*, but it is so only in parts. In *La Loi* Vailland shows as well his considerable ability to exteriorize his problem, or, to borrow a phrase from Mauriac, to transpose the reality of his situation into the fictional world of his novel—a feature which reappears with an altogether different though no less significant effect in *Monsieur Jean*, and makes of this play an important coda to the novel. In the first of two interviews which he gave to *L'Express* critic Madeleine Chapsal, Vailland insisted on the difference between documentary *reportage* and the novel, and in particular on the imaginative qualities of the latter (here *La Loi*) even though it may still relate closely to the author's personal experience.[10] While it is arguable that they may have been prompted to some extent by the feeling of self-defence, Vailland's words should nonetheless be taken as seriously as they were intended, for *La Loi* does indeed mark a turning point in his development not merely in his attitude to the use of imaginative writing or to the kind of problem with which he felt it should concern itself, but also in his narrative and fictional technique as a whole. Indeed it is to this particular aspect of his prize-winning novel that our attention should primarily be given.

In an essay which Vailland wrote about the South of Italy for *Réalités*, he emphasizes in particular the area's remoteness and its uniqueness. He also stresses the closely interlinked, in origin feudal nature of society there in which each individual person has an appointed place.[11] Such vigorous social division is symbolized by the local game, *la legge* to which the novel owes its name. It also provides an image which runs throughout *La Loi* giving it a particular tightness and cohesion not readily to be found in Vailland's earlier work.

Played ideally by seven or eight, *la legge* depends for its effectiveness on the creation of an artificial social situation in which real life roles often become reversed and in which accusations, goadings and tauntings must, by the rules of the game, go unheeded by the person at whom they are directed. One of the group is elected as the *padrone*; he in turn selects a *sotto-padrone*, the choice usually depending on the 'normal' social relationship which exists between them. Having assumed the position of authority, the *padrone* dispenses the wine which accompanies each session and which is paid for collectively, to the other players at his discretion. Once the game has begun it is possible that the same player will act as *padrone* on a majority of occasions; it is equally possible that the role will change hands frequently. Similarly it can happen (as it does in *La Loi* during the one session of the game that is described) that the choice of victim falls regularly upon one person who can then win approval by his acceptance of the ritual and by his refusal to react to whatever accusations are levelled against him, his only chance for revenge being that eventually, he might in turn find himself in the position of authority.

On the large scale of society as a whole the combination of relationships is obviously more complex, but the underlying principle remains the same. As Vailland presents it, the society of Manacore is divided into two sections: on the one hand the household and estate of Don Cesare, and on the other the village itself where Matteo Brigante is, by common assent, allowed to fill the role of an almost permanent *padrone*. Don Cesare for his part (in his attitude to life generally and to politics in particular largely modelled on one colonel Virgilio Panella, with whom Vailland stayed during the summer of 1956) leads an isolated existence expecting and indeed receiving total, unquestioning allegiance from his servants and family. In spite of his seventy-two years he remains in excellent physical condition, and is the best hunter of the region. The latter part of his life has been devoted to a study of the ancient Greek town and civilisation of Uria, long since engulfed under the marshes and bay of Manacore. But gradually disillusioned by people as well as by events, Don Cesare has withdrawn: the analogy Vailland wishes us to make with himself is instantly obvious:

Don Cesare est tellement *désintéressé*, d'année en année, qu'il est devenu lui-même objet pour soi-même. [...] sans amour, sans haine, sans plus aucun désir d'aimer ou de haïr, aussi dépourvu de toute sorte de désir que la défunte cité d'Uria. C'est cela, le désintérêt.[12]

Within his own domain—the limitations of which Vailland will allude to in *Monsieur Jean*—Don Cesare has retained absolute authority, imposing his own justice and values not only on those who belong, but on those too who, like the *agronome* from the north, attempt to interfere with local customs and ways of life. Above all else he has retained his *droit du seigneur*, the right to claim, without challenge, the virginity of any female member of his family or of his household whenever he so desires. But Don Cesare is no despot: his 'law' may be egocentric, but it is always tempered with kindness and generosity, and those in his service love and respect him in true feudal fashion.

The distinction between his society and that of the village, however, is important and especially central to any interpretation of *La Loi* which claims to see it solely as a commentary on Vailland himself at this time. As an individual character—as distinct from a mere presence—Don Cesare occupies very little of *La Loi*. Instead it is on Manacore that the action is focused, a village in which as Attilio remarks 'tout le monde est le flic de tout le monde' (p. 62). All, without exception, are both exploiter and exploited, *padrone* and victim according to time and circumstance. Any expected hierarchy based on rank or professional position is merely a thin disguise—and known to be as such—for the effective 'order' controlled in the main by Brigante and dependant for its continuation on an elaborate system of blackmail and threats. Ironically, Brigante is also presented as a man of firm religious conviction. Social inequality is for him 'une preuve irréfutable de l'existence de Dieu' (p. 207), but he is equally convinced that his own local omnipotence is a divine gift as well, and by exercizing it as fully as possibly he is able to compensate for the socially inferior position in which God has seen fit to place him. The analogy with *la legge* is obvious, and on closer examination it comes as no surprise to find that the characteristics and special requirements for the game, emerge throughout the novel at all levels.

Of these the most noticeable of all perhaps is Vailland's attempt to maintain an appropriate atmosphere of artificiality and even of theatrical convention. As in his essay Vailland insists on the remoteness of Manacore: it is, to use Attilio's words once more '[une] ville dont personne n'a jamais réussi à s'échapper' (p. 45). In fact, of course, its inhabitants are powerless to do so. Like Busard and Marie-Jeanne in *325.000 francs* only more so, their existence is totally conditioned by their environment: even the *agronome* 'finit par adopter la morale du Sud' (p. 331). But while in the earlier novel Vailland was intent on the one hand to expose certain social and economic conditions and on the other to explore the relationship between two people and their reactions within and to these conditions, in *La Loi* he is concerned more with the complexity of the situation itself. There is no suggestion that the underlying principles which govern society in Manacore should be changed; that people should behave in any way other than one which admits acceptance of them. As in the game the rewards and penalties are equally well known: 'Tout se paie; c'est la loi' (p. 207). By agreeing to participate people wittingly allow themselves to be trapped, they are lured by the temptation of acting *padrone* for however brief a time, aware that eventually they must in turn become victims. The gamble fascinates them: Attilio pursues Guiseppina in full knowledge of the ridicule he risks incurring; Donna Lucrezia for all her romantic imaginings, is well aware of the consequences if her affair with Francesco is discovered; Justo exposes Brigante to the police knowing that the racketeer will have his revenge; and even Brigante is himself momentarily humiliated by Mariette and to a lesser extent by Pippo and his *guaglioni*. Behind all this there is a provincialism of the most deep-rooted kind, epitomised above all by the local inhabitants' unquestioning acceptance of tradition and supersitition—the virginity cult and its links with Uria, the gift of *la voix* (p. 117), or even male supremacy —and shorn up by an insistence throughout the novel on the presence of the sea ('la mer qui n'a pas bougé depuis des mois' (p. 13)) the winds (the *libeccio* and the *sirocco*), and the sun 'le *solleone*, le soleil lion' (p. 158). Furthermore, having carefully built up his setting and atmosphere in this way, Vailland ensures that the theatrical nature of the intrigue is not missed by his repeated references to the prisoners and to the *disoccupati*, the silent witnesses of the social game that is being played out before them.

In his Introduction to the first volume of Vailland's *Œuvres Complètes*, Claude Roy requotes a letter which he wrote to his friend on 1 July 1957 and in which he defined *La Loi* as 'le livre d'un maître artisan [...] une machinerie de haute précision'.[13] While admiring the novel, Roy nonetheless saw such technical manipulation to be evidence of a weakness, an oversimplification and hence betrayal of real life. Yet if we consider *La Loi* as a large scale projection of the game to which it owes its title, a carefully controlled structure may be seen to be essential. Certainly there are weaknesses: the theft of the Swiss tourist's wallet for example—the full details of which are not provided until later on in the book—is simply a device used, as in a bad detective story, to draw a number of hitherto unexplained threads neatly together; the few pages which serve as an epilogue (whatever wider significance Vailland might wish them to carry) are also embarrassingly artificial. But the mainspring of the novel's unity is to be found in the most elaborate expression of its underlying image, in the working out and description of the relationship between Donna Lucrezia and Francesco, and in particular of the central episode of their rendez-vous.

Our knowledge of Donna Lucrezia and more so of Francesco before this episode is limited, though, as is usual with Vailland, indicative of their subsequent behaviour and development. Donna Lucrezia in fact is the first of the novel's major characters to be described: 'Donna Lucrezia est superbe, à demi allongée sur le lit, appuyée sur un coude, la poitrine découverte dans l'échancrure du déshabillé, la crinière noire, répandue en désordre, qui lui descend jusqu'aux reins' (p. 8). And a few lines later: 'Elle est à l'évidence donna, *domina* comme l'impératrice des Romains, la maîtresse, la patronne'. In spite of her humble background she has a style—and indeed certain intellectual interests—which set her apart from the rest of the villagers. She holds no religious beliefs and has little time for the niceties of social behaviour; she is, to use Anna's word, '*fière*'. Throughout the novel she is described as 'grande et belle', though when she appears for the second time the suggested sensuality of the opening pages has gone: 'Sa lourde chevelure est maintenant roulée en un strict chignon. Elle porte une robe à col fermé et à manches longues, *dans son style habituel*' (p. 40).[14] But such severity is only a façade. Growing disillusion with marriage and with her husband Alessandro, both as an intellectual companion and as a man of political integrity, have, over the years brought Donna Lucrezia to the point where the urge to escape (symbolized in the initial scene by the open window) has reached a climax. The opportunity to do so has presented itself in the person of Francesco Brigante.

Having lived very much in the shadow of his powerful father, Francesco, whatever his potential qualities may be, is an immature young man. At twenty-two he is six years younger than Donna Lucrezia (and seems significantly to be even more) the difference between their ages playing an important part throughout their relationship and in particular in the description of their meeting in the cave. Before he meets Donna Lucrezia, Francesco's experience of women has been strictly limited to brief visits to brothels in Foggia or Naples and to immature, pubescent dreams. It is hardly surprising, therefore, that he should romanticize their relationship, identifying her with the duchess Sanseverina in Stendhal's *La Chartreuse de Parme* which Donna Lucrezia has lent him. (Needless to say since Sanseverina is 15 years older than Fabrice it is an identification which Donna Lucrezia herself has neither envisaged nor welcomes!) Indeed so absorbed are they both by their personal interpretations of the affair that apart from a solemn declaration of love on both sides it has progressed no further than a single chaste embrace: 'Aujourd'hui pour la première fois ils vont se rencontrer seul à seule. Ils n'ont pas encore échangé un seul baiser' (p. 142).

While for an eventual interpretation of their relationship such preparatory information, however limited, is necessary, it is the structure and setting of the central episode which are initially impressive. Vailland traces the journey each has to make in order to arrive at the cave in which Donna Lucrezia has arranged they should meet. As he does so he alternates recollective passages (which serve both to define his characters more sharply and also to provide the reader with more information concerning their relationship) with descriptive ones. This pattern, leisurely at first, accelerates in tempo as the cave and hence the climax of the scene is approached. At the same time description depends for its effect on the manner in which it reflects the psychological state of the two characters. Donna Lucrezia, believing that this is the first major gesture in her search for independence, for example, 'marche à grands pas tranquilles' (p. 165);[15] Francesco on the other hand, on whom our attention is now directed more closely, carries his apprehension with him:

> Il grimpe, suant et soufflant, entre les pins qui protègent mal du soleil-lion, dans les parfums qui entêtent, poursuivi par les taons. Il a maladroitement choisi la pente la plus raide. Il n'est pas entraîné à courir la pinède en plein midi. [...] Souffler lui fait perdre son assurance [...] (pp. 162–63)[16]

Moreover, Vailland takes care to create the impression that Donna Lucrezia and Francesco are approaching a situation from which escape will be impossible: they move downwards towards the beach, around them access to the outside world is everywhere forbidden:

> côté mer, l'horizon est strictement clos par le banc des nuages que pousse le libeccio et que maintient le sirocco, gris, gris-noir, gris-blanc, plomb, cuivre. Côté terre, la montagne se dresse sans faille, derrière les collines à chèvres, les jardins et la pinède, monumentale falaise aux coulées rougeâtres, crêtée, à mille mètres, d'un trait sombre, une antique vétuste forêt aux arbres multicentenaires, la forêt qu'on nomme majestueusement *Umbra*, de l'Ombre. (pp. 158–59)

Finally the cave is reached: 'c'est comme la bouche de la falaise une gueule béante' (p. 177): inside it is dark and humid—a womb.

The way in which the whole process of enclosure resolves itself in this particular image is, of course, vital for an appreciation both of this central episode, and of the relationship between Donna Lucrezia and Francesco as a whole, which eventually has to be seen as one of mother and son. It is also important at this point to notice the part that is played by the elaborate piece of medieval fishing apparatus, the *trabucco*, which can be seen from the cave. Already in *Héloïse et Abélard* and in *325.000 francs*, Vailland's willingness to indulge a personal liking for technical complexity was apparent, but the descriptions of the elaborate system of pulleys controlling the entrance to Abélard's room or of the repetitive movements of the machines in the plastics factory, are not simply gratuitous stylistic exercises. In *325.000 francs* in particular the description of the machine is, as we have seen, directly related both to the general pattern and movement of the book as a whole and to the relationship between Busard and Marie-Jeanne in particular. So, too, in *La Loi*, The *trabucco* and the methods by which fish are caught (especially the technique of *rappel* whereby one fish is used as a bait to lure others into the nets) relate both to the social patterns of life in Manacore as a whole and to the immediate situation involving Donna Lucrezia and Francesco. The *trabucco* serves the same purpose as a carefully selected piece of scenery in a play; it has a certain interest in its own right, but more importantly it mirrors, even symbolizes, the action that is going on around it. But while in a play any connection to be made must depend to a large extent on the alertness and sensitivity of each member of the audience, in a novel the author is able to control his reader's reactions more closely. We find, for example, that the description of the cave ('la bouche de la falaise, une gueule béante') is echoed by that of the nets as they are wound up to catch the fish: 'au début de la pêche, le filet est ouvert dans la mer, comme une mâchoire. Quand les cabestans tireront les câbles, la partie immergée remontera vers la surface: la mâchoire se refermera' (p. 173). In this way the comforting image of the womb becomes modified by a suggestion of aggression. On examination of the scene as a whole it quickly becomes apparent that not only are these two elements present from the beginning of the scene, but they are also vital for a proper interpretation of it.

Donna Lucrezia as we already know is older than Francesco; it is she who has initiated the meeting, and, most significant of all, once inside the cave her gestures are entirely maternal: 'Elle lui prend la tête et l'attire contre son flanc' (p. 185); 'Elle caresse sa tempe, son front. [...] Il abandonne sa tête sous la caresse légère de la main de Lucrezia, contre la chaleur de son ventre' (pp. 186-7)[17]

At the same time she is also a forbidding figure—'Il n'ose pas jeter par terre la grande et belle femme, strictement vêtue' (p. 184)—and his submission and respect, it is hinted, are due as much to this as to the influence of other, more deep-rooted causes. It is not surprising, of course, that Recanati should make much of this scene. The references to the jaws (not only of the nets and cave but of the fishes imagined by Francesco as well (p. 181)), Francesco's references earlier in the novel to his dreams with the pursuant figures of his father and Donna Lucrezia herself, are ideal fodder for his kind of psychocritical analysis. But, as in *325.000 francs*, it is also relevant and indeed necessary to situate them within the context of the novel and of the particular situation which Vailland has created. Certainly Francesco may be afraid of Donna Lucrezia for reasons which he will not (or cannot) admit, but it is important to see this as part of Vailland's plan to show how each of them lives in an imaginary world entirely of his or her making. Francesco continually thinks about and refers to Donna

Lucrezia as his *maîtresse*; she about him as her *amant*. She imagines his thoughts towards her to be entirely pure, while her vision of their life together once they have eloped is one of middle-class gentility. In fact Francesco's thoughts are, as we know, far from pure—only fear holds him back from attempting to seduce her—while in true romantic style he sees himself happily labouring on building-sites in order to earn enough money for them to live on. (It is arguable, of course, that this is no more than an immature, unacknowledged subconscious urge to prove his virility.) And so on: the similarity between this technique and Stendhal's in *La Chartreuse de Parme*, especially in his account of Sanseverina's efforts to implement Fabrice's escape from prison, is striking, and, in view of Francesco's original identification of Donna Lucrezia with the duchess, ironic.

To place such emphasis on a single episode in this way may at first appear to direct our attention away from other equally fascinating, though less developed, features of the novel: Brigante's pursuit and attempted rape of Mariette or the affair between Alessandro and Guiseppina, for example. Yet any comparison will show that all such relationships depend for their vitality on the same principle taken by Vailland, as we have seen, from the local game. (It is also worth noting that in each of them it is always the woman who acts as *padrone*.) Furthermore they are all neatly self-contained, a quality which again is illustrated in particular by the central episode which, by the way it is described, appears as an interlude, an escape, however brief, from the dull reality of everyday life in the village. Of necessity it has to end, and, as though waking from a dream, Donna Lucrezia and Francesco are obliged to consider instead the mundane details of the latter's proposed trip to Turin, even though, ironically, this will never materialize:

> Ainsi restèrent–ils longtemps, sans bouger, se taisant ou répétant les mêmes mots. Quand il rouvrit les yeux, le filet était de nouveau immergé, les hommes de vigie à cheval sur le mât, et les autres hommes endormis sur le rivage.
> —'J'ai reçu, dit-il, la réponse du directeur de la maison de Turin.' (p. 188)

This fundamental pattern of anticipation and part realization followed by disillusion and deflation which all the characters in the book experience is once again precisely that of the local game. Certainly Mariette and Brigante (and Pippo too in as much as he is dependent on the latter's patronage) continue as *padrone* planning, with the construction of new roads, to exploit Manacore as a tourist centre. But they do so only at the expense of a certain style. Contact with the outside world inevitably cheapens and the destruction of Manacore and all that it represents is inevitable. When, for example, the original statue of the Venus d'Uria is discovered, Mariette thinks only of placing it next to her modern god, the television set.

From this compromise with its resultant loss of values and of dignity only Don Cesare escapes. Yet he is not subject to the same circumstances and pressures; his world is not that of Manacore. In spite of the successful elaboration throughout *La Loi* of the dominant image of the game, the separate nature of the two social units remains (as it did in *Beau Masque*, for example) a basic and important flaw. Moreover those readings of *La Loi* which interpret it as evidence of Vailland's 'withdrawal' at this time tend to look for their evidence in the Vailland–Don Cesare identification only. Certainly, as we have seen, there is good reason for this, much of the information we are given concerning Don Cesare being only thinly disguised autobiography. The lines already quoted on Don Cesare's 'désintérêt' for example, or the pages shortly before his death in which Vailland recounts the various stages of his life placing particular emphasis on his period of political involvement, could have been lifted almost unaltered from Vailland's private diaries. But Don Cesare, like Bernis, belongs to another age. For him there can be no alternative but death. Like the boat which stutters to a halt in the bay as he gazes out of his window for the last time, his life simply stops. It is tempting, of course, to see in the portrait of Don Cesare and particularly in his stoic indifference to the modern world a neat parallel with what Vailland described much later as his need to cultivate a 'buste de pierre' (*Ecrits Intimes*, p. 794); but it is rather as an expression of deep regret at something which *he now realizes* is no longer possible in the terms in which he had once conceived it, rather than one of despair, that it should be interpreted. This is not to say of course that the problem of the 'homme de qualité', has ceased to interest Vailland, simply that it will no longer have the same *political* orientation that he had given it in different degrees and with varying success since the portrait of Drouet in *L'Histoire d'un Homme du peuple sous la Révolution*. As has been suggested, the problem will now become much more personalized and private, turned in upon itself and affecting, too, the form and style of Vailland's imaginative writing. (With the complex use of a single image, and with the overlapping of various periods of action and absence of chapter division indicating precise linear development, *La Loi* looks forward to the more static and circular *La Fête* and *La Truite*.) But *La Loi* was by no means Vailland's last word on the subject during the crucial period of 1956–57. *Monsieur Jean*, largely neglected by his critics, offers us an interesting and valuable postscript on the subject and particularly on the attitude presumed by the critics to be lurking behind the portrayal of Don Cesare.

With the exception particularly in May and June of his reports on the Mille Miglia and the twenty-four hour race at Le Mans for *France–Soir*— both notable for Vailland's interest in the highly developed procedures and artificial style of the motor-racing world—very little journalistic activity followed *La Loi*. Already in April his private diaries were describing instead his ever increasing readiness to indulge in a life of seclusion and private pleasure in which erotic experiences, alcohol and music, especially the stylized form of the Quartet, play an important part. The sole reference to events of the previous year comes in an entry for 28 April 1957:

> Exactement un an après mon départ pour Prague-Moscou d'après le xxe congrès, ai pu passer la soirée entière à parler des malheurs des partis communistes, sans amertume, ni tristesse. Il se vérifie de plus en plus qu'on échappe à la passion politique comme à celle d'amour. (*Ecrits Intimes*, p. 529)

It was about this time that Vailland began also to work on his new play, *Monsieur Jean*. As its title suggests it is a modern-day reworking of the Don Juan theme.

At the age of forty Monsieur Jean epitomises the competitive capitalist society of the Western World. Having exploited the system to the full he has now become so much an integral part of it that one slip will, like a false move in a chess game, cause the whole structure to crumble about him. The slip occurs somewhat ludicrously in the form of a new invention, 'Le Requin-Volant', which he and his principal associate the Commandeur have developed with the aid of government money. On its trial run (when it is piloted by the Commandeur) the rocket disintegrates (note the naïve phallic symbolism here and the use of the initial letters R.V.) and a series of absurd consequences develops from which Jean only escapes when the portrait of the Commandeur (Stalin) cynically placed on the wall behind his desk after the latter's death, falls on him and breaks his neck. Of equal importance in the play, as we might expect, are Jean's amorous adventures. With the complicity of his wife Leporella, he amuses himself with a continuous stream of secretary-typists and switchboard operators. His office, 'une cellule de moine' can be sealed off from the rest of the building at the touch of a switch, while a system of lights enables Leporella and Marthe, his permanent secretary, to know whether or not he is to be disturbed. In his affairs with women as in business, Jean is both hypocritical and cynical. Like his celebrated prototype he is prepared to exploit without conscience every one and everything which comes into his path, and his death, however absurd, has the same ambiguous mixture of defiance and divine justice about it as the original.

While it is arguable that *Monsieur Jean* has more life and movement than either *Héloïse et Abélard* or *Le Colonel Foster plaidera coupable* it can hardly be termed a dramatic success, and the fact that it has never been publicly performed in France must come as no surprise. Certainly it contains a certain farcical element which deserves some attention, but Vailland and his preoccupations are never absent from the play for long,

so much so that Jean Recanati in particular has been led to see it as yet
another expression of what he considers to be Vailland's withdrawal at this
time from any kind of public acitivty.[18] Such an interpretation ignores,
however, both the way in which in *La Loi* Vailland had managed to exteriorize his personal dilemma, and a new element of conscious rejection and
of self-satire that undoubtedly runs through *Monsieur Jean*.

Although he makes little of it Picard at one point compares *La Fête*
to Camus' *La Chute*;[19] a more profitable analogy can be made with
Monsieur Jean. Even though it clearly has none of the subtlety and
sophistication of Camus' last novel, *Monsieur Jean* fills much the same
role. In it Vailland enumerates, analyzes and frequently ridicules positions
and opinions which he has previously held. There are also clear links
to be made with characters and situations in earlier works. In the first
act, for example, we find Jean talking about his relationship with the
workers in his factory, in words which recall Valerio Empoli in *Beau
Masque*, or Morel in *325.000 francs*—a Morel is in fact mentioned elsewhere in the play, as is one Letourneau and a Durand:[20] 'Je n'ai jamais
mis les pieds dans nos fabriques depuis la mort de mon père. Nos ouvriers
pour moi: une abstraction. Moi pour nos ouvriers: une abstraction. Avec
des abstractions, on ne se bat pas; on construit des équations et on les
résout.'[21] And it is not surely due—as it might have been in the case of, say,
Gide—to a lack of imagination that Vailland should have chosen Noblet as
the name for the personnel manager to whom these words are addressed. In
a way, perhaps, such references are like the allusion in *La Chute* to
L'Etranger, but the implication is much stronger. Vailland is here offering
us a satirical commentary on his attitude during the Resistance and later
during the early fifties. Such an interpretation is given increasing weight
as the play progresses. Jean maintains also in Act I and again in Act II
that women have been and continue to be for him the only relief in a
world which would otherwise be 'plus aride que les déserts de la lune' (p.
26). Predictably, the fascination he exerts over them is irresistible: 'Je
peux toujours les avoir, parce que je suis lucide, dénué de scrupules, riche
—c'est très important—et merveilleusement dissimulé derrière la fable
qu'on a bâtie sur mon nom' (p. 54).

Like Camus' Clamence, Jean has been content to benefit from the
public image created about him, but the very fact that he recognizes this is
in itself a form of critical self-awareness. Moreover, unlike Camus who is
ultimately bound by the monologue form of Clamence's confession,
Vailland is able to strengthen this critical view of Jean (and thereby of
himself) through Leporella ('De quel louche spectateur es-tu en train de
guêter les applaudissments?' (p. 77)) and to a lesser extent through Marthe.
With the appearance of Hélène—who with her blue eyes and blond hair
recalls not only the Hélène of *Les Mauvais Coups* but is yet another incarnation of that elusive *fille merveille* figure as well—Jean appears for a

while to repent. Not only does he swear eternal love in true Don Juan fashion, but claims too that Hélène has brought him to see the error of his ways and that henceforth frankness and honesty will characterize his behaviour. He has, he maintains, (not unlike Rodrigue in *Bon Pied Bon Œil*) a new faith in Man. But his conversion, predictably, is utterly false. As he confesses to Leporella: 'Tu n'a pas compris que je ne prenais le déguisement de l'humaniste que pour mieux pouvoir me servir des hommes?' (p. 106). The implied criticism is bitter.

Viewed in this way it would be easy to interpret the play as little more than a thinly disguised and obvious piece of, at times, biting self-criticism, which, whatever Jean's final words may be, ends on a note of despair and frustration. But as in most cases of this kind of self-exposure there is as well a marked degree of ambiguity in many of the statements made both by Jean himself and by Leporella. Clamence may indeed be penitent by the end of *La Chute*, but this does not prevent him from taking a certain delight, if only retrospectively, in those very faults to which he has now admitted. Similarly there is in Jean's confessions a suggestion that he by no means regrets what is past, while his objective (to adapt Leporella's words) to be 'l'homme le plus libre de ce siècle hypocrite (qui ose) proclamer les désirs que les autres mettent tout leur soin à cacher' (p. 79), is one which he continues to pursue to the end. When, therefore, we come to his final speech, which is addressed directly at the audience, we find that regret is tempered by a certain defiance. In it Jean identifies himself with those select few in whom 'la vigueur et le foisonnement des désirs se rencontrent, rarement avec le plaisir de les satisfaire' even though they have been obliged to '(se) dissimuler sous quelque masque' (p. 111). But, he continues, his mistake has been that he has

> trop négligé le masque. J'étais en train d'y remédier.
> Finie la comédie.
> La chute n'en est peut-être pas mauvaise: j'étais juste sur le point de ne plus rien désirer.
> Vous autres, aliénés sublimes, continuez de croire que le sort de l'humanité et la rotation de l'univers dépendent de vos manigances, moi, je vous tire ma révérence. (p. 112)

Taken in a very superficial way it is perhaps possible to see in *Monsieur Jean* (as indeed Recanati has done) further proof for Vailland's withdrawal at this particular moment in his life. Not only is this a general interpretation not entirely borne out by other evidence, however, but even on that of the play alone, with its heavy irony and deliberate satire, it is somewhat unreliable. It is also possible that Vailland was writing very much with his tongue in his cheek, that the reception of *La Loi* had been such that he could not resist the temptation to substantiate it. The true interpretation is probably somewhere between the two. There is no doubt that about the time when he came to write *Monsieur Jean* Vailland had been at an extremely low pitch—physically, mentally, and morally. There is, to be sure, a bounce and vigour about the play which could suggest the contrary, but there is also, as we have seen, much bitterness not far beneath the surface. In spite of its unquestionable superficiality and theatrical implausibility *Monsieur Jean* is saturated with regret. It is a final melodramatic farewell (and there is also considerable melodrama we should note in the description of Don Cesare's death) to a particular and as Vailland had become aware, unrealizable attitude.

Chapter Six

The Final Mask

La liberté dans la solitude.
Ecrits Intimes.

In 1973 Elisabeth Vailland strongly refuted the view that her husband had
ever become quite as politically alienated after 1956 as many of his critics
have suggested. According to her his interest in the political situation never
wavered, his final article 'Eloge de la politique' and the readiness and enthusiasm with which he accepted an offer from the *Nouvel Observateur* to
visit South America providing adequate proof.[1] Nonetheless, the fact remains that during the first seven months of 1958 when Vailland and
Elisabeth went on a long boat journey which took them to Mauritius,
Madagascar, Africa and above all to Réunion,[2] his private diaries reveal
how conscious he was of the new mask he had adopted. The military coup
in Algeria, for example, or contacts with people and places with which in
the past he had been politically connected, are either recorded only
marginally or rejected altogether. Egypt in particular which only a few
years before had aroused his strongest sense of political allegiance is now
quite consciously avoided: 'Les affaires d'Egypte ne m'intéressent plus
[...] à ce stade nouveau dans lequel je suis [...] entré, [...] on ne se pose pas
la question de prendre parti'.[3] Whatever Vailland may have continued to
think about Communism as a political creed, we find him, during this
same period, accusing the French Communist Party of having abandoned
its true revolutionary role. Indeed at a time when he was still a member he
wrote: 'les communistes français se sont démobilisés peu à peu depuis 45,
complètement depuis 1956. [...] La direction du P.C. français est faite de
vieux bolcheviks et de jeunes ambitieux qui se sont fourvoyés dans un rêve
(dans le rêve des grognards de la garde)' (*Ecrits Intimes*, p. 573). It is true
that by comparing (as Ballet has done)[4] such remarks as these with
certain entries in Elisabeth's diary, it would appear that Vailland's attention was much more caught by political events than he was prepared
perhaps to admit. Having deliberately created this impression about himself, however, Vailland was unlikely to risk having it destroyed, and it is
from this position of aloof isolation that he continued for the next seven
years to castigate at regular intervals and at times severely his former
political colleagues.[5]

While it is not in this conscious rejection of political *engagement* that the real interest of these final years lies, the removal of something which had for so long provided a stimulus for his work proved at first difficult for Vailland to accept. As Duc remarks in *La Fête*: 'je ne sais pas du tout ce que je veux. J'avance à tâtons'.[6] For a man of Vailland's temperament complete withdrawal and inactivity was unthinkable, and for a while he worked in the cinema notably with Roger Vadim on an adaptation of Laclos' *Les Liaisons dangereuses*. In 1958–9 he also began work on a commentary on Suetonius' *Lives of the Caesars* (*Les pages immortelles de Suétone*) and wrote a short but important essay *Sur la clôture, la règle et la discipline* which he added to a new edition of *Le Regard froid*.

As Recanati has rightly observed,[7] *Les plus belles pages de Suétone* is a re-exploration of the bolchevik myth with Stalin and the problem of corruption as its inspiration. The pattern from simple honesty through power to self-indulgence and excess, which Vailland maintains is discernible in each of the Caesar's reigns, is predictable. It is one to which he had already alluded, of course, in his *Eloge du Cardinal de Bernis*, but he adds now a new element, that of gratuitousness and self-observation recalling Diderot's *Le Paradoxe sur le comédien* ('distraction de soi d'avec soi') and his own *Expérience du drame*. Having analyzed the process which leads to corruption Vailland draws a strict analogy with the theatre:

> Toutes ses [of the Caesar] actions prennent [...] caractère de gratuité qui ne trouve d'analogie que sur la scène, dans le jeu de l'acteur, qui est simultanément le héros dont il joue le rôle et lui-même se regardant jouer; rien ne tire plus à conséquence; l'Empire tout entier est devenu une immense scène où César joue pour lui-même une pièce dont il est l'auteur et l'unique acteur, ses partenaires n'étant plus que des choses.[8]

The same emphasis on a private, insulated world also occurs, as its title suggests, in *Sur la clôture, la règle et la discipline*, in which it is defined as '(une) société coupée de la vie sociale, suprême artifice de la vie de société, société gratuite'.[9] Such a society had existed already in the eighteenth century and Vailland's own predilection for it can be seen not only in that other essay included in *Le Regard froid*, *L'œuvre de cruauté*, but also in the various references scattered throughout his work to particular instances in the modern world: for example, the sexual rituals of the Dutch colonisers or the Australian aboriginal corroborree which he describes in *Boroboudour*, or the *bringues* in which Le Bressan participates in *325.000 francs*. More consistently we find him returning too to the ways in which the clinic and the brothel (and Vailland's ideas here resemble those of Genet) are places in which an individual can either submit to a rigorous discipline or create an unreal, even fantasy world in which to escape, while in *Sur la clôture, la règle et la discipline* he adds to these the boat (p. 227) the setting for the first draft of his next novel, *La Fête*.

One further element that is particularly evident in this final period is Vailland's insistence on his maturity—not simply as a person but as a novelist as well. In his diaries and in his 1957 interview with Madeleine Chapsal we find him returning frequently (in the language of the early fifties) to the idea of his development by stages, with that final one now having been reached in which the individual and society about him merge in one. But in reality there has been an important shift of emphasis. As we have seen from his contemporary essays, Vailland's preoccupation with the need to create an insulated, private world and with the individual to act within it as an individual ('la seule souveraineté sans aliénation se borne au gouvernement de soi-même' (*Ecrits Intimes*, p. 632)) makes such statements sound as false as the language in which they are expressed appears dated.[10] Yet Vailland also experienced the need to give greater expression to his convictions than occasional essays and diary entries even though the latter were, from early 1958 and the trip to Réunion, written with an eye to their posthumous reception. The result was *La Fête*, which he began in 1959 and in which he hoped to explore in the setting of a boat journey the idea of perfect happiness in the form *amour-passion* as it is experienced by two characters, a doctor, Philippe Legrand, and Jeanne Treffort. As the final version of *La Fête* reveals, this first project was ultimately abortive, however; indeed it seems likely that had he continued with it, he would rapidly have become caught up in a series of somewhat arid discussions in contrived circumstances. Fortunately Vailland was rescued (as is Duc in *La Fête*) by an actual event—a brief affair with the young actress wife of a friend—which became transposed to form the substance of the final published work. For Recanati the whole gestative process, reality and fiction alike, is direct proof of Vailland's development since 1947 and *Les Mauvais Coups*: 'L'histoire vécue (et racontée dans *La Fête*) vient de lui offrir l'occasion d'une vérification de lui-même.'[11] Certainly there is much in the novel to encourage such an interpretation, but Recanati would appear to have overlooked an important statement made by Vailland in his diary a year before: 'Le propre du Souverain (et de l'artiste ou de l'artiste comme seul souverain ou du souverain comme artiste) est de faire des œuvres apparemment inutiles: pour donner à son royaume immédiatement la forme qui apaise-épuise son désir' (*Ecrits Intimes*, p. 574).

Not only can a work of art and in particular a novel portray the kind of situation which Vailland envisages in *Sur la clôture, la règle et la discipline*, it is also in its own right an example of the gratuitous self-indulgence that it is the 'sovereign's' privilege to enjoy. Not only the subject matter, therefore, but also the style and form in and through which it is contained and expressed become significant. In *La Fête* (and as we shall see in a similar but far more successful way in *La Truite*) Vailland attempts in Gidean fashion to draw his reader into this situation by having Duc, his principal character, as the author of the novel of which he is that character. This double role, however, is not revealed until the final lines of *La Fête* and in consequence it is only retrospectively that certain judgements about the book and about what Vailland has attempted can be made. As we shall see, this and the inadequate distinction (eventually recognized by Vailland) between himself and his character results in the novel's failure.

Given Vailland's views on the need to ritualize human relationships and given, too, the rational way in which his own affair was conducted, it is hardly surprising that the most characteristic feature of *La Fête* should be its theatrical nature. Each one of a quartet of characters—Duc, his wife Léone, Jean-Marc and Lucie Lemarque—acts out a part which in relation both to the setting and to the three others is always strictly limited and controlled. In addition each individual scene adds a further dimension to the permanent themes of sovereignty and of the *fête* which are finally brought together in the last chapter. As in earlier novels, however, such control is not without its dangers; precisely because Vailland is so intent on creating a sense of complete artificiality and ritualization, (a 'société coupée de la vie sociale') it is difficult not to allow even the most contrived of situations. Thus the duel between the Citroën and Peugeot cars, the visit to the marble factory, the discussions about jazz or the search for the *orchis bifolia* in the opening chapter, can all, like the individual episodes in *Les Mauvais Coups*, for example, be seen to have specific related functions. Even the unquestionable and far more disturbing transparency of certain names—of Duc (*dux*) himself, of Lucie (*lux*) and of Léone (*lionne*) for example—can, by the same token, be accepted.

The similarity between Duc and Vailland is everywhere apparent. There is a heavy insistence on the emergence of 'un nouveau type d'homme (qui) était en train de se forger'[12] while references to past experiences are numerous: to the period of adolescence and to the Grand Jeu adventure, to the Resistance, to his first meeting with Elisabeth and to his more recent visit to and arrest in Egypt. At first it appears that such recollections are entirely gratuitous yet on examination they may all be seen to refer to periods in Duc's (Vailland's) life when the presence, hostile or otherwise, of other people limited and conditioned his behaviour in such a way that it stifled all potential expressions of personal freedom. Moreover it is noticeable that the one incident to which Duc gives most attention is the announcement that his Egyptian friend Kamal has been arrested once again. From it he develops a long reflection on torture (pp. 127–33), the ultimate form of physical oppression. These pages of *La Fête* are particularly significant, for the act of torture, while being the most odious form of victimization possible, is, for all that, a ritual, a carefully managed situation, contrived to bring about the highest degree of suffering which the victim can endure. (It is interesting to note that like Sartre in *Qu'est-ce que la littérature?* Vailland here refers to the tortured victim as *le patient*, once more drawing an analogy with the clinic.) But as Duc goes on to reflect, the distinction between the ecstatic experience of absolute pain and that of absolute pleasure is so fine as to be immeasurable: 'la douleur peut se changer en plaisir et inversement et la souffrance [...] peut être une joie; il était arrivé à des martyres de tomber en extase au milieu des supplices' (pp. 128–9). What Duc is looking for, therefore, is a situation in which pleasure rather than pain will be the ultimate experience:

> Trouver le rite, le cérémonial, la disposition de l'esprit, l'hygiène, la diététique qui transmuent en joie absolue, ou au plus près de la joie absolue, certaines activités (ou absence d'activité) qui s'y prêtent plus particulièrement: l'écriture d'un poème, le plaisir d'amour ou, il croyait alors toucher à l'essentiel, l'éveil, la veille, au sens ou la veille s'oppose au sommeil le plus profond. (p. 129)

In order to be able to set about this with any hope of success, two prerequisites are essential—on the one hand correct social and material conditions and on the other a state of alert awareness. These are already enjoyed, to varying degrees, by three of the four principal characters—Duc, Léone and Jean-Marc. They appear to have no financial worries, their style of life is of their own making, and they all enjoy that 'maîtrise et possession de soi-même' which is the hall-mark of sovereignty (p. 179).

Duc in particular has cut himself off from the outside world. Newspapers no longer interest him, he maintains (p. 134): he happily asserts as well that he has 'de moins en moins envie de sortir de la maison' (p. 55), and even when he is obliged or chooses to do so he is 'protected' by the upholstered luxury of his car (p. 53). Yet, unlike the others, Duc also experiences moments of dissatisfaction; for him the state of sovereignty can become as burdensome as any other: 'Je me sens lourd, dit-il, enfermé dans ma souveraineté, comme si je traînais avec moi, accroché à mes hanches, un navire de haut bord' (pp. 80–81). The realization, however momentary, of 'le bonheur absolu' is the vital and necessary proof not only of the quality of the state itself, but of his own capacity for experiencing it as well. The opportunity is presented in the person of Lucie who, in spite of her potential (her sturdy peasant origins are referred to on several occasions!),[13] is the one exception in the quartet of characters. Although she is married to Jean-Marc, Lucie continues to live a life of dull regularity, the pattern of which is dictated by her work, the metro and domestic routine. It is from this that Duc plans to lift her and in so doing develop those unique qualities within her which will raise her to the status of sovereign as well. This relationship is carefully prepared from the opening chapters. Duc's search for and eventual discovery of the *orchis bifolia* in Chapter One or the manner in which the various kinds of marble are worked according to their individual qualities in Chapter Two, are both accounts of the way in which objects become unique, and distinguishable

from others. Duc's ambition is to expose and, as a writer, to give definition
to Lucie's *singularité*, '(à) ce qui la distingue absolument d'une autre'
(p. 63). What we have in *La Fête*, therefore, is an account of the way in
which Lucie is gradually made to change from passive object (*être agi*) to
active participant (*agir*) in the *fête*, and at the same time of Duc's direction
of a situation which, so he believes, remains always within his control.

By the early descriptions of her Lucie is unquestionably one of
Vailland's *filles merveilles:* 'Lucie revient vers eux. Elle est longue et
mince [. .] (ses yeux) sont bleus et non gris-bleu, comme il l'avait d'abord
cru [...] Elle porte les cheveux dénoués, flottant sur les épaules [...] Ils
sont nets, légers, aériens. Ils flottent en désordre' (pp. 19–20). She is a
natural being, scorning the artificiality of jewelry and responding in an
unsubtle, instantaneous and emotional way ('Je sens les choses, dit-elle'
(p. 14)) to objects, persons and situations alike. In spite of her physical
qualities, she is, intellectually and emotionally, still a child: 'Lucie, à
vingt-huit ans, est encore une adolescente' (p. 131). Like Frédérique in
La Truite Lucie is yet unformed, an insect emerging from its cocoon:
'Il [Duc] s'émeut un instant à la pensée de Lucie, pas tout à fait sortie du
cocon, accomplissant à tâtons son premier vol, avec encore des soies
accrochées aux facettes de ses yeux, se cognant à chaque objet dans son
inventaire pathétique du monde' (p. 12). Short-sighted, she lacks an
awareness of life about her, 'avançant à tâtons, en trébuchant' (p. 15), but
more importantly still she has been, and continues to be, inhibited by the
pressures and requirements of her working-class family background.
Marriage to Jean-Marc has done little to alleviate matters. Financially
dependent on her husband's parents she is, in spite of his encouragement
to escape,[14] utterly conditioned. Her relationship with Duc, therefore, is
potentially as meaningful to her as he imagines it to be to him in that it
offers her, however briefly, an opportunity to escape.

The pattern of Lucie's development can be divided into three separate
parts. In Chapter One she is described as a natural, instinctive creature;
at the same time her curt reactions to Duc's thinly veiled allusions to an
imagined affair with her already suggest that her ingenuousness will
provide her with fragile protection only against his advances. In the
second phase (Chapters Four—Eight) the relationship develops rapidly.
As in the opening chapter, we find Duc once more observing Lucie; she is
the passive object: 'Léone, Jean-Marc et Lucie étaient assis dans des
fauteuils, un demi-cercle, le dos au tourne-disques, et Duc, par terre, un
peu de côté, de manière à observer les trois autres' (p. 106). But it is not
until Chapters Five ('Duc attaqua Lucie dans la matinée' (p. 114)) and
Seven in which she agrees to model for a series of photographs that the
real manipulation of her begins. At first she is the inaccessible, forbidding
figure already glimpsed in Donna Lucrezia in *La Loi*: 'Lucie, dans une
robe de chambre de soie légère, bleu pâle, ouverte sur une chemise de

nuit blanche, fermée aux poignets, fermée au cou par un col rond, et tombant jusqu'aux pieds' (p. 114). When he kisses her Duc is met by cold indifference: 'Elle ne s'écarta pas, elle ne le repoussa pas, mais elle garde les lèvres closes, immobiles. Les lèvres de Lucie étaient froides' (p. 116). This first physical encounter is described by Vailland as a kind of silent stylized choreographic sequence culminating in the deliberately ambiguous position of the crucifix:

> Ils étaient face à face, proches à se toucher mais sans se toucher. Il prit les mains—en se retournant, elle avait allongé les bras au corps— et souleva les bras tendus jusqu' à hauteur des épaules, lui clouant les mains au mur. (p. 116)
> Il tint ainsi Lucie, les bras en croix [...]—Tu me plais. Ma crucifiée, ma tendre crucifiée, ma fête ... (p. 117)

Here Lucie is passive. Although it is arguable that she tacitly accepts Duc's advances, she can still maintain that her innocence is preserved: as soon as she agrees to participate in the photography session, however, she has allowed herself to be compromised: 'elle a accepté d'être l'objet [...] la victime désignée' (pp. 144–5). It is now only a matter of time before she will voluntarily acknowledge her own part in the ritual that has been set in motion: 'Ce matin, tu tenais mon visage comme un objet dans tes mains. J'étais honteuse, mais j'aimais cela. Je voudrais n'être tout entière qu'un objet dans tes mains' (p. 149). Although she is still a long way from being the ideal partner described in Sur la clôture, la règle et la discipline, Lucie is no longer the mocking creature of the first chapter. Certainly there remain inhibitions from which she has yet to escape; passive willingness and acceptance have still to be changed into active participation. Only within a carefully preserved and enclosed setting—'une fête d'amour exige un lieu clos'[15]—is it possible for this essential transformation to take place.

Before such conditions actually materialize in the final stage of Lucie's development in the form of the hotel to which Duc takes her, we are prepared for them by earlier references to the same idea, albeit not always in the same context—the artificially controlled development of Duc's plants, the boat on which Philippe Legrand and Jeanne Treffort meet, Alexandre's chateau in Majorca or Cleopatra's palace. The most striking example, however, and the one which is intended to prepare Lucie for her fête, is the lunch with Alexandre with which the second stage in her development closes. Here Alexandre is represented as an archetypal sovereign figure who metaphorically gives his blessing to the fête which Duc ('C'est vraiment mon seul fils' (p. 174)) and Lucie have promised one another. In this scene he assumes the role of a feudal lord, discharging his bounty and wisdom to all about him with a generosity and absence of self-interest which, significantly, will be lacking from Duc's behaviour.

Having prepared the way for the *fête* of the closing Chapter, Vailland now moves quickly to it, providing, towards the end of Chapter Nine, a description of the hotel in which it is to take place and which, with few alterations, could have been lifted directly from *Sur la clôture, la règle et la discipline*:

> [...] un château isolé qui dominait un vallon entouré de murs, un parc où alternaient pelouses et bosquets. [...] La cour intérieure du château est vaste. Aucune voiture n'y était rangée. Cailloutis blanc, bien râtissé. Une porte vitrée tourne silencieusement sur ses gonds. Un valet muet vint au-devant de Duc et le conduisit au salon de réception, désert. [...] Un couloir long et étroit, c'était ce qu'il avait imaginé comme accès à leur tombeau. La chambre était basse, la fenêtre ouvrait sur un vaste paysage [...] c'était une fenêtre étroite [...] qui pouvait être quadruplement fermée par des volets, des vitres, des rideaux et des doubles-rideaux. Personne dans le parc. (pp. 195–6)

The scene is prepared; only the actors need now to appear. Moreover they have parts to play which are theatrical projections of those already indicated in the earlier part of the novel. Thus Lucie, on arrival, is once more the hesitant and apprehensive creature of Chapter One. At the station she kisses Duc: 'On embrasse son amant quand on le retrouve à la gare. Elle fait son devoir' (p. 199); at the hotel she is the inert, passive model of the photographs assuming that she is there solely for Duc's pleasure:

> —Faut-il que je me déshabille? demanda-t-elle. Il ne répondit pas.
> —Je suis venue pour cela, dit-elle. N'est-ce pas pour cela que tu m'as fait venir?
> Elle se déshabilla à grands gestes, sans aucune sorte de coquetterie. Puis elle s'étendit sur le bord du lit, les mains croisées sur l'aine, les épaules creusés, les cuisses serrées, les yeux clos. (pp. 199–200)

In the course of the following twenty-four hours under Duc's direction—as in the earlier chapters a mixture of patient physical application and amateur psychoanalysis—Lucie's inhibitions gradually disappear until it is she who, having become Duc's equal, takes the initiative:

> Maintenant c'était elle qui exigeait et guidait. [...]
> —Je voudrais t'humilier, dit-elle, ou bien être humiliée par toi. (p. 215)

Yet however successful the *fête* may be, it is also short-lived. The physical changes which Lucie experiences are as fleeting as Duc's picture of her as a future Parisian business-woman is empty fiction (p. 220). Before long the need for her to return to Paris obliges them to accept once more the reality of the everyday world from which they have temporarily escaped, and their relationship reassumes the awkwardness it had when Lucie first arrived:

'ils étaient devenus gauches, ne pensant plus qu'à la séparation. Lucie portait, comme à l'arrivée, les cheveux noués dans un foulard; les épaules de nouveau se creusaient' (p. 222). The ticket-collector who, like the prompter, had ushered her into the world of the *fête*, now serves to send her back to the metro, the office and the routine of her marriage with Jean-Marc.[16] The spell for Lucie at least is at an end.

Superficially, therefore, the whole affair would appear to have reached its expected conclusion, the *fête* of the closing chapters being an enactment of the debate outlined in the preceeding ones. Duc has proved and retained his sovereignty: Lucie has been initiated into the ritual of the *fête*, even though there is no guarantee that she will have the opportunity to enjoy it again. On reflection, it is difficult not to interpret Duc's actions as being any more than a piece of egocentric self-indulgence, condoned by Léone and Jean-Marc and so presented as to persuade us of the benefit Lucie must ultimately derive from it. No longer would it seem should she envy the relationship which Duc and Léone enjoy, for example.[17] Yet there also appears to be a qualitative difference involved which forces us to look more closely at what Vailland is trying to do in this novel. For Duc to be able to prove to himself—and to others—the real quality of his sovereignty requires the kind of adventure which he enjoys with Lucie. This, we are invited to believe, lifts him out of the rut of mundane, day-to-day reality. Elsewhere in the book this same idea is picked up in various guises—in the references and allusions to historical and imaginary figures like Mark Antony whose career as retold by Plutarch Duc debates with Jean-Marc (and note the name association here); in Philippe Legrand and Jeanne Treffort, the transparently named characters of Duc's abandoned novel; and in Alexandre whose name in turn evokes the Greek leader of the fourth century B.C. It is intended, of course, that Duc should be equated with them, hence his heavy insistence on their shared motivating force, *amour-passion*. Yet whereas they have all, ultimately, become victims of this passion, Duc remains supremely in control, ready where necessary to prove himself again.

Had *La Fête* concluded with Lucie's departure to Paris and with Duc's return to Léone and the village, it would have been tempting to interpret it as just one more piece of thinly disguised autobiography. As we have seen, however, Vailland's intention was more ambitious, and by revealing in the final paragraph that it is *La Fête* itself which is Duc's novel he attempts to separate himself from Duc and portray him as objectively as any other character. Yet the lateness of the disclosure, together with the highly personal nature of *La Fête*, are too great an obstacle. Certainly Vailland does succeed to some extent in creating a critical distance between himself and his principal character who has to be seen together with and not separate from those about him. Indeed in so doing Vailland showed that he was only too aware of the dangers of sovereignty as he interpreted it. But in as much as *La Fête* was to be an example of what he had called 'des œuvres apparemment inutiles: pour donner à son royaume immédiatement la forme qui apaise—épuise son désir', it must be considered to fail. In 1961 Vailland recognized this, attributing it to his inability to distinguish sufficiently between his principal character and himself: 'Duc (était) à la fois moi-même et un autre, [...] j'aurais dû en parler comme d'un "confrère"' (*Ecrits Intimes*, p. 654). While certain themes, especially the treatment of Lucie's *singularité*, are related to the problem and reappear in *La Truite*, Vailland has nonetheless failed to get inside *La Fête*, to become part of the process of its creation. The problem haunted him, however. An interest in the plastic arts, particularly in the sculptures and paintings of his friends Costa Coulentianos and Pierre Soulages,[18] making him increasingly aware of the problem surrounding the relationship between the artist (writer) and his work (novel) and which he was attempting to resolve. On the 17 April 1963 Vailland wrote in his diary: 'me voici seul devant le roman à faire ou ne pas faire—faire un roman d'un seul geste comme une toile de Soulages—*mais il faut s'y enfermer*'.[19] By the early summer he had embarked on *La Truite*.

On a first reading it is tempting to find in this last novel a more refined and controlled treatment of some of the themes—sovereignty and development in particular—that had been central in *La Fête*. Furthermore, Vailland unequivocally projects himself into the novel as an author-character (the *confrère* figure referred to in his diary) in an attempt to avoid the kind of confusion which had flawed the earlier novel. In the portrayal of Frédérique there is much that recalls that of Lucie. Like her, Frédérique also belongs to the *fille merveille* tradition: she is described as '[une] merveilleuse enfant', 'elle procède comme un rêve réel',[20] while Saint-Genis is only really moved by her presence when, on their visit to the Indian reserve, 'elle marchait si vaillamment dans l'herbe coupante du plateau' (p. 351)![21] There is also the same notion of development and potential in the first description of her:

> [Frédérique] contourna le bureau, ce qui l'obligea à se rapprocher de nous et à se montrer de face. Je fus frappé par un air d'extrême jeunesse, la plage lisse sous les yeux, le regard contradictoirement vif et noyé, comme pas tout à fait dégagé de l'animalité de l'enfance. Elle s'éloigna de dos, la hanche un peu lourde, l'omoplate arrondie, mais maintenant que je l'avais vue de face je ne m'en attristais pas: ce qui eût été chez une femme épaississement ne pouvait être chez elle qu'inachèvement, *baby fat*, dernières soies du cocon dont elle était en train de se dégager. (pp. 239-40)

Her childlike qualities are again like Lucie's, acknowledged by her preference for soft drinks and milk to alcohol (the first reference to her drinking alcohol only comes when she leaves for America with Saint-Genis), by

Roger Vailland. (In the background is a painting
by Pierre Soulages). Meillonas, August 1963.
Photo: Garanger.

Roger Vailland writing *La Truite*, Meillonas,
November 1963. *Photo: Garanger*.

her uninhibited enjoyment of card games and television (even if she cannot understand the language in which the programmes are broadcast!) and by her questions about any new experience or situation in which she finds herself. But the similarity goes no further. Even though she ultimately becomes an active and equal partner in the *fête* which she shares with Duc, Lucie is essentially an object to be manipulated by him at his will and for his pleasure. Her freshness and innocence, therefore, are transitory qualities and are underlined only in as much as they are indicative of her potential. In contrast in *La Truite*, Frédérique emerges as a much more positive character in her own right. Her childlike qualities are given further dimensions by references to her as an elemental being ('Elle est un élément comme le fer, le soufre' (p. 438) '[qui] date d'avant toute civilisation' (p. 433))[22] and by the descriptions of her as an animal: 'Je me suis aperçu que je pensais à Frédérique en termes d'animal. [...] un animal d'une branche divergeante de l'évolution, un tarsier de Malaisie, un lémurien de Madagascar' (p. 307). Like an animal, too, she is able both to sense danger before it arrives and to await impassively for the right moment to act. Above all else though she is, in spite of marriage and various adventures, a virgin, a fact which together with the ritualistic practices of the group to which she belonged as a child, make of her a primitive, potentially savage and almost mythical creature: 'vierge magnifique, vierge royale, vierge redoutable ...' (p. 406). Indeed, all of these qualities are implied and neatly summarized by Isaac's likening her to a trout, an image for which we are prepared by various references throughout the book, and in particular by the description of the vicious 'truite solitaire' in the tank in the Monte-Carlo bar (pp. 285–6).

   Such a total picture of Frédérique, however, only becomes possible retrospectively once the novel has been read. Unlike *La Fête*, in which there is a fairly easily discernible pattern to Lucie's development (largely of course because the novel is as much concerned with the manner in which Duc uses her), *La Truite* offers an irregular account of Frédérique's emergence. Like the author, we first see her in action and only gradually thereafter piece together enough evidence to enable us to understand her behaviour in the opening scene. Even then her *singularité* is far from defined: to use the author's words, while we are given various examples of how she appears to others and acts in various situations (her *exposant*), her ultimate stature (her *quantité*) remains uncertain (pp. 341, 358). Even after the confessional fourth section of the novel, 'Le Récit de Frédérique' which serves partly to explain those actions which we have already seen her commit, we are inevitably ignorant as to how she will or would react in quite different circumstances.

   It is this uncertainty which gives *La Truite* its fascination. At first it is tempting to see Frédérique as a catalyst figure, provoking and encouraging certain reactions in those who come into contact with her, with these

F

reactions gradually being explained by the author as more evidence becomes available. With the author as character, however, recording his own reactions, such an interpretation soon becomes too facile. Moreover in *La Truite* Vailland is equally concerned with the relationships (the 'rapport des forces') which exist between other characters (including himself) even though these may, basically, have been prompted by Frédérique's presence in their lives.

Frustrated by what he described as a 'malentendu total' displayed by the novel's reviewers, Vailland attempted on several occasions to define just what *La Truite* was about. In his diary for 29 July 1964, for example, he writes:

> si cela ressemble à quelque chose, c'est à moi-dans-le-monde au moment ou je l'écris [...] et il ne s'agit ni du moi ni du monde, ni de subjectivité ni d'objectivité, mais du rapport vivant, vécu à un moment donné et en fonction de toutes les expériences vécues, de moi et du monde, à un moment donné ... (*Ecrits Intimes*, p. 762)

More significantly, in an entry at the beginning of the month, we find: 'C'est un rêve, avec des personnages et des actions, comme dans les rêves, organisé (dans une unité organique) comme les rêves que l'on se rappelle, rêvé, raconté, et commenté, par moi, dans mon style (*Ecrits Intimes*, p. 744).

Also during the time he was writing *La Truite*, we find Vailland returning again and again in his diaries to the problem of language. For him the idea of precise, accurate description was no longer sufficient; language instead should be seen to be as intrinsically important to the stature of a novel as the subject it is describing. As a result there is in *La Truite* an impression of fluidity, of Vailland (or the author-character) searching both for a definitive system of relationships between his characters and for a language in which to describe it, and which is by definition suitable for no other purpose. He arrives, of course, at neither. Nonetheless there is both an overall plan and an internal cohesion (as in *La Fête*) which enable Vailland rightly to refer to the novel's 'unité organique'. The five-part structure, though deployed in a different manner from earlier work in that the pattern does not neatly conform to that of the classical play, is still very much in evidence. Much as in *325.000 francs* the first part of the novel presents a situation which in miniature prefigures the rest of the action; Parts II and III relate the effect which this first scene has on two of the characters, Rambert and Saint-Genis in particular; Part IV is a confession made by Frédérique to the author in which she provides him and the reader with information about the formative years of her childhood and adolescence, and also relates in her terms and hence gives a further dimension to the relationships already described in the two previous parts; Part V draws the threads together, relates the author's reaction to the situation in his role as author and outlines the new element introduced in the figure of Isaac and in his relationship with Frédérique. While there is therefore one situation presented initially and at the end another that is (to use Vailland's word) 'qualitatively' different from it, there is little sense at any point between the two of climax or even positive movement. As in *La Fête*, however, in which each episode and even the accounts of certain historical events relate to the central themes of sovereignty and freedom, so too in *La Truite* there is an emphasis on ritual and on observation which may ultimately be seen as expressions of what precisely Vailland was attempting.

From the opening scene in the bowling alley we are introduced to a self-contained world with its ways of behaviour, styles of dress and language:

> Comme la plupart des autres joueurs, comme nous-mêmes, il [Galuchat] portait chemise blanche, les manches relevées sur le coude, cravate sombre, rentrée dans la chemise entre le deuxième et le troisième bouton, et pantalons noirs assez longs pour que le plis cassât légèrement sur la chaussure *special bowling*; tenue de rigueur pour les championnats, pas obligatoire en temps ordinaire, mais généralement observée au Point-du-Jour, surtout le mardi soir, considéré ici, bien que cela ne soit pas dans le règlement, comme soirée de gala. La jeune femme, comme la plupart de nos compagnes, en jupe de toile avec pli creux sur le ventre et pull de teinte unie. L'anonymat du bowling m'enchante. Impossible de deviner du premier coup d'œil le milieu, le rang, la classe, la caste. C'est encore plus fascinant que le métro. La première fois que je suis allé dans un bowling, un soir de championnat, en province, pas une seule femme en piste, tous les joueurs jeunes, pas tout à fait, entre trente et quarante, tous en tenue, et dans les gestes, le maintien, sur le visage un air de connivence, comme s'ils participaient à un rite qu'il était interdit de dévoiler. (pp. 238-9)

Similarly Rambert's new enthusiasm for cabinet-making not only demands a skill that comes of constant practice but also has its own language ('des termes du métier ...' (p. 273)) and properties in the shape of highly technical and intricate pieces of machinery (some of whose names Vailland invents! (p. 270)). Saint-Genis and in particular Isaac belong to the completely enclosed world of the high finance of the American Paper and Boxes Company (the APBC) with its carefully controlled hierarchy in which those at the very top—in the language of the company the *tamanoirs*[23] —enjoy a life of luxury and silent power that separates them from ordinary people:

> Les tamanoirs, quand ils descendent à Los Angeles, s'installent aux quinzième et seizième étages, c'est-à-dire au sommet du building.

Ils y ont des appartements (au seizième) où ni Saint-Genis ni Mamoussian n'ont jamais pénétré; ils y reçoivent leurs amis, tout à fait en dehors des cercles habituels de l'APBC. Leurs bureaux (au quinzième), de grandes pièces sans classeur, ni dossier, ni sous-main, ni machine à écrire (ni œuvre d'art), où se déplacent en silence de belles secrétaires, entre trente et quarante ans, élégantes, entretenant des fleurs toute l'année sur les tables vides. (p. 335)

Most marked of all of course, is the *Société Secrète des Vraies Luronnes*, the *SSVL*, formed by Frédérique and her friends Christiane and Michèle as teenagers, initially as a mark of their revulsion with and protest against the sordid habits of their parents and the local boys' obsession with sex. Before long, however, the society lost its defensive character and became much more positive, taking a perverse delight in the plight of its victims and verging at times on crime. With their chant and dancing, their 'langage de plus en plus codé' (p. 380), a system of rewards and punishments and their skills in judo, itself a highly sophisticated form of self-discipline and self-defence, the members of the *SSVL* soon became 'des sauvages, un clan en guerre avec le monde entier' (p. 381). Eventually of the three only Frédérique remained faithful to the society's code, her vicious treatment of Verjon (whose betrayal of her to her father two years earlier they had sworn in a session of sympathetic magic to revenge (p. 376)) becoming the ultimate expression of her amoral, essentially savage (and virginal) nature. (Indeed, so intent does Vailland seem to be here that the naïve, phallic symbolism of Verjon's leg which Frédérique breaks, and of the stuffed fish which she spitefully hurls into the lake, is one of the novel's few weaknesses and recalls the similar infelicity of the poker scene in *Les Mauvais Coups*.)

Whatever form the theme of ritual is given in *La Truite* it is, as has already been suggested, accompanied by that of observation (the verbs *regarder*, *observer* and *remarquer* are frequently to be discovered throughout the book). Saint-Genis and Frédérique spy on the Indians (whose reserve is in itself another enclosed private world); Rambert is watched by his compagnons as he attempts to persuade Galuchat to join them at their *piste*; the offices of the ABPC are built 'd'acier et de verre' open, like a giant vivarium to inspection by those outside (p. 333); while most of all it is the author who studies his characters and their relationships, attempting to understand and, ultimately therefore to classify them, just as he and Frédérique study the trout in the aquarium. In many ways this particular incident is a key one. As Picard has suggested, the glass wall of the aquarium is like the study window in *Un Jeune Homme seul* through which Eugène-Marie Favart watched the factory girls in the avenue de Laon.[24] But the emphasis is quite different. In the earlier novel the window-barrier related directly to Vailland's personal experience; in *La Truite* the whole notion of observation is part of the practice of writing, part of the consideration of what Vailland himself described as 'moi-dans-le-monde au moment où j'écris'. Writing itself, therefore, becomes a ritual and like any other ritual carries within it its own potentially destructive force since ultimately there can be no place left for invention. This, perhaps the most significant and pessimistic point to be made by *La Truite*, is illustrated in particular by Rambert, who has allowed himself to become so totally possessed by Frédérique that he is no longer in control of the particular situation into which he believes he has placed her, even though he claims (and indeed convinces himself) that he is. The implication, too, is much wider. Frédérique and Isaac are in fact the only characters in the novel positively to have escaped. Frédérique on account of the way in which she retains her animal-like qualities and total detachment ('un être inatteignable, intouchable, totalement dépourvu de scrupule et cependant, jusqu'à présent, absolument incorruptible' p. 442)) and Isaac by the way in which at the age of eighty-two he studies advanced mathematics in an attempt to communicate with his grand-daughter: 'pour trouver un langage commun avec sa petite-fille, pour briser la clôture' (p. 442). Even so there is a suggestion by the close of the novel that such efforts are ultimately fruitless and that it is only a matter of time before Frédérique and Isaac too join the ranks of those (to which Rambert and Lou already belong) who have what Vailland describes as *le voile*:

> C'est un voile noir, sans fente, et chaque geste qu'ils font pour s'en débarrasser (sans savoir qu'ils veulent s'en débarrasser, persuadés qu'ils sont de continuer de se mouvoir sur leur lancée, dans la même cadence), chacun de ces gestes par définition désordonné puisqu'il échappe à tout ordre (ne répond à rien, n'agit sur rien), les précipite vers la mort. (p. 422)

Certainly, as totally disinterested creatures they may be presented as ideals, as sovereigns, but in a society that is being reduced daily to an increasingly meaningless and anonymous series of letters and numbers such qualities, ultimately, are useless. As Saint-Genis remarks about Frédérique in the closing words of the novel: '—Qu'elle tienne, [...] qu'elle tienne...Mais pour quoi faire?' (p. 445).

Given the fact that Vailland has projected himself so completely into *La Truite*, and given, too, the way in which the act of writing has been turned into as much a ritualized performance as any other, the sam question ('pour quoi faire?') must also be posed about it. That Vailla intended that it should be is suggested by the way in which having Rambert, the author-character himself experiences driving back to *le voile noir*: 'c'est le voile noir qui enveloppe Rambert et dont que' évidemment s'est accroché à moi' (p. 431)[25]. This incident ca seen to be relevant and understood when we remember Vailland's aims in writing *La Truite*, and when, too, we add to them his growing concern for language. Nowhere perhaps is Vailland's control of his material quite so evident nor so assured as in this last novel: the scattering of key words throughout, the use of the central image of the trout and of the aquarium in the Monte Carlo bar, the theatrical form of sections of the dialogue between the author and Frédérique, the technical details concerning the bowling alley, high finance or the breeding of trouts, for example, the successful way in which the author-character is obviously related to, but quite separate from Vailland himself.[26] But precisely because it is so controlled, because it is, as he calls it in his diary, 'un rêve [...] organisé', it is also the perfect and final expression of his attempt to use himself as material: 'En m'introduisant comme auteur-enquêteur dans *La Truite* [...] j'essaie d'utiliser aussi moi-dans-le-monde comme matériau' (*Ecrits Intimes*, p. 763).

It is tempting with hindsight to suggest that even while he was preparing *La Truite* in 1963 Vailland was, if only subconsciously, aware that he was suffering from a terminal illness. Certainly the diaries for the period beginning in January 1964 are haunted by the presence of death, either directly, in the open references to ill-health, or in more sinister accounts like that of his meeting in Montparnasse with what he saw as a harbinger of his death, the *putain-noire*. (Indeed 'black', frequently to be found in his work as a symbol of anguish and fear, becomes, in the last months of his life, an obsession.)[27] Yet predictably Vailland refused to acknowledge openly that he was ill; illness was a form of weakness, and indication that personal sovereignty had been abandoned. Already in *La Truite* we read in the author's reflections on Rambert: 'Vrai malade: celui qui a abandonné sa souveraineté à la maladie et au médecin, inextricablement liés' (p. 365). In the February before his death Vailland was admitted to a clinic in Neuilly for an exploratory operation and the words now apply directly to him: 'je commençai, malgré cet apparent général respect dû au luxe, de me sentir en ces lieux devenu objet [...] de n'être plus [...] un homme, mais un objet, ce malade'.[28] Yet publicly he continued to reject the inevitable. Indeed, plans for a new novel, a fresh contract with his publishers Gallimard, the proposed trip to South America, and, more personally, the manner in which (according to his diaries) he enjoyed a large number of sexual experiences with both prostitutes and friends, could all be interpreted as efforts to convince the world (if not himself) that there was nothing essentially wrong with him. Even death—though his obsessive concern for it is in itself revealing—could be turned to advantage by suicide, the ultimate proof of his freedom and sovereignty, and a natural extension to the kind of total fusion between himself and his context (*moi-dans-le-monde*) which he had sought to exemplify in his last novel.[29] Ultimately he was cheated. He decided that he would commit suicide on 16 October 1965, his fifty-eighth birthday, unless there was any marked improvement in the state of his health; five months before the day arrived Roger Vailland died of cancer.

Conclusion

From this survey of Vailland's life and work it should become evident that for all his varied experiences and for the enthusiasm with which they were explored, he was a man whose whole personality may, as was suggested in the Introduction, be defined in terms of a simple contradiction. On the one hand the need to express his desire to be alone, aristocratically apart, personified in his work by the libertine, *homme de qualité, vrai bolchevik* or even the *fille merveille* figures; on the other, the sense that he should share in what he saw to be a constant struggle against the threat of mediocrity and mass oppression. From his various attempts to reconcile these two forces a pattern emerges, charted particularly in his novels, which takes him from a sense of anticipated self-fulfillment to one of frustration and even complete disillusion. Indeed his life, rather than dividing itself neatly into various seasons as he liked to claim, might be more usefully seen as a series of scenes in a play in which Vailland as the principal actor is constantly reappearing but each time wearing a different mask: or, to use the image which he employed in *La Truite*, a number of different situations (*exposants*) which, put together, would form a *quantité* that was Vailland.

But it is not only thematically that we find such close links between Vailland's life and his work. For all that Elisabeth Vailland has claimed that he was not 'un homme de lettres',[1] and for all that his own views on the role and importance which literature held in his life varied considerably according to time and circumstance, he never wavered in his belief that his work—like Soulages' paintings—should be seen as a unified body. Even in 1956 when, despairing and utterly disillusioned, he returned from Moscow, we read in his diary: 'je suis un homme d'œuvre et la première ligne de ma première œuvre ne prendra tout son sens que quand j'aurai mis le point final à la dernière'.[2] Writing, too, therefore was as much a role as any other, and, indeed, a more permanent one.

In the preceding chapters, I have attempted where necessary or relevant, to give some indication of the features of Vailland's style as they applied to individual novels. In view of his own total view of his work some general but by no means exhaustive remarks should also be made.

Without question the most striking characteristic of his novels is their theatrical qualities. (Indeed it is arguable that the novels are much more theatrically successful than any of his plays!) Frequently Vailland returned to the idea of internal unity and cohesion, taking as his prototype the classical play with its unities[3] and carefully controlled five-part structure. Nowhere perhaps is this better expressed than in an interview which he gave to Marcel Mithois a year before his death:

je pars toujours d'une histoire composée de cinq panneaux sensible-
ment égaux. Les cinq moments de la tragédie. Je conçois assez le
roman comme le récit d'une tragédie. Je ne crois pas cette division
arbitraire. [...] On peut retrouver dans tous mes romans ces cinq
parties. C'est le mouvement aristotélicien: la première partie est
l'exposé d'une situation qui renferme une contradiction. Deuxième
acte: la contradiction se transforme en conflit. Troisième acte: le
développement du conflit. Le quatrième acte aboutit à la crise. Le
cinquième acte c'est le dénouement, c'est-à-dire l'exposé de la
situation nouvelle qui résulte de ce dénouement.[4]

While this division is more skilfully concealed in some novels (*Les Mauvais
Coups* or *325.000 francs*) than in others (*Drôle de jeu, Beau Masque, La
Truite*), it is not the only indication of manipulation and control on a large
scale. In *Un Jeune Homme seul* and *Bon Pied Bon Œil*, for example, we
also find two major interreflecting parts; *Beau Masque*, Part III, which
spans the same period of time as Part IV, is as we have seen, written in an
epistolary form; in *Beau Masque*, *325.000 francs* and *La Truite* (though
with different intentions and effects) Vailland introduces himself as an
author-character. Within these structural devices Vailland is also to be
found indulging in a number of theatrical effects on a smaller scale: the
setting of a scene with an economy of detail which is instantly followed by
dialogue and action (Marat's arrival at Etiamble in *Drôle de jeu*; the opening
lines of *Les Mauvais Coups*; and on a bigger scale the gradual piecing
together of a number of small scenes to form a composite picture of the
village at the beginning of *La Loi*); the intricate and acutely-observed set
pieces in which language and subject harmonize (Milan's pursuit of the
crow in *Les Mauvais Coups*, the elderly couple in the metro in *Bon Pied
Bon Œil*; the love scene between Pierrette and Beau Masque in *Beau
Masque*; the Jewish couple observed by Marat on his journey to Lyon in
Drôle de jeu; the bowling alley in *La Truite*); the ironic distance established
between the reader, with his total view of the action, and a character as part
of it (Lucrezia's reaction in *La Loi* to Attilio's revelation that Francesco has
been taken to the brothel by his father, which only serves to increase her
love for him; Antoinette's belief in *Bon Pied Bon Œil* that Roderique has
need of her support while he is in prison or the account of her seduction
of him earlier in the same novel); the way in which physical appearances,
like costume, indicate moral qualities (Juliette and Marie-Jeanne in
325.000 francs; Marchand in *Un Jeune Homme seul;* Lucie in *La Fête*); the
detailed technical description of certain pieces of equipment which relate,
usually symbolically, to the action (the *presse-à-injecter* in *325.000 francs;*
the *trabucco* in *La Loi*, the mechanism controlling the skittles in *La Truite*).
Inevitably, such features are not always successful. Neither is Vailland's
unhappy habit of interrupting his narrative with occasional pompous or

sententious reflections like those on love and war in *Drôle de jeu* or on sleep in *La Loi*. No less disturbing are the long confessional passages to be found in various forms especially in the early novels, and his diatribes against the *professions libérales* in *Un Jeune Homme seul*, religion in *Drôle de jeu*, or against bicycles and the status of women in *La Loi*. Moreover, for a writer who professed such concern for control, either there are too many loose ends (what happens to Rodrigue's mother in *Bon Pied Bon Œil*, for example?) or sometimes the various strands of the intrigue are brought together in a hurried and summary fashion, as at the end of *La Loi*, and with insufficient concern for an appropriate degree of verisimilitude, as in *Drôle de jeu*. Yet on balance the strengths outweigh the weaknesses. Some novels—*325.000 francs* and *La Truite*, for example—stand in their own right as finished products; others are more usefully seen in conjunction with those written at approximately the same time and relating to a common problem, notably the quartet *Bon Pied Bon Œil, Un Jeune Homme seul, Beau Masque* and *325.000 francs*. At its worst there is a self-indulgent and repetitiveness about his work which results in its being forced and over-written; at its best it is characterized by a tautness and an allusive quality which links it inseparably with his life and personal preoccupations, and gives a fascinating exposition of his reactions to the events of his time.

How Vailland would have developed and what kind of work he would have produced had he lived is difficult to say. At the end of his life, as the closing words of *La Truite* ('à quoi bon?') suggest, he seemed once more disillusioned. And in March 1965 we find him, Stendhal-like, claiming in his diary that his work had been almost totally misinterpreted: 'ce complet malentendu sur mon "œuvre" car j'écris pour aujourd'hui 200 en France 2000 dans le monde lecteurs, cette frange, et je suis lu par proportionnellement énormément plus pour de mauvaises raisons...'.[5] Perhaps such feelings were largely occasioned by ill-health. Perhaps, as his widow maintains and as he himself suggested in 'Eloge de la politique', he was about to move into a new period of political *engagement* in which Sorel's picture of the aristocratic socialist would have best fitted him. Perhaps, too, the political novel of which he had so often dreamed and which obsessed him during the last weeks of his life would have finally been written. Perhaps... We can only speculate. It seems more likely, however, in view of the position he had reached, that any new enthusiasm would have been relatively short-lived and that any political novel would have thrown up the same insoluble problems as those which had emerged ten years earlier. In an interview which he gave to Francis Jeanson shortly before his death, Vailland repeatedly returned to the paradox which had obsessed him in one form or another throughout his life, namely of resolving personal aims and ambitions with the discipline required by shared or corporate action, what he termed as 'l'impossibilité de faire un'.[6] It was an honest recognition of the inevitable; perhaps the final mask had at last been discarded.

Notes

Introduction

1. *Ecrits Intimes*, p. 486. See also p. 489. Full details of Vailland's work and of all secondary material mentioned in the Introduction are to be found in the Bibliography, pp. 169–74.
2. Perhaps the best known is the film of *La Loi* directed by Jules Dassin in which Gina Lollobrigida played the part of Mariette, Pierre Brasseur that of Don Cesare. Vailland so disapproved of Dassin's direction, however, that he refused to have anything to do with the film.
3. See, for example, D. Caute, *Communism and the French Intellectuals* (London, 1964), Part Two, Chapters 5 and 6.
4. Mention should also be made of the *Lettres à sa famille* collected and edited by Max Chaleil in 1972.
5. A critical edition of *325.000 francs* has been prepared by D. O. Nott and published by The English Universities Press Ltd., 1975.

Chapter One

1. Vailland and Ballet, p. 32.
2. See *Un Jeune Homme seul, Œuvres Complètes*, (hereafter *O.C.*,) III, p. 16, in which Michel Favart's refusal to resit the examination is seen as a weakness and 'Appel à Jenny Merveille', *Ecrits Intimes*, pp. 163-4: 'Lui, préparait le concours d'entrée à l'Ecole Polytechnique. Il a échoué. C'était la deuxième fois. C'est un concours très dur. [...] Il s'est découragé. Il s'est présenté en octobre à un concours pour être ingénieur au service Ministère de la France d'Outre-Mer. C'est beaucoup moins difficile. [...] Il a été reçu. Il s'est marié six semaines plus tard. Il a obtenu un poste à Madagascar. Ils sont partis tous les deux...'.
3. 'L'Enfant couvert de femmes', *Entretiens*; p. 23.
4. *Ecrits Intimes*, p. 103, Cf. Geneviève Vailland: 'Sans doute apparaissait-il comme un petit garçon très choyé, très pomponné (il avait un col raide, une grande lavallière) et les autres garçons n'ont pas dû tellement aimer ça'. *Entretiens*, p. 24.
5. Just how committed to freemasonry Georges Vailland had been is difficult to say, but it seems likely that he was motivated simply by some kind of idealism. However strong his anti-religious belief had been, it had not prevented him from accepting a religious marriage service (though no doubt his wife's persuasive powers counted for much).
6. Geneviève Vailland, *Entretiens*, p. 23.
7. It is interesting to note that *Un Jeune Homme seul* was the only one of his novels of which Vailland did not send a personal copy to his sister. See *Entretiens*, p. 26. Cf. M. Picard, *Libertinage et Tragique dans l'œuvre de Roger Vailland*, pp. 26 and 34.

8. *Entretiens*, p. 26.
9. Picard, p. 61.
10. Vailland's poem, *En vélo*, is reproduced in *Ecrits Intimes*, p. 25.
11. *Ecrits Intimes*, p. 26. Cf. Geneviève Vailland, *Entretiens*, p. 28.
12. *L'Adolescence à Reims*. Unpublished fragment written 1943-4.
13. 'Révolution, Révélation', article intended for *Le Grand Jeu*, No. 4. Quoted in Michel Random, *Le Grand Jeu*, Vol. I, pp. 23-4.
14. Lecomte, who always liked to assume a superior role, was known as Papa or Coco de Clochilde for example. Vailland was Dada or François.
15. *Le Surréalisme contre la Révolution*, *O.C.*, VIII, p. 252: 'Une tête de pleine lune, deux yeux ronds sans prunelles, une fente oblique en guise de bouche et deux embryons d'ailes à la place des oreilles. A longueur de journées nous dessinions des Bubus sur les murs, sur le sable, sur le papier. C'était Bubu qui présidait à nos orgies de tétra-chlorure de carbone, à toutes nos tentatives pour atteindre à la torpeur des bêtes larvaires'.
16. *Pour et contre l'existentialisme*, pp. 169-70.
17. See below, p. 78. Cf. *Les Mauvais Coups*, *O.C.*, II, p. 42: 'A l'adoles-cent que je fus, la condition des travailleurs manuels apparaissait à la fois enviable, car je souffrais de la solitude bourgeoise et redoutable, car j'étais persuadé qu'elle exige un entraînement en quelque sorte natif et que pour ma part je n'avais pas assez de vigueur pour en affronter les rudesses et les incertitudes.'
18. Letter to René Maublanc, *Ecrits Intimes*, p. 31.
19. *Une Génération dans l'orage, Notre avant-guerre* (Paris, 1968), p. 41.
20. Paul Guth, *Quarante contre un* (Paris, 1947), p. 285.
21. *Lettres à sa famille*, p. 32.
22. *Lettres à sa famille*, p. 35. Mme Labou was one of his pet names for his mother. Further references to this work are given after quotations or allusions in the text.
23. Daumal and Lecomte had already suggested *La Voie* as a title. Pierre Minet's recollection that the change occurred shortly after the Vailland family's departure to Antibes in July 1926 is almost certainly incorrect, however, even though he was present at the meeting (Roger Gilbert-Lecomte, *Correspondance* (Gallimard, Paris, 1971), p. 121 note 1). In a letter to Lecomte written on 2 August 1927—wrongly dated 1926 in the *Ecrits Intimes*, pp. 32-7—Vailland refers on a number of occasions to La Voie (no italics). Random's date of November 1927 seems most likely: M. Random, *La Grand Jeu*, Vol. I, p. 37.
24. *Un Jeune Homme seul*, *O.C.*, III, Part I, Chapter 6.
25. *Entretiens*, p. 49. Had she also been Adamov's mistress? *Ibid.*, p. 68.
26. E.g. *Lettres à sa famille*, pp. 104, 105, 110. Vailland was careful to make his relationship with Mimouchka sound as innocent and 'respectable' as possible.
27. *Ecrits Intimes*, p. 26.
28. For the fullest accounts to date see Michel Random's study, the text of the three issues of *Le Grand Jeu* together with other related documents reproduced by the *Cahiers de l'Herne* (Paris, 1968), and volumes of

memoirs like Pierre Minet's *La Défaite* (Paris, 1947). Much, however, remains to be done.

29. Lecomte, *Correspondance*, pp. 179–92.
30. *L'Herne*, pp. 72–3 and pp. 77–8.
31. *Mémoires d'une jeune fille rangée* (Paris, 1958), p. 260.
32. *L'Herne*, p. 78. Cf. *Un Jeune Homme seul, O.C.*, III, p. 100.
33. *L'Herne*, pp. 96–100.
34. Quoted in Random, II, p. 151.
34. Random, II, p. 152.
35. Random, II, p. 151.
36. Compare his claim to Paul Guth that at the time '(il avait) été d'une bonne foi, d'une puerilité désarmantes'. Guth, p. 287.
37. *Ecrits Intimes*, p. 498.
38. Recanati, pp. 81–3.
39. See, for example, *Ecrits Intimes*, pp. 498–500.
40. *Lettres à sa famille*, p. 206. Marianne Lams has suggested, perhaps rather fancifully, that it was to do with mines or armaments. *Entretiens*, p. 53.
41. There is, to be fair, one reference to this (*Lettres à sa famille*, p. 212) though it seems to have had little effect on his attitude.
42. Interview with Madeleine Chapsal, *L'Express*, July 1957.
43. *Lettres à sa famille*, p. 270. Cf. pp. 271–2.
44. B. in *Drôle de jeu* ('à trois heures du matin, sur le pont Saint-Michel, une femme qui s'appelle B. m'est apparue pour la première fois' *O.C.*, I, p. 362); Roberte in *Les Mauvais Coups*.
45. Serialized in *Le Peuple* in 1937. First published in book form in 1947.
46. Picard, pp. 38–9.
47. Picard, pp. 187–8.
48. *O.C.*, II, p. 84: 'Bien vite nous nous sommes détestés de trop nous aimer et d'être pour ainsi dire enchaînés par le besoin que nous avions l'un pour l'autre.'
49. *Entretiens*, p. 35.
50. *Drôle de jeu, O.C.*, I, p. 207.
51. *Ecrits Intimes*, p. 70.
52. *O.C.*, X, p. 440 (*Le Nouvel Observateur*, 26 November 1964).

Chapter 2

1. *Ecrits Intimes*, p. 73.
2. *Ecrits Intimes*, p. 123. The newspaper *L'Echo de Paris* which, particularly after the first World War, was one of the principal organs for the expression of Republican Nationalism, discontinued publication in 1942.
3. *Lettres à sa famille*, p. 298.
4. 'L'aventurier du journalisme', *Entretiens*, p. 62.
5. *Ecrits Intimes*, p. 84.
6. See below pp. 90–91.
7. *Ecrits Intimes*, p. 93. One specific link to be made concerns the novelist Céline. In Chapter VI (Première Journée) of *Drôle de jeu* Chloé refers

to the flat above hers: 'Céline habite au-dessus. Chaque fois qu'on fait du bruit chez moi, il croit qu'on s'apprête à le tuer' (*O.C.*, I, p. 111). In an article published in the *Tribune des nations* (13 January 1950), 'Nous n'épargnerons plus Louis-Ferdinand Céline', Vailland recounts how he and his Resistance colleagues had discussed the possibility of assassinating the whole of Céline's *Je suis partout* group. Elsewhere (*Magazine littéraire*, February 1969) Vailland is reported as having refused to participate: 'Je ne tuerai pas un écrivain'. Céline rejected the whole story as absurd, claiming instead that he and Robert Champfleury to whom the Resistance flat belonged, but whom Vailland never mentioned, were close friends. In fact Champfleury originally offered Céline the opportunity to join the *maquis*.

8. *O.C.*, I, p. 58. Cf. an unpublished *Avant-propos* to the novel: 'je n'ai jamais eu l'intention de faire un tableau de la Résistance ou des portraits de Résistants'.

9. Unpublished *Avant-propos*.

10. *Drôle de jeu*, *O.C.*, I, p. 124. Further references to this work are given after quotations or allusions in the text.

11. Chloé also illustrates another of Vailland's favourite theories—the sharp distinction between the highly polished and mature Parisian (or any capital) figure, and the unformed provincial. See p. 301: 'C'est un phénomène essentiellement parisien: Chloé est à l'opposé de la provinciale, elle ne peut être née que dans une grande capitale...'.

12. Compare Frédérique's remark on the *maquis* in *La Truite*, *O.C.*, XII, p. 383: 'Des jeunes gens avec des mitraillettes, qui chantaient parce qu'ils avaient tué des Allemands dans les bois'.

13. See p. 267:
     '—Pourquoi Frédéric est-il communiste? demande Marat.
     —Pour les mêmes raisons qui, en d'autres temps, l'auraient fait entrer au couvent, parce que le Parti a une doctrine aussi précise qu'un dogme et exige de ses membres une discipline absolue.'

14. The description of Thucydide, Mathilde's executioner, is very like one of Vailland himself! See pp. 366–7.

15. See below Chapters Three and Four.

16. Compare Pierre Berger's comments on *Un Jeune Homme seul*. See below, p. 89.

17. See Vailland and Ballet, p. 39: 'Un jeu poussé si loin qu'il engageait l'existence du joueur'.

18. While I have not included a particular section on Vailland's style, a number of relevant comments will be found throughout. Some general points are also made in the Conclusion.

19. *O C.*, X, p. 317.

20. *O.C.*, X, p. 318–19.

21. *O.C.*, X. p. 327. There may well be a direct allusion here to Nizan's own pamphlet *Les chiens de garde* (1932) in which he attacked the bourgeois intellectual for his refusal to commit himself to any kind of political activity, for his moral smugness and his overriding concern for material security.

22. *Pour et contre l'existentialisme*, p. 171.
23. Unpublished 'Projet de conférence: Surrealism—From anti-militarism to the underground'. Cf. *Quelques réflexions sur la singularité d'être français*, O.C., VIII, p. 26. *Le Surréalisme contre la Révolution* was prompted by the 1947 Surrealist exhibition and the accompanying catalogue, *Le Surréalisme en 1947*. Much of what Vailland has to say about the movement and indeed about all forms of *mystification* are very similar to Sartre's remarks in Chapter IV of *Qu'est-ce que la littérature?*
24. *Pour et contre l'existentialisme*, p. 175.
25. *De quel monstrueux souci leur âme et dieu font-ils le poids?* (Unpublished)
26. *Quelques réflexions sur la singularité d'être français*, O.C., VIII, pp. 21–2.
27. *Marat*.
28. *Ecrits Intimes*, p. 106.
29. *Ecrits Intimes*, pp. 106–13 and compare *Les Mauvais Coups*, O.C., II, p. 24.
30. O.C., IV, p. 78.
31. See 'L'Homme mystifié', *Ecrits Intimes*, p. 125.
32. O.C., IV, p. 51.
33. *Les Mauvais Coups*, O.C., II, p. 10. Further references to this work are given after quotations or allusions in the text.
34. It is also worth noting that in the Spring of 1947 Vailland accompanied a friend Fernand Lumbroso, who was leading a theatrical tour, to Egypt. During the voyage Vailland gave up drugs of his own volition and for the last time.
35. Particularly by the insertion of adverbs—*gentiment, tendrement* for example—into an unexpected context.
36. Compare p. 146: 'les souvenirs troublés qui font que dans mes rêves elle [Roberte] m'apparaît souvent sous les traits de ma mère'.
37. Compare Recanati, *Roger Vailland, Œuvres Complètes*, II, p. 385: 'La crise a atteint le point où, capitulation, mort ou rupture, elle doit se dénouer'.
38. Picard, p. 114.
39. *Roger Vailland, Œuvres Complètes*, II, p. 386.
40. Claude Roy, *Nous* (Paris, 1972), p. 247.
41. *Ecrits Intimes*, p. 141. Further references to this work are given after quotations or allusions in the text.
42. Claude Roy, pp. 248–9.
43. Claude Roy, p. 250.
44. 'Elisabeth Vailland raconte...', *L'Express* (July–August, 1972), No. 26.
45. *Ecrits Intimes*, p. 194. See Elisabeth Vailland, 'Roger Vailland au jour le jour', *Entretiens*, p. 162.
46. *Bon Pied Bon Œil*, O.C., II, p. 167. Further references to this work are given after quotations or allusions in the text.
47. Chloé, of course, reappears in Rodrigue's dream. See below pp 59–60.
48. In fact in a 'crêmerie'!
49. Bott, p. 143.

50. See p. 185; p. 199; pp. 281–2; p. 326 and *Drôle de jeu*, *O.C.*, I, p. 294; 'Au fond, tu es encore au stade de la révolte individuelle: c'est de ta génération. Moi je suis discipliné'.

51. The scene could be interpreted with Antoinette in the role of the mother and Rodrigue in that of the child. His version, in which he takes the initiative, would then be one further example of his attempt to rid himself of the mother image.

52. Note the war vocabulary and the fact that she signs the letter with her maiden name, Antoinette Larivière.

53. Aragon too made much of this kind of mythical figure both in his novel *Les Communistes* (1949–51) and in his essay on Gabriel Péri who was shot by the Germans in 1941. See 'La Passion de Gabriel Péri' in *L'Homme communiste*, Vol. I (1946).

54. Recanati, p. 145.

55. *Ecrits Intimes*, p. 203: 'Plus décidé que jamais à ne plus travailler qu'avec le peuple organisé dans le P.C.' (3 May 1950).

56. Bott, p. 149.

Chapter 3

1. From his letters to Elisabeth it would seem that Vailland tired of the project before long. *Ecrits Intimes*, p. 328, p. 332, p. 343. Even so he appears to have completed the text which contains nine fairly substantial chapters. A small extract was published in *Le Nouvel Observateur*, 3 October 1957.

2. *Ecrits Intimes*, p. 225.

3. *Ecrits Intimes*, p. 203.

4. Compare an unpublished text *Notes sur la liberté*: 'La liberté [...] c'est aussi pouvoir s'aliéner; user et abuser de soi-même, se consommer'.

5. *La Cruauté dans l'amour*, *Le Regard froid*, *O.C.*, VIII, p. 88.

6. *La Cruauté dans l'amour*, pp. 92–3. Cf. *Ecrits Intimes*, p. 424.

7. *Entretiens*, pp. 163–4. Cf. *Ecrits Intimes*, p. 259.

8. *Le Regard froid*, *O.C.*, VIII, p. 93.

9. 'Je parviens à m'avancer et le Pope passe tout près de moi. Le corps et les membres sont entièrement cachés. Seules, les mains jointes et la tête coiffée de la mître apparaissent au-dessus du trône. Un visage blanc comme les étoffes blanches. Un visage immobile, impassible, sans expression, un visage déhumanisé, c'est à dessein. Un regard vide, ou tourné vers l'intérieur, ou fixé vers le ciel, comme vous voudrez, enfin un regard volontairement privé de tout contenu. Un visage rigide comme le visage d'un mort ou comme le visage d'un dieu. Cela passe très lentement.'

10. *Ecrits Intimes*, p. 271. Further references to this work are given after quotations or allusions in the text.

11. *Le Colonel Foster plaidera coupable*, *O.C.*, IV, Act I, Scene 2, p. 194.

12. Act IV, Scene 1, p. 292: 'Citoyen, j'ai le droit de n'être pas d'accord avec la politique de mon gouvernement. Soldat, j'exécute les ordres que je reçois.'

13. There is more than a hint of an analogy here between Masan and the prisoners and Christ with the two thieves.

14. *Ecrits Intimes*, p. 316: 'le prix lui-même, cela me semble impossible pour les raisons politiques'.

15. *Boroboudour*, *O.C.*, VI, pp. 48–9. Further references to this work are given after quotations or allusions in the text.

16. Compare p. 98: (The Indonesian officer's answer to Vailland's claim that he was not a colonialist) 'vous êtes Blanc...il faudra encore quelque temps avant que mes compatriotes admettent qu'il arrive que des Blancs soient aussi des hommes'.

17. Vailland recounts a chance meeting with a Siamese student: 'A une réflexion que je fis, le Siamois comprit que je sentais cela exactement comme lui et que mon cœur battait à l'unisson du sien. Je rencontrai son regard, qui était devenu fraternel jusqu'à la tendresse. C'est le souvenir le plus émouvant que je rapporte d'un voyage de quarante mille kilomètres sur trois continents'.

18. See, for example, Claude Roy's account of Vailland's decision to leave Paris, *Nous*, p. 256 and Recanati, p. 349.

19. Introduction to *De l'amateur*, *Le Regard froid*, *O.C.*, VIII, p. 101.

20. Recanati, p. 349.

21. *Un Jeune Homme seul*, *O.C.*, III, p. 10. Further references to this work are given after quotations or allusions in the text.

22. Note the repeated *elle* in this passage.

23. Those who belonged to the 'professions libérales'—doctors, lawyers, architects, for example—were not only assured of financial independence, but also enjoyed a social distinction often envied, of course, by those in the salaried and working classes.

24. We should also note how towards the end of the novel when Victoria, who is by now demented, attempts to interfere and protect Eugène-Marie, a similar language is used. See p. 208: 'mon tout petit, mon fils à moi toute seule, rien que nous deux [...] je sais bien que tu souffres, mon pauvre petit, mais je ne t'en veux pas, *on s'en fiche tous les deux de l'Espagnole, dadi dada dadeu, nous deux, babi baba babou, on se fiche de tout*'. Vailland's italics.

25. See p. 28: 'le vieillard et l'adolescent se trouvent [...] tout près l'un de l'autre, comme des complices'.

26. See p. 116: 'à Paris, ce sont les *tantes* qui se font faire des costumes comme le tien'.

27. Victoria of course is highly regarded by the Vichy administration: 'Une femme bien. Membre du Secours national et de plusieurs œuvres paroissiales' (p. 152).

28. See above, pp. 35–7.

29. Eugène-Marie also suffers periodically from bouts of unspecified illness. Domenica is reported as saying: 'Plus les crises sont violentes, plus il est près de la guérison. Je suis sûre de lui' (p. 161).

30. Not surprisingly there are similarities between the descriptions of Domenica in the novel and those of Elisabeth Naldi in *Ecrits Intimes*.

31. See p. 216: 'Favart se redressa, ses bras s'allongèrent le long du corps, le

cou se raidit, le pas devint aisé, amples et un peu solennel, et plus personne ne s'étonna qu'il fût en tête de tous, le premier des hommes de la famille'.

32. See p. 202: 'Je ne m'intéresse ni à mon gouvernement ni à ceux qu'il me fait exécuter. Seules m'importe la rigueur et l'élégance de l'exécution'.

Chapter Four

1. 'Class and Art' in *Leon Trotsky on Literature and Art*, edited by P. N. Siegel (New York, 1970), p. 64.
2. See above, p. 71.
3. Unpublished letter to Vailland, 4 November 1951.
4. *Ecrits Intimes*, p. 445. Cf. *Expérience du drame, O.C.*, V. p. 134.
5. *Choses vues en Egypte, O.C.*, VI, p. 210. An account of Vailland's Egyptian experience is also to be found in *La Fête (O.C.* XII, pp. 133–138).
6. It is worth comparing the description of the vice-omdeh in *Choses vues en Egypte* with that of Madru in *Un Jeune Homme seul*: 'Le vice-omdeh qui nous reçut cet après-midi-là, [...] est un homme d'une quarantaine d'années, grand, maigre, légèrement voûté. Il porte au plus haut point les qualités caractéristiques du peuple égyptien; les belles proportions, le regard vif et intelligent, le sourire bienveillant, l'air de bonté' (*O.C.*, VI, pp. 221–2). Madru 'se tient droit, solidement posé sur ses pieds largement écartés. Le cheminot est légèrement voûté, la poitrine un peu creuse, le visage maigre, mais les épaules massives comme les arcs des cathédrales romanes' (*O.C.*, II, p. 80). Cf. as well Albéran in *Bon Pied Bon Œil, O.C.*, II, p. 369.
7. *Choses vues en Egypte, O.C.*, VI, p. 245 and p. 254.
8. *Expérience du drame, O.C.*, V, pp. 117–18.
9. *Expérience du drame*, p. 145.
10. 'Roger Vailland nous parle de théâtre', *Théâtre populaire*, May 1957, p. 5. Interview with Bernard Dort.
11. 'Roger Vailland nous parle de théâtre', p. 7.
12. *Laclos par lui-même, O.C.*, IX, p. 13. See Baudelaire's notes on Laclos' novel in C. de Laclos, *Œuvres Complètes* (Paris 1951), p. 717.
13. I am grateful to Professor H. T. Mason for allowing me to consult material which is to appear in his book *French Writers and their Society, 1715–1800*.
14. *Laclos par lui-même*, p. 51.
15. *Expérience du drame*, p. 190.
16. 11 November 1954.
17. *Beau Masque, O.C.*, VII, pp. 188–9 and p. 208. See p. 334. Further references to this work appear after quotations or allusions in the text.
18. See p. 403: '...trois siècles ayant convaincu Florence, Lyon, Paris, Hambourg et Londres, que les Empoli étaient invincibles'.
19. See Pierrette's earlier remark, p. 92: 'c'est tout simplement un gosse malheureux'.

20. My italics.
21. Part of this lecture which has remained unpublished is reproduced in *Entretiens*, p. 258.
22. In an interview with Régis Bergeron in *L'Humanité*, 7 February 1955 Vailland described Beau Masque as 'bienveillant et *débrouillard*, mais frivole et un peu *anar*'.
23. *Ecrits Intimes*, p. 475.
24. *Ecrits Intimes*, p. 458. See Vailland's article in *Les Lettres françaises*, 24 September 1953.
25. Letter to Elisabeth Vailland, 7 May 1955, *Ecrits Intimes*, p. 466.
26. Interview with Madeleine Chapsal, *L'Express*, 12 July 1957.
27. 'Vailland, militant communiste: témoignages de militants de l'Ain', *Entretiens*, p. 92.
28. *325.000 Francs*, *O.C.*, III, pp. 297–8. Further references to this work appear after quotations or allusions in the text.
29. It should be noted that while *un busard* is a bird of prey (cf. *milan*), *buse* also means 'a stupid person'.
30. *Ecrits Intimes*, p. 475.
31. Note the contrast between Juliette's surname, *Doucet* and the repeated description of Marie-Jeanne as *sèche*.
32. My italics. See p. 281: 'A onze heures, elle rangeait son ouvrage; c'est alors qu'il aura la permission de s'étendre près d'elle sur le lit'.
33. E.g., *Ibid.*, p. 342; p. 402; p. 413.
34. *Ecrits Intimes*, p. 712.
35. *Ecrits Intimes*, p. 549.
36. Quoted in *Entretiens*, p. 93.

Chapter Five

1. *Ecrits Intimes*, p. 753.
2. *The Observer*, 10 June 1956.
3. *La Fête*, *O.C.*, XII, pp. 10–11.
4. *L'Express*, July–August 1972.
5. *Ecrits Intimes*, p. 498: 'Je courais, la main dans la main avec Roger Gilbert-Lecomte, sur l'herbe rase d'un plateau incliné vers l'ouest; je savais que c'était l'ouest, à cause du soleil couchant, et un plateau, non une plaine, comme on sait ces choses-là dans les rêves, sans doute parce que je savais que nous allions arriver sur le bord supérieur d'une falaise. Nous courions à foulées lentes, très allongées, presque un vol. J'étais au comble du bonheur'.
6. See, for example, the entry for 24 October 1956. *Ecrits Intimes*, pp. 515–516.
7. *Eloge du Cardinal de Bernis*, *O.C.*, VIII, p. 161. Further references to this work appear after quotations and allusions in the text.
8. My italics.
9. Predictably the Communist Press was less enthusiastic. André Wurmser, writing in *La Gazette de Lausanne*, for example, referred to *La Loi* as 'un recul dans l'œuvre du romancier'.

10. Chapsal, *L'Express*, 12 July 1957.
11. Interestingly, a number of observations on the social and political problems in this society which Vailland makes in his article are excluded from the novel. Alessandro's social-democratic inclinations are referred to for quite different reasons, while the episode concerning the mason Mario only serves to underline the manner in which the inhabitants of Manacore are trapped, at all levels of society.
12. *La Loi*, O.C., XI, pp. 98–9. Further references to this work appear after quotations and allusions in the text.
13. Claude Roy, pp. 46–7.
14. My italics.
15. See also p. 176.
16. See also pp. 152; 159; 164–5.
17. Note, too, the way in which she decides for him how he is to go to Turin in order to see the lawyer.
18. O.C., V, p. 362.
19. Picard., p. 494.
20. Lamballe, too, is contained in Lambert—Lavalle, Pierrette in Pierrot—Charlotte.
21. *Monsieur Jean*, O.C., V, p. 25. Further references to this work appear after quotations and allusions in the text.

Chapter Six

1. See Vailland and Ballet, pp. 5–11.
2. An account of this trip *La Réunion* was eventually published in 1964.
3. *Ecrits Intimes*, pp. 538–9. See p. 779: 'je ne suis jamais arrivé à m'intéresser à l'Algérie'.
4. Vailland and Ballet, pp. 65–7: 'notre attention est entièrement concentrée sur l'Algérie, sur la France' (14 May 1958); 'aujourd' hui tout est en suspens, nous attendons le déroulement des événements en Algérie et en France' (15 May); 'nous dînons et restons suspendus à la radio... nous sommes anxieux et hésitants' (17 May); 'une blonde...agréable... Roger ne m'en a pas parlé, nous sommes trop pris par la politique...A deux heures du matin, nous en parlons encore Roger et moi' (27 May).
5. See, for example, *Ecrits Intimes*, pp. 661, 707, 815.
6. O.C., XII, p. 152.
7. *Roger Vailland, Œuvres complètes*, IX, p. 318.
8. *Suétone: Les Douze Césars*, O.C., IX, p. 252. See *Ecrits Intimes*, p. 712.
9. O.C., VIII, p. 228.
10. See, for example *Ecrits Intimes*, pp. 559–60.
11. *Roger Vailland: Œuvres Complètes*, XII, p. 454.
12. *La Fête.*, O.C., XII, p. 139. Further references to this work appear after quotations or allusions in the text.
13. E.g., pp. 38 and 181–2.
14. See p. 121: 'Je pense qu'il est temps que tu apprennes à te conduire comme une femme'.

15. P. 150. Compare p. 146: 'Une fête [...] exige un temps séparé du reste du temps et un lieu qui lui soit particulier, limite, séparation qui donnent à la fête sa réalité comme la forme au corps de son être'.

16. See *Ecrits Intimes*, p. 815: 'Depuis lors [1956] je ne peux plus souffrir en particulier les cheminots (comme je l'ai sournoisement montré dans *La Fête*), des gars qui s'engagent à 18 ans à poinçonner des tickets jusqu' à l'âge de la retraite...'.

17. Whatever the implications of Duc's description of their life together—and in spite of her name—Léone is, in fact, totally subservient. Although in the scene with Jean-Marc she claims that she is contented (this is her form of sovereignty) we should remember that Duc *as novelist* is putting the words into her mouth.

18. See, for example, the essays *Comment travaille Pierre Soulages* and *Les Sculptures de Coulentianos* in *O.C.*, VIII.

19. *Ecrits Intimes*, p. 722. My italics.

20. *La Truite.*, *O.C.*, XII, p. 267 and p. 359. Further references to this work appear after quotations and allusions in the text.

21. Compare p. 256: 'Frédérique rit [...] rire clair, sonore, enfantin'.

22. Although Saint-Genis knows that according to her passport she is twenty-three, there is considerable doubt about her real age.

23. Note the link between these (the ant-eaters) and the image of the offices as a vivarium.

24. Picard., p. 446.

25. Compare *Ecrits Intimes* p. 742: 'Une peu inquiet sur l'autoroute au retour: j'ai senti le voile (noir)'.

26. Picard (p. 511) also notes the change from the linear pattern of the earlier novels to one which is 'en étoile; elle s'articule autour de la secrète Frédérique. En toile d'araignée'.

27. See Picard, pp. 515–18.

28. *Ecrits Intimes*, p. 820. Compare p. 821.

29. *La Truite*, p. 776: 'ce Roger Vailland en train (dans le moment présent) de réfléchir et d'écrire, qui va mourir en 19... et qui peut à chaque instant décider de mourir, mort qui pour moi anéantira dans le même instant (atomisera) le monde tout entier et moi-même'.

Conclusion

1. Vailland and Ballet, pp. 5–6.

2. *Ecrits Intimes*, p. 492.

3. See, for example, *Ecrits Intimes*, p. 674: 'Une œuvre d'art c'est l'organisation, la mise en forme d'une certaine matière dans un certain cadre. c'est-à-dire dans certaines limites de temps, d'espace ou de mouvement'.

4. 'Les secrets de l'écrivain', *Réalités*, March 1964.

5. *Ecrits Intimes*, p. 832, 20 March 1965.

6. The interview has not been published. A recording of it was generously lent to me by Elisabeth Vailland.

Bibliography

1. Books

Listed here in order of publication are Vailland's principal works. Details of the various essays collected together in *Le Regard froid* and of all unpublished material which has been consulted are to be found in the notes.

Suède 1940, Sagittaire (Paris, 1940). (Written under the pseudonym of Etienne Merpin.)

La Dernière Bataille de l'Armée de Lattre, Editions du Chêne (Paris, 1945).

La Bataille d'Alsace—novembre–décembre 1944, Jacques Haumont (Paris, 1945).

Léopold III devant la Conscience belge, Editions du Chêne (Paris, 1945).

Drôle de jeu, Corrêa (Paris, 1945).

Quelques Réflexions sur la Singularité d'être français, Jacques Haumont, (Paris, 1946).

Esquisse pour le portrait du vrai libertin, Les Entretiens de Madame Merveille avec Octave, Lucrèce et Zéphyr, Jacques Haumont (Paris, 1946).

Un Homme du peuple sous la Révolution, Corrêa (Paris, 1947). (Written in collaboration with Raymond Manevy and first serialized in *Le Peuple* in 1937.)

Héloïse et Abélard, Corrêa (Paris, 1947).

Le Surréalisme contre la Révolution, Editions sociales (Paris, 1947).

Les Mauvais Coups, Sagittaire (Paris, 1948).

Pour ou contre l'existentialisme, Editions de l'Atlas (Paris, 1948). (Debate with J.-B. Pontalis, J. Pouillon, F. Jeanson, J. Benda, E. Mounier.)

Bon Pied Bon Œil, Corrêa (Paris, 1950).

Le Colonel Foster plaidera coupable, Editeurs Français réunis (Paris, 1951). (A second edition with an Introduction by René Ballet was published in 1973 by Editions Grasset et Fasquelle, Paris.)

Boroboudour, Corrêa (Paris, 1951).

Un Jeune Homme seul, Corrêa (Paris, 1951).

Choses vues en Egypte, Editions Défense de la paix (Paris, 1952).

Expérience du Drame, Corrêa (Paris, 1953).

Laclos par lui-même, Seuil (Paris, 1953).

Beau Masque, Gallimard (Paris, 1954).

325.000 francs, Corrêa (Paris, 1956).

L'Eloge du Cardinal de Bernis, Grasset et Fasquelle (Paris, 1956).

La Loi, Gallimard (Paris, 1957).

Monsieur Jean, Gallimard (Paris, 1959).

La Fête, Gallimard (Paris, 1960).

Les Liaisons dangereuses 1960, Julliard (Paris, 1960).
Les Pages immortelles de Suétone—Les Douze Césars, Corrêa, Buchet-Chastel (Paris, 1962).
Le Regard froid, Grasset et Fasquelle (Paris, 1963).
La Truite, Gallimard (Paris, 1964).
La Réunion, Editions Recontre (Lausanne, 1964).
Ecrits intimes, Gallimard (Paris, 1968). (Edited by Jean Recanati.)
Lettres à sa famille, Gallimard (Paris, 1972). (Edited by Max Chaleil.)
Œuvres Complètes, 12 volumes, edited and with notes by Jean Recanati.
Editions Rencontre, Lausanne, 1967–8.

Vol. I   'Profil gauche de Roger Vailland' by Claude Roy. *Drôle de jeu.*
Vol. II   *Les Mauvais Coups, Bon Pied Bon Œil.*
Vol. III   *Un Jeune Homme seul, 325.000 francs.*
Vol. IV   *Héloïse et Abélard, Le Colonel Foster plaidera coupable.*
Vol. V   *Monsieur Jean, Expérience du drame, Batailles pour l'Humanité, Les Liaisons dangereuses 1960.*
Vol. VI   *Boroboudour, Choses vues en Egypte, La Réunion.*
Vol. VII   *Beau Masque.*
Vol. VIII   *Le Regard froid, Le Surréalisme contre la Révolution, Comment travaille Pierre Soulages, Les Sculptures de Coulentianos.*
Vol. IX   *Laclos par lui-même, Suétone: Les Douze Césars, Sur 'Manon Lescaut'.*
Vol. X   *Un Homme du peuple sous la Révolution, La guerre au jour le jour, La dernière bataille de l'armée de Lattre, Ecrits politiques, 1945–47, Eichmann et ses juges, Léopold III devant la conscience belge, Avant le Vingt-quatre Heures du Mans, Lisez Flaubert, Eloge de la politique.*
Vol. XI   *La Loi.*
Vol. XII   *La Fête, La Truite.*

2. Prefaces

Mémoires de Jacques Casanova di Seingalt, Club du Livre du mois (Paris 1957).
Les Liaisons dangereuses de Choderlos de Laclos, Club du Livre du mois (Paris, 1955). (Reproduced for various editions of Laclos' novel in subsequent years.)
Anthologie libertine du XVIIIe siècle, Jacques Haumont (Paris, 1960).
Tableau des mœurs du temps dans les différents âges de la vie, Cercle du livre précieux (Paris, 1959).
Les Pléiades de Gobineau, Livre de poche (Paris, 1960).
Manon Lescaut de l'abbé Prévost, Editions Lucien Mazenod (Paris, 1967).

3. Articles

During his life Vailland wrote over 2,500 articles for the following news-papers and reviews: *Action, Les Allobroges, Arts, L'Avant-Garde, Les Cahiers de la Télévision, Clarté, Confluences, Confessions, Constellations, L'Express, Europe-Auto, France-Observateur, France-Soir, France-U.R. S.S., Le Grand Jeu, Horizons, L'Humanité, L'Humanité-Dimanche, Les Lettres françaises, Libération, Livres de France, Le Monde, La Nef, La Nouvelle Critique, Le Nouvel Observateur, Paris-Midi, Paris-Soir, Présent, Réalités, La Revue de la Compagnie, Transatlantique, Spectacle, Théâtre populaire, La Tribune des Nations.*

Selections of some of the most important of these articles are to be found in: *Œuvres Complètes.* Vol. X; *Roger Vailland* (R. Ballet and E. Vailland); *Lettres à sa famille; Ecrits Intimes.*

4. Editions

325.000 francs. Edited with an Introduction and Notes by David Nott, English Universities Press Ltd, London, 1975.

5. Translations

The following novels have been translated into English:
Drôle de Jeu: Playing with Fire, Chatto and Windus, London, 1948.
La Loi: *The Law*, Jonathan Cape, London, 1958.
La Fête: *The Sovereigns*, Jonathan Cape, London, 1960.
La Truite: *A Young Trout*, Collins, London, 1966.

STUDIES OF VAILLAND

1. Books

BALLET, René, and VAILLAND, Elisabeth, *Roger Vailland*, Seghers (Paris, 1973). (Collection: Ecrivains d'hier et d'aujourd'hui.)

BOTT, François, *Les Saisons de Roger Vailland*, Grasset (Paris, 1969).

BROCHIER, Jean-Jacques, *Roger Vailland. Tentative de description critique*, Losfeld, (Paris, 1969).

CHALEIL, Max (ed.) *Entretiens: Roger Vailland*, Editions Subervié (Rodez, 1970).

PICARD, Michel, *Libertinage et Tragique dans l'œuvre de Roger Vailland*, Hachette (Paris, 1972).

RECANATI, Jean, *Esquisse pour la psychanalyse d'un libertin. Roger Vailland*, Buchet-Chastel (Paris, 1971).

The following contain useful chapters or sections on Vailland:

BRASILLACH, Robert, *Une génération dans l'orage...journal d'un homme occupé*, Plon (Paris, 1968).

CHAPSAL, Madeleine, *Les écrivains en personne*, Julliard (Paris, 1960).
(Text of the interview in *L'Express*, 12 July 1957.)

GUTH, Paul, *Quarante contre un*, Vol. I, Corrêa (Paris, 1947).

ROY, Claude, *L'Homme en question*, Gallimard (Paris, 1960).
(Basically the same text as that of Roy's article in *Les Temps modernes*).

ROY, Claude, *Nous*, Gallimard (Paris, 1972).

2. Articles

Many of the articles to have appeared to date are little more than extended reviews. In addition to the important collection in the *Entretiens* series the following are of particular interest:

BONNET, Y. and HUSSON, A. 'Roger Vailland', *Tendences*, No. 62. December 1969.

BOTT, François. 'L'Homme de proie', *Lui*, July 1964 (Interview).

BUIN, Yves, 'Vailland. Homme du XVIIIe ou écrivain du XXIe siècle', March 1964.

CHAPSAL, Madeleine, *L'Express*, 12 July 1957, 19 April 1964 (Interviews).

CHOUBLIER, Claude, 'Roger Vadim et Roger Vailland révèlent comment a été conçue et réalisée l'adaptation des *Liaisons dangereuses*', *La Nef*, October 1959 (Interview).

DORT, Bernard, 'Roger Vailland nous parle de théâtre', *Théâtre populaire*, No. 24, May 1957 (Interview).

ENGLER, Winfried, 'Idyllen bei Zola und Vailland', *Zeitschrift für Französische Sprache und Literatur*, LXXII, October 1962.

FLOWER, John, 'Roger Vailland: *325.000 francs*', *Modern Languages*, LIII, June 1972.

GEORIS, Michel, 'Roger Vailland à la recherche de l'homme de qualité', *Le Thryse*, November—December 1967.

LAUFER, Roger, 'Le héros tragique dans les romans de Roger Vailland', *AUMLA*, No. 22, November 1964.

MITHOIS, Marcel, 'Les secrets de l'écrivain', *Réalités*, No. 218, March 1964.

PIATIER, Jacqueline, *Le Monde*, 16 February 1963 (Interview).

PICARD, Michel, 'Le Thème des mères chez Roger Vailland', *Revue d'histoire littéraire de la France*, July—August 1971.
'On n'est pas sorti de l'auberge, roman et épreuve de réalité d'après *La Fête*', *Littérature*, No. 6, May 1972.

ROLLAND, Jacques-Francis, 'Vailland le clandestin', *Le Nouvel Adam*, March 1969.

ROY, Claude, 'Esquisse d'une description critique de Roger Vailland', *Les Temps modernes*, December 1957.

SCHAEFFER, Marlyse, 'La dernière interview de Roger Vailland', *Candide*, 16 May 1965.

SICARD, Alain, 'Réflexions sur l'œuvre de Roger Vailland', *La Nouvelle Critique*, February 1966.

VAILLAND, Elisabeth, *L'Express*, No. 26, July—August 1972 (Interview with Bernard Chardère).

SELECTED SECONDARY MATERIAL (Books and Articles)

ADERETH, Maxwell, *Commitment in Modern French Literature*, Gollancz (London, 1967).

ANDREU, Pierre, 'Les idées politiques de la jeunesse intellectuelle de 1927 à la guerre', *Revue des Travaux de l'Académie des Sciences morales et politiques*, Second Semester (1957).

ARON, Robert, *Histoire de Vichy, 1940–44*, Fayard (Paris, 1954).

BEAUVOIR, Simone de, *Mémoires d'une jeune fille rangée*, Gallimard (Paris, 1958).

BENDA, Julien, *La Trahison des clercs*, Pauvert (Paris, 1965).

BERL, Emmanuel, *Mort de la morale bourgeoise*, Pauvert (Paris, 1965).

Mort de la pensée bourgeoise, Grasset (Paris, 1929).

BERNARD, Jean-Pierre, *Le Parti Communiste Français et la question littéraire, 1921–1939*, Presses universitaires de Grenoble (Grenoble, 1972).

BOISDEFFRE, Pierre de *Une anthologie vivante*, Perrin (Paris, 1965).

BROMBERT, Victor, *The Intellectual Hero: Studies in the French Novel, 1880–1955*, Faber and Faber (London, 1962).

CAUTE, David, *Communism and the French Intellectuals*, André Deutsch (London, 1964).

The Illusion, André Deutsch (London, 1971).

DAUMAL, René, *Lettres à ses amis*, Gallimard (Paris, 1958).

'Le Grand jeu' in *Cahiers de l'Herne* (see below).

DOMENACH, Jean-Marie, 'Le P.C.F. et les intellectuels', *Esprit*, May 1949.

GILBERT-LECOMTE, Roger, *Correspondance*, Gallimard (Paris, 1971).

HAMILTON, Alistair, *The Appeal of Fascism*, Blond (London, 1971).

HOWE, Irving, *Politics and the Novel*, Horizon Press (New York, 1955).

KUNNAS, Tarmo, *Drieu la Rochelle, Céline, Brasillach et la tentation fasciste*, Les Sept Couleurs (Paris, 1972).

LOUBET DEL BAYLE, Jean-Louis, *Les Non-Conformistes des années 30*, Editions du Seuil (Paris, 1969).

MANDER, John, *The Writer and Commitment*, Secker and Warburg (London, 1961).

MINET, Pierre, *La Défaite*, Sagittaire (Paris, 1947).

NADEAU, Maurice, *Histoire du Surréalisme*, Editions du Seuil (Paris, 1947).

Documents surréalistes, Editions du Seuil (Paris, 1948).

NIZAN, Paul, *Les Chiens de garde*, Maspero (Paris, 1965).

Aden Arabie, Maspero (Paris, 1971).

PLUMYENE, Jean and LASIERRA, Raymond, *Les Fascismes français*, Editions du Seuil (Paris, 1963).

POLITZER, Georges, *Fin d'une parade philosophique*, Pauvert (Paris, 1968).
  La Philosophie et les mythes, Editions Sociales (Paris, 1969).

RANDOM, Michel, *Le Grand Jeu*, 2 vols. Denoël (Paris, 1970).

REDFERN, Walter, *Paul Nizan: Committed Literature in a Conspiratorial World*, Princeton University Press (Princeton, 1972).

SARTRE, Jean-Paul, *Politics and Literature* (Translated by J. A. Underwood and John Calder), Calder and Boyar (London, 1973).
  Qu'est-ce que la littérature?, Gallimard (Paris, 1948).
  Situations, Vol. VII, Gallimard (Paris, 1965).

SIEGEL, Paul (ed.), *Leon Trotsky on Literature and Art*, Pathfinder Press (New York, 1970).

SOREL, Georges, *Réflexions sur la violence*, Rivière (Paris, 1936).

TOUCHARD, Jean, 'L'Esprit des années 30' in *Tendances politiques dans la vie française depuis 1789*, Hachette (Paris, 1960).

TROTSKY, Leon, *Literature and Revolution*, University of Michigan Press (Ann Arbor, 1960).

VANDROMME, Pol, *La Droite buissonnière*, Les Sept Couleurs (Paris, 1960).

Cahiers de l'Herne, No. 10, 'Le Grand Jeu', Minard (Paris, 1968).

Hermès, No. 5, 'La Voie de René Daumal du *Grand Jeu* au *Mont Analogue*', Association Les Amis d'Hermès (Paris, 1967).

Index

References to notes are given only when attention is drawn to important bibliographical information or when they contain useful illustrative
material.